CALIFORNIA
HISTORY

Also by Gordon Morris Bakken

The Development of Law on the Rocky Mountain Frontier, 1850–1912 (1983)

The Development of Law in Frontier California: Civil Law and Society, 1850–1890 (1985)

Rocky Mountain Constitution Making, 1850–1912 (1987)

California Legal History Manuscripts in the Huntington Library: A Guide (1989)

Practicing Law in Frontier California (1991)

Surviving the North Dakota Depression (1992)

Learning California History, co-authored with Brenda Farrington (1999)

Law in the Western United States, editor (2000)

Racial Encounters in the Multi-Cultural West, co-authored with Brenda Farrington (2000)

Environmental Problems in America's Garden of Eden, co-authored with Brenda Farrington (2000)

The Gendered West, co-authored with Brenda Farrington (2000)

Law in the West, co-authored with Brenda Farrington (2000)

The Urban West, co-authored with Brenda Farrington (2000)

Where is the West?, co-authored with Brenda Farrington (2000)

CALIFORNIA HISTORY

A Topical Approach

Gordon Morris Bakken, editor
California State University at Fullerton

Harlan Davidson, Inc.
Wheeling, Illinois 60090-6000

Library of Congress Cataloging-in-Publication Data

California history : a topical approach / Gordon Morris Bakken, editor.
    p. cm.
Includes bibliographical references and index.
    ISBN 0-88295-971-9 (alk. paper)
  1. California—History. I. Bakken, Gordon Morris.
    F861.5 .C35 2003
      979.4—dc21
                                                                  2002008871

Cover photograph: The vineyards of Zaca Mesa Winery in the Santa Ynez
Valley of Santa Barbara County. *Photograph by Kirk Irwin, copyright
© Kirk Irwin*
Cover design: DePinto Graphic Design

Manufactured in the United States of America
04 03 02 1 2 3 4 SB

CONTENTS

CONTRIBUTORS

Lisa E. Emmerich is Professor of History and Coordinator of the American Indian Studies Program at California State University at Chico. She has written extensively on American Indian women, health care for American Indians, and federal assimilation policies. Her most recent article, "'Save the Babies': American Indian Women, Assimilation Policy, and Scientific Motherhood, 1912–1918," appears in Susan Armitage and Elizabeth Jameson, eds., *Writing the Range: Race, Class, and Culture in the Women's West* (1997).

Ronald C. Woolsey is the author of the critically acclaimed *Migrants West: Toward The Southern California Frontier.* He has just completed an important biography of Will Thrall, a mountain evangelist who was considered the John Muir of southern California. The book is slated for publication in 2003. He teaches at Citrus College in Glendora, California.

John Joseph Stanley, M.A., is a deputy sheriff and currently serves as the Vice President of the Association for Los Angeles Deputy Sheriffs. He is a past winner of the California State Bar Association award for the best essay in California legal history. Most recently, he contributed four articles to *Law and the Western United States*. Currently he is preparing an article on jail matrons for a forthcoming book on the history of women in law enforcement.

Wayne N. Engstrom is Professor of Geography at California State University at Fullerton and is presently working on a reconstruction of the nineteenth-century physical geography of the southern California coastline.

Gordon Morris Bakken is Professor of History at California State University at Fullerton, where he has taught since 1969. He and Brenda Farrington co-authored *Learnng California History* (1999) as well as the six-volume *The American West* (2000).

Danelle Moon is an archivist/librarian in Manuscripts and Archives, Yale University Library, and teaches U.S. History and Women's History as an adjunct history professor at Central Connecticut State University. Prior to her work as an archivist, she worked as a professional public historian and as an independent researcher and scholar. She is currently writing an article on the professionalization of women librarians in the West. She holds an M.A. in history from California State University Fullerton and an M.L.S. from Southern Connecticut State University.

John Anderson is a California native and lifelong resident. He is currently a doctoral candidate in the History Department of the University of Southern California. He received his Bachelors degree at UCLA and his Masters in Public History at California State University at Fullerton.

Nancy J. Taniguchi is Professor of History at California State University at Stanislaus and is the author of *Necessary Fraud: Progressive Reform and Utah Coal*. She is currently working on two books, one an American history centered on the region of the Old Spanish Trail where it runs through Utah, and the other called "Connecting California."

Ricardo Griswold del Castillo is Professor of Chicana and Chicano Studies at San Diego State University. His books include *The Treaty of Guadalupe Hidalgo: A Legacy of Conflict*, *La Familia: Chicano Families in the Urban Southwest, 1848 to the Present*, *The Los Angeles Barrio, 1850–1890: A Social History*, and, with Arnoldo De León, *North to Aztlán: Mexican Americans in United States History*.

Victor W. Geraci is Associate Professor of History at Central Connecticut State University in New Britain, Connecticut, and the author of a forthcoming book on the Santa Barbara County wine industry with the University of Nevada Press.

PREFACE

Having taught the course in California history at a state university for twenty-three years, I have long sought a reader that might engage students of different backgrounds, and of all levels. Supplementary textbooks that present strings of historiographical debates and reproduced documents are excellent tools for instructors and history majors, but they tend to bore, even overwhelm, most students. Such compilations hardly speak to the broad range of interests today's students bring to the study of California history. Finally, time constraints—especially for one faced with taking a course presented within the confines of a single semester or quarter—and limited student budgets make lengthy and expensive supplements unattractive.

With this in mind, I present *California History: A Topical Approach*, a collection of ten scholarly but easily readable essays to complement any standard textbook on California history. A glance at the table of contents reveals that the following works compose an eclectic mix. A look at the list of contributors confirms that the authors, some of them new scholars, some of them experts in their field, write from different perspectives. Nevertheless, the essays relate to one another in interesting and unexpected ways and sound common themes—connections readers will enjoy discovering.

A topical approach to the study of history conveys a sense of relevancy sometimes lost in textbook treatments. While some of the essays that follow go deeper than survey coverage to consider central events in California history in detail, others treat subjects simply not found in survey textbooks. All of them raise new questions.

Asking questions drives historical inquiry and gives meaning to its products. Therefore, I hope that readers will leave these pages with a new appreciation of the breadth and complexity of California history, as well as with questions of their own.

Gordon Morris Bakken
Department of History
California State University at Fullerton

CHAPTER ONE

Managing the Gold Rush: California Indians and California History

Lisa E. Emmerich

Rising above the northern Sacramento Valley, Mount Shasta looms more than 14,162 feet above the surrounding countryside. This majestic volcanic peak, the second tallest of the Cascade Range, is a place of multiple identities. To travelers along Interstate Highway 5, it is the sentinel of the Oregon-California border. To outdoor enthusiasts, Mount Shasta is the site of year-round recreational activities: downhill and cross-country skiing in the winter and mountaineering and backpacking in the summer. And to members of local American Indian communities, the mountain is a place of enormous spiritual import. For northern California tribes like the Karuk, the Achumawi, the Maidu, and the Wintu, the mountain's springs, meadows, forests, and snow-bound upper reaches are all sites and sources of religious power.

Recently, the image of Mount Shasta has gained yet another identity—gaming symbol. With the passage in 1988 of the Indian Gaming Regulatory Act (IGRA), many California Indian tribes decided to pursue economic development through gaming enterprises. The Redding Rancheria of Wintu, Pit

Redding Rancheria members attending a tribal conference, 2001. *Courtesy of Win-River Casino, Public Relations Department.*

River, and Yana Indians opened the Win-River Casino in Redding, California, in 1993. Attracting patrons from northern California and southern Oregon, along with travelers of the Interstate 5 corridor, the casino boasts plush surroundings and twenty-four hour gambling. Video slots, video poker, blackjack, and high-stakes bingo entice all those willing to part with a roll of quarters, or considerably more money, for an opportunity to hit the jackpot. Glitzy commercials advertising Win-River feature pictures of smiling winners and their loot set against a striking graphic backdrop of an eagle circling—what else?—Mount Shasta.

Mount Shasta's two different faces represent more than the intersection of the sacred and the commercially profane; they offer a hint of the complicated history of California Indian peoples. Scores of California tribes in the last decade have themselves gambled on the construction and opening of bingo halls and casinos as a means of achieving tribal prosperity. And thanks to gaming profits, many of these communities have been able to raise their members' living standards, provide health care, promote education, support the revival of traditional culture, and expand tribal land bases. Indeed, these monies have helped put California tribal communities on the local, state, and national political "map," in some cases for the first time in history. It is inescapably ironic that this Indian-authored "gold rush" has largely coincided with observations of the sesquicentennial of the 1848 Gold Rush and subsequent statehood.

In the century and a half since James Marshall first saw the glitter of gold in the millrace at Coloma, Indian tribes in California have experienced dramatic, often devastating, transformation as well as dynamic resurgence. Yet their contacts with outsiders began long before gravel from the icy waters of the American River changed history. Just as surely as spring floods, summer fires, and winter snows affected the daily lives of most Native communities, so too did the arrival of Spanish explorers and missionaries, Russian fur traders, Mexican settlers, and American expatriates. Bringing with them an insatiable demand for resources and lands, alien religious systems, oppressive legal codes, and an overweening ethnocentrism, these foreigners irrevocably changed California and the lives of its Indian inhabitants.

To tell the story of California Indian endurance and survival, it is important to start at the very beginning, in the oral traditions of communities who knew and cherished the world as a familiar cultural landscape. For the Konkow Maidu of the northeastern Sacramento Valley, Earth Initiate and Turtle help bring the world into being. Among the Cahuilla in the south, Mukat and his brother Tamaioit become the creative forces that shape life. And the Pomo peoples of the north central California coast know that the hands of Marumda and Kuksu gave their land its distinct features.[1] Each Native nation had, and still has, its own unique understanding of the origins and life cycle of the physical and metaphysical space that was, and remains, home.

California, home to many such peoples, was a place of remarkable diversity and rich resources. More than 100 million acres were bounded to the east by the Sierra Nevada, to the south by the desert expanses, to the west by the Pacific Ocean, and to the north by the redwood forests. Along the coast, ocean currents and storms determine the climate; farther inland, elevation shapes weather both in the mountain ranges and in the rain shadows thereof. A Mediterranean climate prevails in most of the rest of the region: cool, damp winters precede dry, hot summers. In the valleys and the foothills, the rainy season brings with it verdant greenery and brilliant wildflowers. These give way, as the temperatures rise, to the browned-over shrubbery and tinder-dry grasses that color California's famed golden hills.

In this colorful natural setting, with its varied climates and topographies, Native peoples adapted to the many different ecological niches and learned to modify them for their own uses. In doing so, they made the most of the rich resources around them. California Indians were sophisticated agriculturists and horticulturists as well as expert hunters and fishers. They routinely used techniques such as weeding, pruning, tilling, and sowing to encourage the growth of indigenous plants they used as foodstuffs and medicines. They also employed tools like fire and irrigation to mimic effectively the annual floods and fires that contoured the landscape and affected the productivity of plants. Hunting and fishing were usually considered as appropriate tasks for the men of the community. Women were responsible for gathering, foraging, and overseeing whatever cultivation took place. It was not uncommon, however, for all members of the community to collaborate in stockpiling provisions at certain times of the year, for food collection was labor-intensive. These efforts ensured both sufficient food for the entire group and reinforced communal ties.

Such a remarkable refectory, both natural and manipulated, helped make pre-contact Native California a stunning mosaic of bioregions supporting indigenous cultures.[2] More than 300,000 inhabitants, speaking hundreds of different dialects, made it one of the most densely populated, most culturally diverse areas within indigenous North America.[3] Northern coastal tidelands gatherers like the Yurok and Miwok took shellfish, game, and acorns as their primary food supplies. Farther south, groups like the Chumash and the Gabrielinos used plank canoes to augment their diets of game, shellfish, and acorns with large sea fish and sea mammals. Inland along California's great rivers like the Sacramento and the Klamath, annual runs of salmon and steelhead supported communities like the Karuk, the Wintu, and the Maidu, who also relied heavily on acorns and game. In those areas where year-round lakes fostered more sedentary lifestyles, groups like the Pomo and the Yokuts exploited fish, waterfowl, and other aquatic food sources. The Sacramento and San Joaquin Valleys supported communities like the Patwin and the Nisenan, who enjoyed a mixed subsistence base that included salmon, acorns, and game. Farther inland, in the foothills of the Sierra Nevada, tribes like the

Nomlaki, the Yana, and the Shasta relied heavily on game. Even farther east, where the climate and topography echoed that of the Great Basin, Paiutes and Washo hunted game and gathered piñon nuts. In the south, where desert areas dictated vastly different subsistence patterns, the Yuma and the Mohave cultivated corn, pumpkin, and beans near the Colorado River.[4] Where resources were abundant, as throughout most of the Central Valley and along the coast, smaller tribal landholdings supported dense populations. Where food was scarce, along the eastern slope of the Sierra Nevada and the northeastern high deserts, for example, even small populations required larger land bases. Regardless of community size or location, though, California Indians knew their physical surroundings intimately.

For all the cultural and geographic distances separating them, California Indian peoples were linked by certain common experiences. For the most part, they lived in small groups within clearly defined territorial boundaries. These autonomous "village communities" ranged anywhere in size from 50 to 1,000 inhabitants and were usually governed by a "headman."

Community members ran the social and economic spectrum, with the affluent, the comfortable, and the struggling living side-by-side. Marriages among village residents further enhanced the ties that bound individuals to their communities. Religious traditions gave these people a common sense of identity as well as a sense of purpose. Religious leaders, usually men but sometimes women, supported their communities by conducting ceremonies to heal the sick, promote the maintenance of individual and communal harmony, and mediate relations between the people and spiritual forces shaping their lives.

Life for California Indians was scarcely predictable; individuals and their communities were affected by natural phenomena like floods, fires, and droughts, as well as by human-made disasters like war. But the rhythms of life familiar to each community doubtless gave them faith in the persistence of their cultures and societies.

In every case, the transformation of these singular Indian communities may be traced to one of four colonial experiences. Depending upon tribal affiliation and location, traditional life ways changed at the hands of Spanish settlers and missionaries, Russian fur traders, Mexican settlers, or the conglomeration of Americans who stormed into California during the Gold Rush. Coming in successive waves, the strangers sought imperial possessions, converts to Christianity, laborers, natural resources, individual wealth, and private property. In a three hundred-year-long mad scramble that began with Spanish contact and concluded in the killing fields of the Gold Rush era, the Indians of California suffered greatly, their indigenous cultures all but destroyed.[5]

The determination of the Spanish in Mexico to find the elusive passage around the "island" of California began the transformation of the world and lives of California Indians. Though speculation abounded, the upper reaches of this mysterious area went unexplored until 1542, when Juan Rodríquez Cabrillo led an expedition that charted the coast from present-day Baja California to Oregon. His journey gave Spain an unambiguous claim to the lands of Alta (Upper) California. This claim went unchallenged until Sir Francis Drake of Great Britain stunned the Spanish authorities by sailing up the coast of California in 1579 and brazenly laying claim to the land in the name of Queen Elizabeth I. A subsequent expedition led by Sebastián Vizcaíno in 1602 reasserted Spanish rights over the territory.

For more than a century after these first encounters with Europeans, life in California Indian communities continued much as before. Accounts of the physical appearances of the strangers, their vessels, and their behavior slowly made their way into tribal oral traditions and were carried forward by subsequent generations. Though these narratives may have alerted Indians to the mysterious foreigners who had made their way along the coast years before, nothing could have prepared them for the coming onslaught. Only dreams and prophecies could see that far into the future. Centuries later, Lucy Young told a story that she had heard as a young child. Speaking to a local historian in 1939, the eighty-year-old Wintu woman explained that long before the Gold Rush, her grandfather had dreamed that the Wintu world of northern California would disappear with the arrival of a strange creature, "White Rabbit." According to her grandfather, "White Rabbit gonta devour our grass, our seed, our living. We won't have nothing more, this world."[6]

The story Young's grandfather told anticipated the arrival of those whose presence and actions would make the familiar world a strange new place. This process began in earnest in 1769, when Captain Gaspar de Portolá and Franciscan missionary president Fray Junípero Serra journeyed north at the head of a column of Spanish troops and religious personnel. Eager to solidify existing claims over California, the Spanish authorities paired the sword and the cross as partners in this endeavor. That pairing would shape the future for the Indians living along the coast northward from San Diego.

The principle mechanisms for the extraordinary changes that Native Californians would experience after 1769 were the *reduccións* (missions), *presidios* (military bases), and *pueblos* (civilian communities). On July 16, 1769, the Portolá-Serra expedition founded the first Alta California mission, San Diego de Alcalá, at the site of present-day San Diego. From this point on, the mission system in California expanded to accomplish two separate but related tasks: extend Spanish control over the Native population and establish Spanish ownership of Native lands. Some Indians readily moved into the Spanish colonial and religious settlements, perhaps seeking safety from slave labor raids or a more certain food supply. In the main, though, "recruitment campaigns" and the civilian and military expropriation of tribal lands after 1769 forced thousands of Indians into the missions.

California Indians quickly discovered that these religious enclaves bore little similarity to their traditional village communities. Missionaries, backed up by the military, wielded authoritarian power. The use of violent force was commonplace. Indians worked to feed and support the mission personnel as well as whatever military forces were stationed nearby, often going without food themselves. Every year, hunger, despair, and the rampant spread of diseases of European origin, such as measles and diphtheria, killed hundreds of Natives at each of the missions. Those who survived were confronted by assimilative strategies that promoted the conversion of the *gentiles* (unconverted Indians), encouraged the *neophytes* (Indian converts) to persist in their new beliefs, and prepared all to receive and accept the "yoke" of Spanish colonial authority

Native Californians rapidly learned that the missions were not the only sites for enforced cultural change. Both the Spanish civilian and military populations of Alta California depended upon Indian labor. The civilian pueblos of Los Angeles, Santa Cruz, and San José grew and flourished because Indians constituted an available supply of inexpensive labor. The presidios also relied heavily upon Native laborers as construction workers and providers of food. Some Indians attempted to maintain a degree of economic and social autonomy as they worked and lived within these communities. Yet, despite their importance to the growth and development of Spanish California, indigenous peoples typically fared poorly in pueblo and presidio alike. Civilians and soldiers regarded them as a workforce that had few rights and could be dominated easily. Unfortunately, succeeding generations of California Indians would find this pattern of economic exploitation and ethnically based discrimination born in the pueblos and the presidios a familiar component of life.[7]

In short order, resentment and hostility replaced whatever initial hospitality the Indians may have extended toward the newcomers. Overt as well as covert forms of resistance to colonial control and forced acculturation developed and proliferated. The Kumeyaay living near the mission in San Diego tolerated the outsiders for less than a month in 1769 before they attacked the site, ultimately destroying the mission in 1775. To the north, the medicine woman Toypurina led an organized attack on the Mission San Gabriel in 1785. Ohlone and Coastanoan neophytes in and around San Francisco fought back against the Spanish system in the 1790s. And at the Missions Santa Barbara and La Purisma, Chumash Indians led by Mariano, Pacomio, Benito, and Bernarde fought for more than a month in the most spectacular episode of Indian resistance in 1824.[8] More typically, gentiles and neophytes fled, returning home or taking refuge in another tribal community. Covert expressions of opposition also spoke eloquently of the desperation of the mission populations. Traditional religious ceremonies and rituals performed out of the sight of the friars offered some comfort to those who could still recall the old ways. Others took more drastic steps. Native women raped or forced into concubinage by Spanish men deliberately terminated their pregnancies and practiced infanticide. Clearly, Indians struggling to survive under this system made hard, sometimes terrible, choices.

At the northernmost reaches of Spanish control, the arrival of the Russians in the first decades of the nineteenth century added a new element to this colonial environment. The Russian-American Fur Company, following the seal and sea otter populations southward from Alaska, made contact with California Indians in the late eighteenth century. By 1809, a more formal relationship among the Russians, their Aleut hunting partners, and the Natives living north of San Francisco had developed. Resources in the area were sufficiently attractive that the Russians decided to establish a permanent outpost and built Fort Rus (Fort Ross) above Bodega Bay in 1812. Relations between the Russians and the Kashaya Pomo, the local Native population, were fraught with tension. Though the Russians did not intend to create a permanent colonial settlement, their coercive labor practices and mistreatment of the Indians ultimately led to hostilities. Russian managers and their Aleut hunting cadres lived on the coast for nearly three decades, hunting and trying to grow food to feed those in the Russian settlements in Alaska. By 1841, over-hunting of seals and sea otters, and increasingly hostile relations with the Pomo, made their venture economically unsound. The Russians left Fort Ross that year, ending their relatively brief presence in California.

Political changes in the early nineteenth century also brought about the denouement of Spanish control over California. In 1821, Mexico won its independence from Spain. The new nation, in turn, claimed California as a territory rich in both human and natural resources. The Mexican era lasted less than three decades but proved equally as perilous for the Indians as the Spanish period had been. Mexico's decisions to secularize the missions, establish large land-grant ranchos, and engage in brutal military campaigns in the interior valleys took a terrible toll on the approximately 200,000 Indians who survived the Spanish era.

For California Natives, emancipation from wardship status in the 1820s and secularization in the 1830s ushered in a period of incredible change. With secularization, Mexican authorities planned to distribute mission land holdings and properties to the resident Indians, as well as to the *gente de razón*, the Hispanized territorial population. What may have begun in 1834 as an attempt to ensure that the "missionized" Indians had some means for economic support and social identity soon failed miserably. The *gente de razón,* not the Indians, benefited from secularization. By the early 1840s, many of the Natives were landless vagrants with neither village nor mission to call home.

To escape this fate, Indians sometimes wound up working on the large land-grant ranches and farms spreading throughout the coastal and central valley regions. Between 1834 and 1846, more than seven hundred private land grants totaling some 8 million acres of land had been made to both Mexican land holders like Mariano Vallejo and foreign immigrants such as the Swiss-born John Sutter.[9] Indians formed the workforce for these enormous agricultural enterprises that transplanted the *hacienda-peon* (plantation) system, much to the benefit of the landholders. As *vaqueros* (cowboys), as household servants, and as day laborers, California Natives made possible the economic success of these farms and ranches. Their labor was so important to the territorial economy that raids on interior Indian communities, undertaken to kidnap more workers, became commonplace during the Mexican era. Vallejo and Sutter both adopted this policy to ensure an adequate workforce.

With the dissolution of the missions and the peon labor system the only alternative available to many Indians, some of the former neophytes and gentiles fled inland to Native communities (relatively) unmolested by the Spanish or the Mexicans. Sometimes, bands of these interior Indians led raids of their own against Hispanic towns and ranches. Horse stealing became an economic alternative for Indians pushed off the former mission lands.[10] The Mexicans became increasingly frustrated by the attacks along the eastern boundary of the narrow corridor of "civilization," and they retaliated with indiscriminate raids of their own against tribal communities.

As the California Indians chafed under Mexican governance, so did the Mexican territorial authorities have to cope with an increasing, and increasingly troublesome, Anglo population of Alta California. Throughout the 1840s, American settlers accomplished what neither the Spanish nor the Mexicans had ever been able to do: effectively colonize California. Their fractious presence soon led to the Bear Flag Revolt. In 1846, a rebellion erupted as Americans aided by John C. Frémont seized control over Alta California and declared the existence of the Republic of California. Fortunately for the filibusterers, their actions in California coincided with the official start of the American war with Mexico. Within two years, the United States took possession of California under the Treaty of Guadalupe-Hidalgo.

The resolution of the war with Mexico in favor of the United States meant that California Indians would encounter yet another colonizing power. But the transition from Mexican to American political domination paled in comparison to the remarkable transformation prompted by a handful of gold-bearing gravel pulled out of the American River. Whatever cultural disintegration, economic exploitation, and territorial dispossession the California Indians had experienced up until 1848 would seem almost trivial during the next two decades. For them, the Gold Rush and its immediate aftermath was a time of utter catastrophe.

The discovery of gold at Coloma in 1848 set in motion an international race by the so-called Argonauts to reach California and exploit the available mineral resources. Before the Gold Rush, ten times more Indians than non-Natives lived in California. By the early 1850s, there were twice as many Anglos as Indians, and the Native population was rapidly declining. Thousands of fortune hunters, each more eager for riches than the last, inundated the Indians living in southern and central mining districts of the western Sierra Nevada and the northwestern district in the Trinity-Siskiyou-Klamath region. These newcomers quickly came to regard the indigenous populations they encountered as obstacles, little different from or better than animals. Even those Indians who did participate in the "diggings" were suspect, because most did so as hired laborers, not as independent workers. There was no room left for the California Indians in this highly individualized, highly competitive, and highly violent environment.[11]

California Indians witnessed conditions deteriorate abysmally over the first twenty years of statehood. The Native population collapsed, declining from approximately 150,000 persons in 1848 to fewer than 30,000 by 1860. Malaria, cholera, and a host of other epidemic diseases played a substantial role in this demographic crash. But two other factors likely had an equivalent influence. The first was starvation. Just as Lucy Young's grandfather had predicted, the White Rabbit took everything. As the gold seekers moved into the Sierra Nevada and the northwestern mountains, they set in motion a process of environmental degradation that even today can scarcely be imagined. Hunting, gathering, fishing, and cultivating systems disintegrated as the outsiders destroyed the natural world of the California Indians.

The kind of destructive violence visited on the landscape in pursuit of gold, blasting and hydraulic operations that broke apart and washed away entire mountains and effected near total deforestation throughout the mining districts, presaged the outright brutality directed against the Indian peoples of the land. What Young's grandfather did not foresee was the horrifying carnage that the gold miners set in motion and the settlers of the latter nineteenth century continued. Violence against Indians erupted early on and stayed a near constant of life in California in its first two decades of statehood. From the infamous massacre of the Clear Lake Pomo in 1850, to the 1863 Chico to Round Valley "Trail of Tears," to the Modoc War in early 1870s, Indians were forcibly evicted from their lands and, in the process, often killed by miners and settlers. "Indian hunting" became an officially sanctioned activity throughout much of California. Newspaper editorials called for the wholesale extermination of the surviving Native population and called on local citizens to do the dirty work. Both the state and the federal governments paid bounties to volunteers engaged in what today we would term "ethnic cleansing."[12]

For the Indians, the Americanization of California during the Gold Rush meant the revocation of their human rights. In 1850, the California legislature passed an act designed to "protect and govern" Indians that severely limited their legal rights and eroded traditional life ways. The act deprived them of clear title to the land. It further denied them legal recourse by preemptively negating their testimony in cases against whites. It criminalized certain traditional subsistence strategies; the use of fire to regenerate grasslands, for example, suddenly was redefined as arson. Finally, and most shockingly, the 1850 legislation created a system of indentured servitude for Indian men, women, and children that was legalized slavery in all but name.[13] The practice of indenturing abandoned Native minors, whose parents often had been murdered to create their orphanage, remained a part of California law until the passage of the Fourteenth Amendment in 1868.[14] "Protection" and "governance," it seemed, could cloak a multitude of sins.

The United States government intervened on behalf of the Indians in this violent chaos in the early 1850s. Between 1851 and 1852, federal representatives negotiated eighteen treaties with Native nations throughout the state. The tribes agreed to surrender their remaining homelands in exchange for secure reservations totaling some 7.5 million acres of land on which, they were assured, they could live unmolested by Americans. Specially appointed federal Indian commissioners would administer to these reservations scattered throughout the state. Congress, however, bowed to the objections of California's state legislature and its congressional delegation in 1852 when they howled over the "unreasonable" generosity shown Indians in the land apportionment. The federal government refused to ratify the agreements and filed the treaties away under an injunction of secrecy that remained in effect until 1905.[15] By the time the United States government revisited the issue of California Indian land policy again in the late 1850s, it was too late to protect tribal landholdings.

Thus, a national government unwilling to grant the Indians any genuine measure of protection through territorial allocations left them at the mercy of an overtly hostile state government and a dangerously violent state population. That any of the Indians of California were able to survive this terrible era is testimony to their remarkable courage, tenacity, and adaptability as individuals and communities. That they sustained themselves and their communities at all during the subsequent decades seems almost miraculous in retrospect. Despite the near-total destruction of land bases, cultures, families, economic systems, and human rights, individuals and communities somehow hung on. Scattered throughout California, Indians were hidden in plain sight from a state and national citizenry that was quick to forget the atrocities visited on Natives during the Gold Rush.

The dismal state of most California tribes remained an open secret from the 1860s until well into the twentieth century. In the late nineteenth century, the saga of the "Mission Indians" became well known when activist Helen Hunt Jackson publicized their plight. These landless descendants of emancipated mission populations, who were scattered throughout southern California, were romanticized in Jackson's 1884 novel, *Ramona*. Responding to Jackson's persistent lobbying efforts, the federal government established a group of small reservations for the displaced mission bands of Indians. Unfortunately, the lands allocated thusly were quite isolated and mostly arid. Thirty years later, it was the tale of Ishi that riveted public attention to the plight of California's forgotten Native peoples. Ishi, the Yahi/Yana man reputed to be the "last wild Indian in America," emerged from the "wilderness" of northern California in 1911. Taken to San Francisco by anthropologist Alfred Kroeber, and ensconced at the University of California Museum of Anthropology as a living history exhibit, Ishi acclimated enough to help scholars study the "vanishing Indians" of the state. His death from tuberculosis in 1916 seemed a fitting conclusion to the story of California's once numerous Indians.[16]

Looking beyond the Mission Indians and Ishi, however, reveals that the end of the nineteenth century and the early decades of the twentieth century were years of struggle and endurance for California Indians. The remnant Native groups fortunate enough to receive the small reservations and tiny rancherias the federal government established in the 1890s found themselves relegated to substandard lands poorly suited to agriculture.[17] But even these marginal lands were vulnerable to squatting by Americans who contested Indian land rights. With implementation of the U.S. government's policy of allotment following the passage of the Dawes Act in 1887, tribal properties were diminished even further. Advocates of Indian assimilation regarded allotment as the "anvil" on which the remaining vestiges of tribalism would be smashed. The Dawes Act sought to Americanize Indians by forcing them to accept private land ownership, thereby breaking up the reservations into small, family-owned units. Robert Spott, a Yurok tribal leader, spoke for many of the state's Indians when he explained to members of San Francisco's Commonwealth Club in 1923 how allotment had beggared his people. "You know very well," he told them, "that we cannot live on that little land [his father's allotment was 10 acres] that we have got."[18] Land policies implemented in the decades after the Gold Rush had, by the turn of the twentieth century, locked most California Natives into unrelenting poverty and political invisibility.[19]

American assimilation policies had as devastating an impact on the surviving Native cultural communities and institutions as allotment had on tribal economies and land bases. Between the 1890s and the early 1930s, de-Indianization was the government's preferred solution to the "Indian problem." Now, Indian children were required to attend federal boarding and day schools in which they were taught to reject their tribal languages and cultures in favor of "American" ways. In a haunting echo of the Spanish period, missionaries once again repudiated traditional religious systems and encouraged conversion to Christianity. Meanwhile, American bureaucrats preached the gospel of economic advancement, modernization, and consumerism. California Indians, like Native peoples around the nation, were forced to adopt the "white man's way." It is no surprise, then, that traditional cultures withered, languages fell into disuse, and religious ceremonies went underground. And certainly nothing they had experienced over the preceding 150 years would have persuaded California Natives that staying "Indian" was a good idea.

A sea change in federal Indian policies during the 1930s and 1940s made some California Indians optimistic about their future. Commissioner of Indian Affairs John Collier, a member of the Roosevelt administration, developed the "Indian New Deal" as the solution to the problems plaguing American Indians. His program promoted the stabilization of Indian communities throughout California and the nation, by ending the ill-conceived policy of allotment, supporting tribal sovereignty, and encouraging cultural renaissance. However, this brief spark of federal interest in the state's Indian population could not begin to undo decades of neglect. Communities characterized as destitute in 1906 by officials of the Bureau of Indian Affairs (BIA), the federal agency responsible for Indian policy, continued to languish in the mid-1940s and remained problem areas long afterwards. Participation in the military and the civilian workforce during World War II brought some California Indians a measure of social acceptance and economic stability. But in the wake of V-E and V-J Days, Indians once again found themselves marginalized politically and economically.

The postwar era found California Indians, like other American Indians, on the receiving end of policies intended to solve the "Indian problem." Each of these tactics, which so eerily harkened back to the "bad old days" of the Gold Rush era and the late nineteenth century, had a significant impact on California Indian communities. Compensation, termination, and relocation were three new federal initiatives that in many ways resembled the disastrous allotment and Americanization policies of the nineteenth century. Under compensation, American Indians could sue the federal government for treaty violations; if they won, they would be eligible for monetary awards. Termination was defined as a libratory policy because it ended the BIA's paternalistic control over tribal communities. Relocation to urban areas promised Indians the social and economic advantages associated with city life.[20] Working together, these three policies seemed to offer American Indians a new measure of freedom and autonomy.

The reality, especially for California Indians, was quite different. The efforts of the Indian Claims Commission to adjudicate compensation claims in California were complicated by the unratified treaties of the 1850s as well as by the great number of different tribal groups seeking justice. A 1944 U.S. Court of Claims case, K-344, had found the federal government liable for monetary compensation for the eighteen treaty reservations that had never been created.[21] But the Indian Claims Commission took on the cases of tribal communities suing for compensation for the other 91 million acres of land lost during the nineteenth century. After twenty-six years of litigation, some 75,000 enrolled California Indians each received $668.51. Thus, the total compensation received by California Indians for the loss of their homelands and all the resources contained therein, $46 million, or less that 50 cents an acre, was roughly equivalent to the value of the gold mined in California during the year 1859 *alone*.[22]

The compensation plan's utter failure to provide adequate remuneration to California Indians for the loss of their homelands was followed by the fiasco of termination. This federal plan to "emancipate" Indians became, in California, a land grab from some of the smallest and least powerful tribal communities. The California Rancheria Act, passed in 1958, resulted in the termination of thirty-six rancherias and the loss of 5,000 acres of Native lands. Public Law (PL) 280, passed in 1953 to give states civil and criminal jurisdiction over "terminated" Indians, was manipulated by state and local welfare agencies to deny Indians benefits because of their change in status. Just as in the Gold Rush, federal policies facilitated both the loss of tribal property and the discriminatory treatment of California Indians.

Relocation, the third component in the twentieth-century push for assimilation, also worked against the best interests of the Indians of California. The BIA relocated thousands of American Indians from reservation communities around the country during the 1950s and 1960s. More than half of this number, 60,000 to 70,000, wound up in California's major urban areas. Many Native Californians were quite uneasy with this sudden influx of Indians from other parts of the United States. The relocatees seemed to threaten what little identity the state's primary Indian population had been able to preserve. Moreover, the emphasis on relocation meant that those California Indians who remained in the unterminated rancherias and reservations received less attention and funds from the BIA.

By the 1960s, then, the Natives of California had experienced another round of federal and state policymaking seemingly designed to ensure their demise as distinct cultural and political entities. Just as a century earlier, the economic impact of these federal policies reverberated within the tribal communities throughout the state. The California State Advisory Committee on Indian Affairs reported in 1966 that the average life expectancy for Indians was 42 years, compared to 62 years for the general population. Infant mortality among California Indians was 70 percent higher than among the general population. On California reservations, somewhere between 38 percent and 42 percent of the homes took water from contaminated sources. Overall, the state reported in 1966 that the median annual income for reservation families was $2,268, a fraction of the income earned by other Californians.[23] A few years later, the California Department of Housing and Community Development called for the BIA to redress past wrongs inflicted on California Indians by offering them federal recognition as sovereign nations, designated land bases, improved educational opportunities, better health care, and greater support for tribal economic development.

Like other American Indians across the country, some California Indians chose activism as a means of dealing with the pervasive sense of marginalization they experienced at the hands of state and federal policy makers. The 1960s and 1970s witnessed a string of dramatic events: the tense occupation of Alcatraz Island in San Francisco harbor by the activist group Indians of All Tribes; the involvement of California Indians in the American Indian Movement's protest activities; the development of American Indian/Native American studies programs at the University of California at Berkeley and San Francisco State College; the establishment of an Indian-centered institution of higher learning, Deganawida-Queztalcoatl (D-Q) University near Sacramento; the Pomo Indian occupation of an island in Clear Lake, California, as well as a surplus U.S. Army base in Middletown, California; and the Pit River tribe's claim over lands held by the Pacific Gas and Electric Company in Lassen National Forest and their subsequent occupation of another site near Burney, California. Newly organized advocacy groups like the American Indian Historical Society, the California Indian Education Association, and the California Indian Rural Health Board all sought to address the most pressing problems facing California Indians.[24]

Given their persistent poverty throughout the twentieth century, it is hardly surprising that many California tribal communities defined economic development as the key to their escape from this marginalized status. And, beginning in the mid-1960s, the chances to do so began to proliferate. President Lyndon Johnson reversed historic federal policy trends in 1968 when he told tribes that the time had come to end paternalism and promote "partnership and self-help."[25] His successor in the White House, Richard Nixon, followed suit and promoted "self-determination," a far-reaching plan intended to empower tribes. The president and his commissioner of Indian affairs, Louis Bruce, sought particularly to assist tribes with the creation of local business opportunities. Congress supported this concept by passing the Indian Financing Act (1974) and the Native American Programs Act (1974). Both pieces of legislation channeled funds into the hands of Native entrepreneurs and tribal governments.

For many Indian nations across the United States, the era of self-determination and the passage of the Indian Financing and Native American Programs Acts marked the starting point for a new future. Now, the Cabazon Band of Mission Indians, one of the southern California groups that Helen Hunt Jackson had championed in the 1880s, explored several different business enterprises. The tribe was somewhat successful at growing and marketing sesame and jojoba in the late 1970s. And customers flocked to the tribe's "smoke shop," where they could avoid paying certain state and federal taxes on tobacco products purchased on sovereign Indian land. Neither venture, however, promised to make enough money to substantially improve tribal living conditions. Then, in the early 1980s, the Cabazon joined several other tribal communities around the country in considering the operation of bingo halls as a revenue-generating venue. Along with the Seminole of Florida, the Pequots of Connecticut, and the Stockbridge-Munsee in Wisconsin, the Cabazon Band recognized that operating gaming concerns could draw numerous customers and generate substantial income for reservations with limited resources.[26] Meanwhile, the Indian Financing and Native American Programs Acts offered loans to tribal communities to fund construction costs for gaming centers. Persuaded that they finally had hit upon a real solution to undoing Indian poverty, the Cabazon opened their own bingo "palace" near Indio, California, in 1982.[27]

The phenomenal success of the early Indian-run bingo halls led quickly to battles among the tribes, the states, and the federal government over the control of this new and extraordinarily lucrative business. In the process of adjudicating these disputes, old policies that determined the legal rights of Indian communities relative to state laws surfaced to complicate further an already complicated issue. At the same time, governors and attorneys general across the United States became increasingly concerned that unrestricted gaming on the lands of Indian nations might transform their states into meccas for compulsive gamblers and havens for organized crime groups. This conflict reached its peak in California, where the once destitute Cabazon Band had parlayed its gaming business into a lucrative economic development strategy. The same tribe that had once looked to jojoba cultivation on a dusty reservation of 1,700 acres as the road to financial solvency had begun to realize tremendous profits with its gaming operation. In 1987, the Supreme Court's decision in *State of California* v. *Cabazon Band of Mission Indians* resolved many of the nagging questions regarding the status of Indian gaming.[28] The Cabazon argued that California had no right to interfere in Indian gaming since the state had already legalized other forms of gambling such as a state lottery. In response, the State of California cited regulatory and criminal concerns over the infiltration of organized crime as justification for invoking PL 280 jurisdiction, dating from the 1950s, to shut down the Cabazon gaming operations. The Supreme Court found in favor of the band, effectively ending the initial round of discussion over the legitimacy of Indian gaming.[29]

In 1988, Congress responded to the Court's support for Indian gaming by passing the Indian Gaming Regulatory Act (IGRA).[30] This legislation created a three-tier classification for gaming in Indian country that ranged from traditional social and hand games regulated by the tribe (Class I) to high stakes bingo, card games, pull-tabs, and lottos (Class II) to the most sophisticated high stakes activities including card and casino games as well as slot/electronic gaming machines (Class III). It also established a regulatory commission authorized to assist tribes and states in resolving conflicts created by the spread of Indian gaming.

In the fifteen years since the *Cabazon* case, gaming in Indian country has mushroomed. In California, tribes of all sizes have made gaming their ticket to financial security. In 2001, some forty-five Indian reservations and rancherias had some form of gaming open to the public.[31] The results of this activity have been astounding. Life has improved dramatically in most of the communities in which gaming is now a centerpiece of economic development. At the Barona reservation east of La Jolla, the "Big Top," one of the largest Indian casinos, has driven down unemployment dramatically among tribal members. Tribal children now have access to high-tech educational tools in grades K-12 and can obtain financial aid for higher education by maintaining a minimum GPA.[32] The San Manuel Serrano Indians, living outside San Bernardino, used casino profits to build a new water supply system for the community and improve tribal housing.[33] Unemployment at the Santa Rosa Rancheria in northern California has dropped from 85 percent to 25 percent and tribal members now live in block homes and mobile units, all thanks to gaming profits.[34] In Redding, Lucy Young's grandfather might well applaud the way the Redding Rancheria of Wintu, Pit River, and Yana Indians have used the profits from the Win-River Casino to finance the expansion of two health care clinics, move tribal members off the welfare rolls, and offer any student who wishes to attend college a complete scholarship.[35]

The proceeds of Indian gaming have also found their way outside the reservations and rancherias into non-Native charities and projects. The Sycuan Kumeyaay community, located east of San Diego, donated $200,000 to support the San Diego Symphony Orchestra in the mid-1990s and provides much needed fire, paramedic, and emergency services to communities outside the reservation.[36] Win-River Casino's support of charities throughout Shasta County resulted in the Redding Rancheria receiving a countywide award in 1997 for the most outstanding philanthropic work.[37]

The Barona casino donated more than $2 million to local community and charitable organizations in San Diego County between 1994 and 1998.[38] The Rumsey Rancheria took over the financing of a California Department of Forestry fire station closed by the state during a budget shortfall during the 1990s. By sharing funds with local governments and other non-Native organizations located near their gaming sites, the California tribes are developing strong community partnerships and building more positive images of themselves as contemporary Indians and good neighbors. Sharing the proceeds of gaming brings positive visibility to Indians living in a state where some still use the epithet "Digger" to describe the state's Indian peoples.

Indian gaming money in California has also found its way into politics. In the 1990s tribal communities contributed to the campaign coffers of local- and state-level candidates in order to offset the opposition to gaming from the highest levels of state government. Former governor Pete Wilson and his attorney general Dan Lungren were adamant opponents to Indian casinos achieving Class III status, by far the most lucrative license but also, in their view, the most problematic. Under existing IGRA regulations, Class III status required that Indian tribes and the various states develop compacts defining the so-called scope of gaming. Both the governor and the attorney general maintained throughout the 1990s that those tribes operating any video machines in their casinos or running any house-banked card games were acting illegally. Consequently, the state refused to negotiate the compacts required under the terms of IGRA for tribes to obtain Class III status.[39] As a result, California gaming tribes were held in a kind of legal limbo for much of the decade as litigation proceeded over the issue.[40] In cases such as *Cabazon Band of Mission Indians* v. *National Indian Gaming Commission, Sycuan Band of Mission Indians* v. *Roache,* and *Rumsey Indian Rancheria of Wintun Indians* v. *Wilson,* the state and the tribes battled out the boundaries of tribal sovereignty and state's rights.

Given the state government's intransigence, the California tribes took their fight for legalized gaming to the voters. Proposition 5, the Tribal Government Gaming and Economic Self-Sufficiency Act, was put on the ballot in the November 1998 general election after a costly and controversial petition drive. The battle over Proposition 5 pitted gaming tribes against non-gaming tribes, California gaming interests against Nevada gaming interests, and citizens against their state leaders. The pro-gaming tribes and the anti-gaming opposition spent a combined total of $91.3 million in lobbying and ads on the initiative, which ultimately passed with 63 percent of the vote during the 1998 election.[41] But in August 1999 the California Supreme Court judged the initiative unconstitutional, forcing tribes back into the legislative process. In March 2000, 64.6 percent of the voters in the state passed Proposition 1A, a similar piece of legislation that allowed the governor to negotiate compacts with federally recognized tribes wanting to operate Class III gaming activities.

For many California Indians, the state government's reluctance to support tribal gaming ventures until voters forced the issue suggested something far more ominous than the publicly stated concerns over the rise of gambling addiction: reservations and rancherias with gaming, roughly half of the state's federally recognized Indian groups, as well as those without gambling enterprises feared that state opposition would erode tribal sovereignty. While, as one tribal attorney noted, "the money is in the machines," there is far more than dollars at stake.[42] As Ken Ramirez from the San Manuel Band of Mission Indians noted, "as long as Indians were dirt poor they [state and federal officials] were willing to grant their sovereign rights. So soon as they improved their lot through Indian gaming, all bets were off."[43] Many Native leaders believed that the hostility between the gaming tribes and the State of California was the direct product of historic conflict over sovereignty. Now they welcomed the chance to defend their communities. Viejas Kumeyaay Band chief Anthony Pico spoke of this during the late 1990s, asserting

> this is the greatest time in the lives of Native Americans. . . . To have the privilege to fight like my ancestors did—for equality, not just for survival. . . . Its [sic] one thing to fight when you have two or three bullets in your rifle. . . . It's another to fight with a stockpile of ammo. . . . We're learning about lobbying, public speaking and laws that affect us, and we're battling for property rights and local control (of gaming).[44]

Ken Ramirez, Anthony Pico, and other California Indian leaders regarded the confrontations over Class III gaming with the state and the federal government in the 1990s as more than mere struggles over money. For them, these events have suggested in ways impossible to ignore that California Indians still must fight to assert their sovereign rights in a state, and a nation, historically antagonistic to their existence. The visibility and the power that have accrued to tribes along with gaming revenues are transforming the political, economic, and social landscape of Indian country. As they do so, California Indians are actively developing and managing their own Gold Rush.

Notes

1   See Malcolm Margolin, ed., *The Way We Lived: California Indian Reminiscences, Stories, and Songs* (Berkeley, CA: Heyday Press, 1981) for a selection of traditional origin histories.

2   See Lowell J. Bean, "Indians of California: Diverse and Complex Peoples," *California History* LXXI, 3 (Fall, 1992): 302–323 and Michael J. Moratto, "Linguistic Prehistory of California," reprinted in Lowell, John Bean and Sylvia Brakke Vane, eds., *Ethnology of Alta California Indians I: Precontact* (New York: Garland Publishing, 1991), p. 61–107.

3   The classic discussion of California demography is Sherburne F. Cook, *The Population of California Indians, 1769–1970* (Berkeley: University of California Press, 1976).

4   See Ralph L. Beals and Joseph A. Hester, Jr., "A New Ecological Typology of the California Indians," Lowell J. Bean and Harry Lawton, "Some Explanations for the Rise of Cultural Complexity in Native California with Comments on Proto-Agriculture and Agriculture," and Sean L. Swezey and Robert F. Heizer, "Ritual Management of Salmonid Fish Resources in California" in Lowell John Bean and Sylvia Brakke Vane, eds., *Ethnology of Alta California Indians I: Precontact* (New York: Garland Publishing, 1991); T. C. Blackburn and M. Kat Anderson, eds., *Before the Wilderness: Environmental Management by Native Californians* (Menlo Park, CA: Ballena Press, 1993); and M. Kat Anderson, Michael G. Barbour, and Valerie Whitworth, "A World of Balance and Plenty: Land, Plants, Animals, and Humans in Pre-European California," in Ramon Gutiérrez and Richard Orsi, eds., *Contested Eden: California Before the Gold Rush* (Berkeley: University of California Press, 1998).

5   Among the most important scholarship on the early settlement, mission, and Mexican periods are the following works: Lowell Bean, *Native Californians: A Theoretical Perspective* (Socorro, NM: Ballena Press, 1976); Rupert F. Costo, *The Missions of California: A Legacy of Genocide* (San Francisco: The Indian Historian Press, 1987); Constance DuBois, *The Condition of the Mission Indians of Southern California* (Philadelphia: Indian Rights Association, 1901); Robert F. Heizer, *The Other Californians: Prejudice and Discrimination under Spain, Mexico, and the United States to 1920* (Berkeley: University of California Press, 1970); and Robert H. Jackson and Edward Castillo, *Indians, Franciscans, and Spanish Colonization: The Impact of the Missions on Californians Indians* (Albuquerque: University of New Mexico Press, 1995).

6   Lucy Young, "White Rabbit Got Lotsa Everything," in Peter Nabokov, ed., *Native American Testimony*, 2nd edition. (New York: Penguin Books, 1999), p. 7–10.

7   For an excellent case study discussion of this kind of economic exploitation, see George Harwood Phillips, "Indians in Los Angeles, 1781–1875: Economic Integration, Social Disintegration," *Pacific Historical Review* (1980): 427–451.

8   See especially Albert Hurtado, "Sexuality in California's Franciscan Missions: Cultural Perceptions and Sad Realities," *California History* LXXI, 3 (Fall, 1992): 370–385, Jackson and Castillo, *Indians, Franciscans, and Spanish Colonization*, George Harwood Phillips, *Indians and Intruders in Central California, 1769–1849* (Norman: University of Oklahoma Press, 1993), and James J. Rawls, "The California Missions: Symbol and Myth," *California History* LXXI, 3 (Fall, 1992): 342–361.

9   See Richard B. Rice, William A. Bullough, and Richard J. Orsi, *The Elusive Eden* (New York: Alfred A. Knopf, 1988), p. 126–127.

10 See Phillips, *Indians and Intruders in Central California, 1769–1849*, p. 94–106 and Albert Hurtado, *Indian Survival on the California Frontier* (New Haven: Yale University Press, 1988), p. 32–54, for discussions of this raiding economy and resistance strategy that the ex–neophytes and gentiles used.

11 The scholarship on the fate of California Indians during the Gold Rush era is substantial. See especially the following sources: Robert F. Heizer, ed., *The Destruction of the California Indians* (Lincoln: University of Nebraska Press, 1993) and *They Were Only Diggers: A Collection of Articles from California Newspapers, 1751–1866, on California Indian and White Relations* (Socorro, NM: Ballena Press, 1974); Jack D. Forbes, *Native Americans of California and Nevada* (Healdsburg, CA: Naturegraph Publications, 1969); James Rawls, *Indians of California: The Changing Image* (Lincoln: University of Nebraska Press, 1984); and Hurtado, *Indian Survival on the California Frontier*. See also Robert F. Heizer, ed., *Handbook of North American Indians, California*, Vol. 8 (Washington, DC: Smithsonian Institution, 1978) for an encyclopedic discussion of the experiences of each tribe.

12 See Edward D. Castillo, "The Impact of Euro-American Exploration and Settlement," in Heizer, ed., *Handbook of North American Indians, California*, p. 99–127.

13 See Robert F. Heizer, "Indian Servitude in California," in Wilcomb E. Washburn, ed., *Handbook of North American Indians, History of Indian-White Relations*, Vol. 4 (Washington, DC: Smithsonian Institution, 1988), p. 414–416.

14 Castillo, "The Impact of Euro-American Exploration and Settlement," in Heizer, ed., p. 108–109.

15 Robert F. Heizer, "Treaties," in Heizer, ed., p. 701–704.

16 For information on the Mission Indians and Helen Hunt Jackson, see Valerie Sherer Mathes, *Helen Hunt Jackson and Her Indian Reform Legacy* (Austin: University of Texas Press, 1990), Florence Connolly Shipek, *Pushed into the Rocks: Southern California Indian Land Tenure, 1769–1986* (Lincoln: University of Nebraska Press, 1987). The classic account of Ishi is Theodora Kroeber's *Ishi in Two Worlds: A Biography of the Last Wild Indian in North America* (Berkeley: University of California Press, 1961).

17 Castillo, "The Impact of Euro-American Exploration and Settlement," in Heizer, ed., p. 117.

18 Robert Spott, "Neglect Along the Klamath," in Nabokov, ed., *Native American Testimony*, p. 313–315.

19 "Report of the California Indian Task Force, 1984" quoted in Carole Goldberg-Ambrose, J. D., and Duane Champagne, Ph.D. et. al., "A Second Century of Dishonor: Federal Inequities and California Indian Tribes" (Los Angeles: University of California, Los Angeles, American Indian Studies Center, 1996), Chapters 1 and 2. This document is available for downloading from the following World Wide Web site: <http://www.sscnet.ucla.edu/indian/ca/Tribes1.html>.

20 The classic case study on termination and relocation is Donald Fixico's *Termination and Relocation: Federal Indian Policy, 1945–1960* (Albuquerque: University of New Mexico Press, 1986). For an extended discussion of the impact of urbanization on American Indians, see Joan Weibel-Orlando, *Indian Country, L. A.: Maintaining Ethnic Community in Complex Society*, rev. ed. (Urbana: University of Illinois Press, 1999).

21 K344, as it is often referred to, awarded a defined group of California Indians the sum of $17,053, 941.98 for the 18 reservations. The United States then subtracted from the judgment the sum of $12,029,099.64, the amount supposedly spent by the BIA on California Indians for their subsistence. California Indians included in the suit ultimately received $150 per person as compensation for the 7.5 million acres of land supposedly guaranteed them in the reservations. K344 did not, it is worth noting, adjudicate claims for the rest of the lands lost during the Gold Rush. See Kenneth M. Johnson, *K-344, or the Indians of California vs. The United States* (Los Angeles: Dawson's Book Shop, 1966) for a full discussion of this case.

22 See Rice, Burrough, and Orsi, *The Elusive Eden*, p. 185. The total dollar amount of gold taken in California in 1859 was $45,846,599.

23 "Progress Report to the Governor and Legislature on Indians in Rural and Reservation Areas," California State Advisory Commission on Indian Affairs, Sacramento: Office of State Printing, 1966, p. 32–40.

24 For information on these events and groups, see: Stephen Cornell, *The Return of the Native: American Indian Political Resurgence* (New York: Oxford University Press, 1988); Troy R. Johnson, *The Occupation of Alcatraz Island* (Urbana: University of Illinois Press, 1996); and Edward Castillo, "Twentieth-Century Secular Movements," in Heizer, ed., p. 713–718.

25 Lyndon Johnson, "The Forgotten American," quoted in James J. Rawls, *Chief Red Fox is Dead: A History of Native Americans since 1945* (New York: Harcourt Brace College Publishers, 1996), p. 60–61.

26 U. S., Supreme Court, *State of California, et. al., Appellants* v. *Cabazon Band of Mission Indians, et. al., Appellees,* No. 85–1708, Motion for leave to file brief amici curiae and brief amici curiae of the Pueblo of Sandia, the Pueblo of Acoma, the Pueblo of Tesuque, and the Pueblo of San Juan in support of the position of the appellees, September 24, 1986.

27 For a detailed discussion of the Cabazon story, see Ambrose I. Lane, Sr., *Return of the Buffalo: The Story behind American's Indian Gaming Explosion* (Westport, CT: Bergin & Garvey, 1995).

28 The first major decision regarding Indian gaming was *Seminole Tribe of Florida* v. *Butterworth* 658 F. 2nd 310, 311 (5th Cir. Unit B 1981). In this, the State of Florida argued that it could intervene in Indian gaming under the auspices of PL 280. The federal court held that the state could not control tribal gaming because elsewhere in the state, non Indian gaming operations were regulated but not prohibited. The "regulation v. prohibition" argument has been the subject of hundreds of law review articles. See William E. Horowitz, "The Scope of Gaming Under the Indian Gaming Regulatory Act of 1988 after *Rumsey* v. *Wilson*: White Buffalo or Brown Cow?" 14 *Yeshiva University Cardozo Arts & Entertainment Law Journal* 153 (1996) and N. Bruce Duthu, "Crow Dog and Oliphant Fistfight at the Tribal Casino: Political Power, Storytelling, and Games of Chance" 29 *Arizona State Law Journal* 171 (1997) for discussions

of the decision in *Bryan* v. *Itasca County* (423 U.S. 373, 1976) and its relationship to this debate.

29 *State of California et. al. v. Cabazon Band of Mission Indians et. al.,* 480 U.S. 202, 107 S. Ct. 1083, 94 L. Ed. 2nd 244, 1987.

30 The Indian Gaming Regulatory Act took as its centerpiece the concept expressed in the *Cabazon* decision that "Indian tribes have the exclusive right to regulate gaming within a State which does not, as a matter of criminal law and public policy, prohibit such gaming activity on Indian lands if the gaming activity is not specifically prohibited by Federal law and is conducted within a State which does not, as a matter of criminal law and public policy, prohibit such gaming activity."

31 At present, there are 102 federally recognized Indian tribes in the state of California. Gaming under IGRA may only be conducted on lands held by those tribes. Information on all aspects of California Indian gaming can be found at the web site of the California Nations Indian Gaming Association, http://www.cniga.com.html.

32 "The Impact of Gaming," taken from the Barona Indian Reservation World Wide Web site: <http://www.barona.com.html>.

33 Joseph G. Jorgensen, "Gaming and Recent American Indian Economic Development," *American Indian Culture and Research Journal* 22, 3 (1998): 164.

34 "The Santa Rosa Rancheria," taken from the Santa Rosa Rancheria World Wide Web site: <http://www.tachi-yokut.com.html>.

35 Interview with Steven Hayward, Marketing Director, Win-River Casino, July 19, 1998.

36 Max Vanzi, "Tribes' Political, Charitable Causes Get Casino Funds," *Los Angeles Times,* May 6, 1996, A3.

37 Interview with Steven Hayward, July 19, 1998.

38 "Barona: Sharing with the Community" taken from the Barona Indian Reservation World Wide Web site: <http://www.barona.com.html>.

39 Those states wishing to stall the Class III compact negotiation process received a tremendous boost in 1996 when the U. S. Supreme Court, in *Seminole* v. *Florida,* held that states could protect themselves from suits by Indian tribes under the 11th Amendment "sovereign immunity" doctrine.

40 See Horowitz, "The Scope of Gaming Under the Indian Gaming Regulatory Act of 1988 after *Rumsey* v. *Wilson:* White Buffalo or Brown Cow?"

41 Lynda Gledhill, "Davis, Lawmakers Move to Save Indian Gaming," *San Francisco Chronicle,* August 25, 1999, A21.

42 Susan Reed, "Officials Threaten to Shut Down Indian Casinos," downloaded from the World Wide Web site: <http://www.cnn.com/US/9704/24/indian.protest/index.html>.

43 Ken Ramirez, "A Letter on Sovereignty," downloaded from the World Wide Web site: <http://www.sanmanuel.com/Kramiez2.html>.

44 Stephen Magagini, "Indians Find New 'Buffalo' in Casinos," *Sacramento Bee,* December 2, 1997, B 12–13.

CHAPTER TWO

Wagon Wheels West: Trailblazers and Settlers in Mexican California

Ronald C. Woolsey

In the twenty-five years before the war with Mexico, the patterns of overland migration to California gradually evolved in purpose and scope. During the 1820s and 1830s, the possibility of new hunting grounds lured trappers and traders to the Far West. What they found was a sprawling landscape of deserts, mountains, and valleys, sparsely populated and teeming with wildlife. By the 1840s, what began as a trickle of interlopers had increased to a steady stream of settlers—persons interested in making a fresh start in a new Eden. Land and settlement had replaced the transient goal of trade and exploration. During these years, some would perish in their attempt to reach California, but those who endured consituted the first wave of American settlement. In a few years hence, these Californians would become embroiled in a larger conflict with Mexico, which, in a more profound way, best characterizes the larger pattern of the westward movement.[1]

During the 1820s, Americans were on the move west toward the Great (Continental) Divide and beyond, committed to a belief in the nation's "manifest destiny," the popular notion that the American people were destined, even ordained by God, to spread across the continent "from sea to shining sea." The possibility of continental expansion was first entertained with the exploits of the Lewis and Clark expedition in 1804–1806.[2] Within fifteen years of that monumental trek, sectional issues complicated the simple dream of westward expansion.

In 1819, Congress became embroiled in a bitterly contested argument over whether to admit Missouri into the Union as a free or a slave state. The next year, the debate over the admission of this western state (west, that is, of the Mississippi River) led to the 1820 congressional compromise over the expansion of slavery.[2] Henceforth, the new state of Missouri would become a popular staging area for new arrivals interested in engaging in the river trade along the Missouri and Mississippi Rivers, as well as a point of departure for those interested in migrating to the Far West.[3]

The Padres at San Gabriel Mission greet Jedediah Smith. *Seaver Center for Western History, Los Angeles County Museum*

Indeed, the westward movement gained momentum in the years following the Missouri Compromise. In 1821, Stephen F. Austin led families from the southern United States into the Mexican province of Texas, where they established slaveholding settlements along the Nueces River and the Rio Grande. Meanwhile, hearty trappers and mountain men traversed the rugged Rocky Mountains, probing the vast Northwest and Canada, during the twilight of the once great era of French fur trade. Now, California and the rest of the Far West, a region of vast resources and a possible nexus for economic trade with Mexico and Asia, emerged as a focal point in United States expansion.

Meanwhile, a young trapper named Jedediah Strong Smith had earned a reputation for bravery and leadership during the early 1820s. The Smith family had moved from Pennsylvania to Ohio during Jedediah's teenage years. He spent his formative years working the farm in the backwoods of Richland County, Ohio.[4] In 1822, young Jedediah left home and was recruited at St. Louis by fur traders William Ashley and Andrew Henry for a party headed west for the Rocky Mountains. The twenty-three-year-old Smith learned his craft in the Montana wilderness, courageously fighting hostile Indians and trapping the feared grizzly bear. During this time, Smith and other trappers had gradually entered the Great Salt Lake region from the nearby Rockies. This southwest expansion of trappers and hunters, coupled with rumors of a mythical Buenaventura River cutting through the heart of the continent, spawned further interest in the potential California and far western markets.

By 1826, Jedediah Smith joined a speculative fur-trapping venture, the Rocky Mountain Fur Company. He agreed to lead a seventeen-man expedition to California in order to establish relations with Mexico and search for beaver pelts and new trading outposts. In August, what Smith termed as the "South West Expedition" set out from the Great Salt Lake on the longest and most ambitious overland journey since that undertaken by Lewis and Clark two decades earlier.[5]

The Smith party traveled over rugged Utah mountains, along the east side of the Sevier River, reaching the lower course of the Virgin River. After struggling across the hot Nevada deserts, the expedition arrived at the Colorado River exhausted and short on supplies. They stayed two weeks at a Mojave Indian encampment, where the party exchanged gifts, bought horses, and recruited two Indian guides. On November 10, 1826, the South West Expedition continued across the Mojave Desert over the San Bernardino Mountains (just south of Cajon Pass) by the Mojave Trail. The party then worked their way north past Mud Springs (present-day San Dimas), reaching the San Gabriel mission before the end of the month.[6]

Smith's group encountered the last vestiges of a soon-to-be dismantled mission system. The gracious padres extended their hospitality to Smith's entire party, which had been disheartened and exhausted by the time it straggled into the mission. The sprawl of the mission ranch, which included nearly 1,000 Indians and more than 30,000 head of cattle, impressed Smith. American Indians had been the backbone of the economy. As scholar George Harwood Phillips observed, "since the Indians did most of the menial and skilled labor in California, they were the economic mainstay of the province."[7]

Smith enjoyed the church celebrations and gaiety of the Mexican California lifestyle, but his primary interests remained to find a central river cutting east toward the Great Salt Lake, exploit new hunting grounds, and establish commercial trade. Now he wrote Governor José Mariá Echeandía for permission to travel north to the Bay of San Francisco, hoping to find the fabled Buenaventura River to carry them directly back to the Great Salt Lake.

Governor Echeandía was alarmed to learn of Smith's presence in California, and with good cause. He felt that Smith's men would only cause trouble with local residents by staying in the province. Echeandía considered dumping the problem on higher authorities by sending Smith to Mexico, but he eventually decided against that idea, fearing that detaining Smith could also complicate matters with U.S. authorities. After two months of failed negotiations, which included a trip by Smith to San Diego to plead his case, Governor Echeandía refused permission for Smith to travel farther into the California interior.

A disappointed Jedediah Smith returned to the San Gabriel mission, gathered his men, then departed under the pretext of returning to Utah as

Echeandía had ordered. Smith was not, however, going to accept the Mexican refusal. Once over the San Bernardino Mountains, Smith and his men abruptly turned north, heading through the Tejon Pass and into the southern part of the San Joaquin Valley, trapping beavers as they moved. As they crossed the valley parallel to the Sierra, a heavy late-spring snowstorm prevented them from returning over the mountains, so they made camp on the Stanislaus River in May, 1827.

Their problems now escalated. The Indians located in the interior had long raided the coastal missions, stealing horses and livestock and aiding mission runaways. Rumors increased with the realization that Smith was still in California and living among the gentiles. Now, Franciscan padres falsely accused Smith's party of having caused trouble by encouraging runaway neophytes at the San José mission. In response, Smith wrote a letter to Father Narcíso Duran at San José, explaining that his party was in the region only until the snows melted enough to allow his men to return home over the Sierra range. When a furious Governor Echeandía received word that Smith was still in California, he immediately dispatched soldiers with an ultimatum for Smith to leave the territory or face imprisonment. Yet Smith and two of his men, Silas Gobel and Robert Evans, had already left California, promising the rest of the party to return by autumn with supplies and reinforcements.

On this resupply mission, Smith and his two companions encountered another late-spring snowstorm on May 25 in which they nearly perished. The men were trapped in the blizzard for another two days and, as Smith recalled, "it required an utmost exertion to avoid the fate of the poor animals that lay nearby almost covered with the drifting snow." Historian Thomas R. Tefft observed that "the weary explorers were not marked for destruction yet: the sun broke through on the 27th and they were able to continue up over Ebbetts Pass to become the first Americans to cross the Sierra."[8]

The weary men finally trudged down out of the Sierras, only to spend three weeks crossing the parched and barren Salt Lake Basin. Finally, in early July, 1827, with the help of Snake Indians, the three men reached Bear Lake, which lies within the great bend of Bear River near the Utah-Idaho boundary along the forty-second parallel.[9]

Smith immediately organized an eighteen-member expedition and set out to return to California. In the meantime, recent conflicts between New Mexican trappers and Mojave Indians had turned the latter hostile. Unaware of these developments, an unsuspecting Smith was attacked near the Colorado River, losing ten men along with precious supplies and horses before the startled group could respond with gunfire. When the attackers retreated, Smith and eight survivors escaped into the desert. Traveling at night to avoid the desert sun, they eventually reached the San Gabriel mission. This time, however, they encountered a cool reception by the wary padres, who had been warned by Mexican officials that Smith's presence was illegal and unwelcome.

Over the next few months, Smith and his men were briefly imprisoned at the San José mission by angry padres who believed that Smith's men had indeed instigated neophyte runaways. During one of his infrequent stays in Monterey, a perturbed Governor Echeandía pondered sending the impudent interloper to Mexico City. Fortunately for Smith, he had managed to develop friendships with a few Yankee traders during his two trips to California. British and American sea traders had long traveled the California coast, trading in whale oil, seal and otter furs, and steer hides. Many of these traders had established trading posts and maintained close business ties with the Mexican government.[10] Governor Echeandía, for one, trusted the judgment of the Yankee traders far more than that of an overland interloper such as Smith. In November 1827, the governor decided to free Smith based on a bond made by a Yankee trader, Captain John Rogers Cooper, who vouched for Smith's return to Utah.[11]

Rejoined with his men and this time intent to leave California, Smith reached the Sacramento Valley after having failed to find a pass through the rugged Sierra range. In the spring of 1828, Smith led his men on a northwestern route toward Klamath, hugging the coastline all the way across the Umpqua River and into the Oregon frontier.[12]

Jedediah Smith's expeditions into California were significant for several reasons. His travels opened three important arteries leading into California. Smith's journeys across the Mojave Desert into southern California, eastward over the Sierra to Utah, and north into the Oregon frontier provided future routes for hide-and-tallow traders and gold seekers. In addition, Smith's willingness to flaunt local authority exposed the weakness of Mexican rule. In the eyes of many Americans, California had a virgin countryside with a sparsely populated interior, one largely undefended and awaiting permanent settlement.

Smith was fortunate. He did not experience serious opposition from Mexican officials, and he freely disregarded Governor Echeandía's orders without suffering adverse consequences. Such would not happen again. The next overland party would face far greater Mexican opposition. Governor Echeandía understood the flagrant disregard that Smith had demonstrated toward Mexican rule, and he was determined not to bear such insolence again.

Within months of Smith's Oregon exodus, Sylvester Pattie and his son James Ohio Pattie led an eight-member group into southern California. The Patties were originally from the backcountry of Kentucky, the land of Daniel Boone. During the early 1820s, they were part of a steady migration of traders, trappers, and settlers traveling to Missouri, by this time a growing hub of commercial activity for the Midwest and beyond. From 1824 to 1826, the Patties took part in several expeditions into New Mexico, Arizona, Sonora, and along the Big Horn and Yellowstone Rivers. In their

California Overland Travelers
1820s – 1830s

† Mission
□ Fort
• Town

–·–·– Jedediah Smith
------- Joseph Walker
——— James Ohio Pattie

California Overland Travelers
1830s – 1840s

† Mission
• Town
—·—·— Ewing Young
-------- Bartelson-Bidwell
———— Workman-Rowland

Clear Lake

Trukee Lake

Sacramento

COAST

SIERRA

Sacramento Valley

Stanislaus

Marsh Ranch

Monterey

Salinas

RANGES

San Joaquin Valley

San Joaquin

Mono L.

Yosemite Valley

NEVADA

Owens Lake

Kern

Tejon Pass

San Fernando

Cajon Pass

Los Angeles

San Pedro

Santa Ana

Temecula

Salton Sea

0   50   100
Miles

travels, they trapped on the Gila River, hunted buffalo on the Great Plains, encountered hostile Indians along the New Mexico and Arizona frontier, and visited the Mexican pueblos of Chihuahua, Taos, and Santa Fe. By November 1826, the Patties and a few men crossed the Gila Trail into Arizona and trapped along the Gila and the Colorado. Yuma Indian raids and desertions reduced the party to a few men. Leaving their furs and whatever else behind, the party then made an exhaustive march across the barren Baja desert, eventually reaching a mission in Lower (Baja) California. There, Dominican padres directed the group toward San Diego to meet with Governor Echeandía. As the Patties had no passports, and the governor was still fuming over the most recent intrusion by Jedediah Smith, he was in no mood to show leniency. Immediately, he had the interlopers thrown into prison.

There, in the impersonal confines of an adobe jail, the dispirited group languished for several months. Isolation, fatigue, and poor treatment eventually killed an already weakened Sylvester Pattie. The other captives, except for James Ohio Pattie, were finally released in order to recover the beaver pelts they had left near the Colorado River. They were expected to return with the valuable furs to San Diego. To ensure that they did just that, the governor kept James Pattie in the jail.

The younger Pattie had nothing but contempt for the Mexican authorities, especially in consideration of the conditions surrounding the death of his father. James probably would have languished in prison himself if not for a stroke of good fortune. A smallpox epidemic had spread among the southern California cities of San Diego, Los Angeles, and San Juan Capistrano. According to his own account, Pattie had brought along with him a supply of smallpox vaccine. Now he used the medicine as a bargaining chip to gain his freedom. The Mexican authorities released him from jail and sent him north to inoculate Mexican inhabitants along the coast as far north as San Francisco, including a brief outing to inoculate inhabitants at the Russian outpost at Fort Ross.

At this point, the circumstances of Pattie's release become sketchy. The governor, relieved that a widespread epidemic had been averted but certainly not enamored with having this American interloper in California, agreed to release Pattie and expel him from the territory. Pattie claimed that Echeandía had promised him a gift of land and cattle for his services, a claim which may or may not be true. Perhaps Echeandía never intended to give Pattie a land grant, or maybe Pattie had misinterpreted the governor. It also is possible that the American was denied a rancho grant because of his refusal to convert to Catholicism, a legal requirement for land ownership under Mexican law. In any event, angry at his failure to gain entry into the ranchero elite, a disgruntled James Ohio Pattie returned to Tennessee and published a memoir in 1831, *Personal Narrative of a Voyage to the Pacific and Mexico*, that detailed his exploits in a land of fertile soil and temperate climate. Regardless of whether Echeandía had ever promised Pattie a land grant, the more important point is that the tense relationship between Pattie and Mexican officials presaged future economic and cultural differences between the United States and Mexico.[13]

Like Jedediah Smith, the Patties had opened a new trail into California. The Gila Trail served to connect New Mexico, Arizona, and California. It would prove to be useful as a secondary route for hide-and-tallow traders as well as gold seekers in the decades to follow. Pattie's animated tales also generated public interest in the Far West, fueling the growing belief among Americans that they had a manifest right to further western expansion.

On the heels of the Smith and Pattie groups came a series of important new interlopers. Many of these trailblazers traveled portions of the routes taken earlier by Smith or Pattie. However, they added new twists to overland trails, rediscovered earlier paths taken by Spanish explorers, and, in a few cases, discovered entirely new routes into California.

In 1829, Ewing Young led forty trappers from Taos, New Mexico, into California. Mysterious and elusive, Young is, nevertheless, singularly important to understanding the overland migration during this era. As writer Kenneth L. Holmes observed, Young "is like a drop of mercury on a smooth table top; you put down your finger, and he is gone."[14] Ewing Young's party traveled south of the Grand Canyon, across the Mojave Desert, over the Cajon Pass, and then on to the San Gabriel and San Fernando missions. The group, which included the celebrated scout Kit Carson, then traversed the San Fernando Mountains and threaded the Tejon Pass. Entering the San Joaquin Valley, Young encountered a company of sixty men from the Hudson Bay Company, which had pushed south across the Central Valley. Peter S. Ogden led the Canadian contingent from Vancouver on the Columbia River south into California. The Hudson Bay men had experienced a successful season of trapping, which, in turn, left the Young group with sparse hunting. Now the two groups decided to combine their efforts. Over the next ten days, they traveled north toward the Sacramento Valley. There the parties divided, leaving Ewing Young to return south toward Los Angeles in October 1830. Mexican officials, unable to convince or force Young's contingent to leave the community, helplessly watched as the rowdy men created mayhem and mischief in the pueblo. Soon, however, Young decided to leave the region for better hunting along the Colorado River.[15]

In 1832, Ewing Young left Santa Fe to make a second foray into California. Retracing his earlier route into Los Angeles, he and his men spent the summer hunting sea otter along the coast. In the fall, Young's group traveled into the San Joaquin Valley, reached Sacramento, and made a wide circle that took them near Klamath and looped back toward Los Angeles. Young then headed south past Temecula, over the Colorado River, and into the Gila Valley.[16]

Ewing Young's travels highlighted to both Mexican and U.S. officials the need to secure the commercial and political nexus between Santa Fe and Los Angeles. Young's experiences proved the feasibility of greater trade and travel between New Mexico and California, opening the Mexican southwest to a complex network of commercial exchange. In addition, the fact that Young had run into agents of the Hudson Bay Company signaled to Americans the urgency of improving relations with Mexican California in order to blunt further British expansion into the Far West.

During the time that Ewing Young was making his important journeys to California along the Santa Fe Trail, two other trailblazers charted a variation of the Smith route from Taos to Los Angles. The Old Spanish Trail provided a relatively safe trip compared to the extreme southern routes across the unforgiving Arizona deserts or the imposing Sierra range running along the eastern border of California. The trail was actually not "old," or "Spanish," and Smith had used a small portion of it. In 1829, Antonio Armijo left New Mexico and traveled into the San Juan Valley, over the Colorado and Sevier Rivers. He then followed Jedediah Smith's general route from southern Utah into California. In 1830, William Wolfskill went from Taos into Utah (near present-day Moab, Utah), across the Sevier River, then south along a path similar to the one that Armijo had taken to Los Angeles.[17]

From 1830 to 1850, the Old Spanish Trail was used by traders and hunters eager to avoid the Indian hostilities or inhospitable climate that characterized the southern routes. The long, winding path covered relatively gentle terrain and promised temperate weather and relatively peaceful Ute tribes, as contrasted with the barren landscape, arid climate, and fiercely territorial Comanche and Apache peoples one encountered farther south. Yet by 1850 the Old Spanish Trail fell into disuse, as gold seekers hastening to the California placers favored more direct routes.

In 1833, Joseph Reddeford Walker charted another important route into central California, one that marked a significant departure from previously known routes. At the head of sixty other trappers, Walker left Utah's Humboldt Valley and blazed a trail across the imposing Sierra Nevada and into the Central Valley. In so doing, he and his men became the first white persons to behold the majestic scenery of the land we know today as Yosemite National Park. Awed by the gigantic sequoias, the group traversed the Tuolumne and Merced Rivers before discovering an important mountain pass (Walker's Pass) through the rugged peaks overlooking the spectacular waterfalls of the Yosemite Valley. Finally, the tired men descended the hills and straggled onto the fertile plain of the San Joaquin Valley. Walker visited the Owens Valley on his way out of California, but the central route he blazed into the province remained his most significant achievement. In later decades, that Sierra crossing proved popular with the so-called argonauts rushing toward the placers.[18]

As a group, the early white settlers in Mexican California reflected a desire to adapt to a new lifestyle rather than to try to dominate or change the existing rancho society. It was a romantic land, popularized in later novels such as those by Helen Hunt Jackson. Her most famous work, *Ramona*, portrays an agrarian, fun-loving people steeped in the elaborate rituals of Catholic traditions yet supporting a social lifestyle centered on the *rodeo* and *fandango*. Mexican California resembled the planter society of the southern gentry or the agrarian world portrayed in the Jeffersonian dream of land and opportunity. And not unlike those societies, Mexcian California featured an economic and political elite along with an exploited working class.[19]

In the early 1830s, the American Abel Stearns opened a trading post at San Pedro. He catered to an early wave of Yankee traders who sailed the California coastline in search of fur seals, otters, and sperm whales. This group also hoped to participate in the hide-and-tallow trade with the Mexican ranchos. Born in Massachusetts, Abel Stearns took to the sea as a young man. He traveled to Mexico and then to Monterey in the hopes of securing land and a respectable life in California. Yet, as a foreigner, he was denied the right of land ownership. Undeterred, Stearns did the next best thing by opening his commercial trading operation on the southern California coast. From this unique vantage point, he could entertain Asian markets in the east, Latin American traders sailing from the south, commercial interests arriving from San Francisco and Monterey, and personally greet the hide-and-tallow merchants coming overland from Taos and Santa Fe. Stearns embodied the pragmatic New England values of frugality and hard work. He built a thriving enterprise in wines, silks, and assorted dry goods.

Stearns embraced Mexican California, spoke Spanish fluently, participated in city politics, and married into a *ranchero* family. Indeed, his marriage to Arcadia Bandini provided him entry into the landed aristocracy, the *Californio* elite. Stearns the trader thus became Stearns the *don*, a land baron and one of the wealthiest men in southern California. Those connections would bring him serious responsibilities in later years. Stearns spent a great deal of his time and fortune helping Mexican rancheros, longtime compadres, during the decades of the 1850s and 1860s when land-title disputes, unscrupulous lawyers and bankers, and unusually severe droughts and floods led to the subdivision of the large estates. Like his contemporary Phineas Banning, Stearns would become a leader in Republican party politics, supporting the Union war effort. Through it all, Abel Stearns maintained his allegiance to two cultures, his capitalist instincts laying the foundation of the most powerful and influential rancho empire in southern California.[20]

A close friend of Stearns, Hugo Reid, also came to southern California during the Mexican period, although his entry into local society was

decidedly different. The Scottish-born Reid came to America seeking opportunity, eventually traveling from the East Coast to California and mar-
rying Victoria, a Gabrielino Indian. Stearns and Reid were friends, although
their lives had taken nearly opposite paths. While Stearns socialized with
the *Californio* elites, Reid languished in the ruins of a mission system destroyed by a policy of secularization that had left the Indian peoples vulnerable to exploitation by the larger society. Reid's simple adobe home near
the San Gabriel mission reflected the Spartan lifestyle of his desperate surroundings, he and his family living among the disease and squalor of an
exploited and largely forgotten people.

Often referred to as the "Scotch Paisano," Hugo Reid was crusty, animated, and forthright, a personality that allowed him to become the con-
science of the more taciturn Stearns. Reid frequently and unabashedly asked
his Yankee friend for medicine, food, clothing, and other necessities in order
to aid the sick at the rancheria, all the while reminding his frugal compadre
that there would be no repayment for his generosity.

American Indians were further impoverished by the annexation of California by the United States, the subsequent Gold Rush, and the accelerated
push for western settlement. Reid, aghast at the deplorable condition of
the Indians, wrote a series of articles for the *Los Angeles Star* that highlighted the nuances of Gabrielino culture. He catalogued the customs,
lifestyles, and practices of local tribes, accentuating their complex political organization and religious practices. Reid captured in print what the
famous artist George Caitlin captured on canvas: a glimpse of the everyday life of American Indians, at work and at play, a people and society living in harmony with their natural environment. Reid's thoughtful articles
led to Indian reform policy and were later important to Helen Hunt Jackson in her research on southern California tribes. Sadly, Reid never participated personally in the Indian reform efforts he helped spawn. He died
at the age of forty, shortly after the publication of his work in 1852.[21]

Reid and Stearns had come to southern California seeking economic
opportunity and had ended up embracing, even defending, the indigenous
peoples they found there. Like other early settlers among them, they greeted
the hide-and-tallow traders, trappers, and travelers who arrived after them
with curiosity and interest, desirous of any news about the United States,
be it on politics, society, or the economy. For these distant settlers, the
southwestern trails served as the conduits that connected them to past roots
as well as current events.

John A. Sutter and Thomas O. Larkin might be considered the northern California counterparts of Stearns and Reid. Yet Sutter and Larkin were
more ambitious, perhaps more nationalistic, and certainly less interested
in assimilation than Stearns or Reid. According to writer Richard Dillon,
John Sutter was "an ordinary man but one who did extraordinary things
in a savage wilderness."[22] In 1834, impoverished and threatened with debt-

ors prison, Sutter left his native Switzerland and a wife and family in order to seek a new beginning in America. After a brief stay in New York, he spent the next few years in a series of mediocre endeavors at commercial trade in Missouri, New Mexico, and the Far West. In 1838–1839, Sutter spent time in Hawaii before sailing to California, where he ingratiated himself with the Mexican officials in Monterey. He proposed establishing an American presence in California with himself becoming a liaison between Mexico and the United States. Mexican authorities were impressed with Sutter's plan, especially because they hoped to use Sutter to thwart any potential threats from the Russians at Fort Ross or the British at Vancouver. As Sutter reasoned, the presence of an influential American might provide the necessary counterbalance against any potential foreign intrusion into northern California.

As a ranchero, merchant, and local politico, Sutter's extensive influence among the *Californio* elite made him a valuable spokesman of American interests at Monterey during the 1840s. With Mexican consent, Sutter built New Helvetia in 1840, a trading post and fort situated in the Sacramento Valley. At first, Mexican officials approved of Sutter's fort, seeing it as a good buffer. Ironically, and much to the consternation of these same officials, as Mexico-U.S. relations deteriorated in the 1840s, Sutter's fort provided the United States with a potential commanding presence in the Far West.[23]

As historians Harlan Hague and David J. Langum noted, Thomas Larkin "was entrepreneur par excellence."[24] Larkin emigrated to California in 1832 and built commercial investments through coastal trade in lumber and assorted goods and services. Although Sutter presented himself to Mexican authorities as the foremost American in California, that position actually belonged to Larkin. In 1843, Larkin became the U.S. consul, an influential position that required close contact with both Mexican and American officials, especially at a time when competing political factions had weakened Mexican rule, produced chaotic policy, and frustrated Yankee entrepreneurs. Indeed, Thomas Larkin would be instrumental in the coming conflict between Mexico and the United States.[25]

By the early 1840s, a new breed of overland traveler had begun to arrive in California, men and women who intended to settle permanently in the Far West. Unlike the Yankee traders who stayed on in California, this wave of Americans expected to assume dominance of the land and cultures in order to recreate an American society similar to that in their home states. Several factors contributed to this gradual transition from traders and trappers to settlers. Underlying this renewed surge in westward expansion was a severe economic depression in the United States during the 1830s. Even as new overland routes west were discovered, a growing U.S. population desired more land. Americans had fully embraced the belief in manifest destiny. Soon, these elements converged with the escalation of the long-simmering conflict between the United States and Mexico.

In 1841, the entrance into California of two significant overland groups made the fulfillment of America's manifest destiny a realizable dream. The Bidwell-Bartleson and Workman-Rowland parties represented a watershed in the permanent American settlement of the region. Many individuals in these emigrant trains went on to become prominent figures in the political and economic growth of California, although each party came to California through different routes and under dissimilar circumstances.

Two factors underlay the origin of the Bidwell-Bartleson party. First, high winds, soil depletion, and poor farming techniques characterized agrarian frontier life, which promoted continual migration west; second, the lively stories spreading east about California's temperate climate and abundant land enticed many wishing to settle permanently in the Far West. As John Bidwell himself put it, "when a man moved out West, as soon as he was fairly settled he wanted to move again, and naturally all question imaginable was asked in regard to this wonderful country."[26]

With just such hopes for a permanent life in the Far West, the Bidwell-Bartleson party set out from Kansas along the Oregon Trail in May 1841. At the Humboldt Sink in Utah, the group divided, with half of the members traveling onward to Oregon and John Bidwell and John Bartleson leading the remaining thirty-two men to California along a route similar to the one Walker had blazed years before. The latter party climbed the rugged Sierra range with only mule meat and berries for rations, persisting even as Indian raiding parties periodically stole one of their horses for food. The emigrants managed to survive, and they marveled at the rock formations, rushing waters, and huge trees that surrounded them. John Bidwell recalled seeing "cedars of uncommon size, pines, the most thrifty, clothed the mountains."[27] He noted that one pine measuring an impressive 206 feet tall was far from the largest tree in the forest. The weary group descended the mountains along the course of rapid streams, steep cliffs, and deep ravines, reaching the San Joaquin Valley in late October, barely ahead of winter snows. They recuperated near Mount Diablo at the ranch of John Marsh, a pioneer who had come to California in 1836. Marsh was familiar with the routes taken by Jedediah Smith and Joseph R. Walker, and he shared with the Bidwell-Bartleson party his knowledge of the countryside.[28]

The Bidwell-Bartleson party marked a turning point in overland migration to California, for the group had successfully traveled the Sierra, increasing hopes for the potential viability of greater migration over the central crossing forged by Joseph Walker in the 1830s. Moreover, the composition of the overland party, mostly settlers rather than traders, signaled a change in the tenor of American westward expansion. Finally, members of the group did indeed make new lives for themselves, with some of them becoming prominent boosters of future expansion. Several of their stories, diaries, and journals were printed in American newspapers and garnered a national readership. In 1842, Charles Hopper and Joseph B. Chiles, former members of the Bidwell-Bartleson party, led a group of ten men back to Missouri via the San Joaquin Valley and along the Old Spanish Trail. Their tales of fertile lands and open country piqued the interest of many potential settlers. Both men would later return to California and become permanent residents of the state.

Meanwhile, William Workman and John Rowland led a twenty-five-member party of traders and trappers out of New Mexico in September 1841. The political situation had become hostile for Americans residing in New Mexico. Intrigue, growing resentment and distrust of Americans on the part of Mexican officials, and rumored threats of an invasion of New Mexico from the upstart Republic of Texas all had made life in New Mexico precarious for settlers such as Workman and Rowland. To them and others like them, southern California, with its long-standing economic ties between hide-and-tallow traders and *rancheros*, seemed like a good haven. John Rowland formerly had worked in the hide-and-tallow trade, visited southern California, and maintained contacts with the likes of Abel Stearns, Hugo Reid, and other white settlers.[29]

In the fall of 1841, weary of the growing indigenous hostility, the Workman-Rowland party fled New Mexico and crossed the Old Spanish Trail, encountering dust, deep fissures, desert winds, and parched land. As it turns out, they had left none too soon, for Mexican officials had prepared to arrest the Americans as rumors of a Texas invasion deepened suspicion of foreigners, intrigue, and cabals. The Workman-Rowland party reached Los Angeles in December. Most of the members were prepared to settle in this distant land full of *ranchos, fandangos,* and *vaqueros.* As scholar Robert Glass Cleland noted, southern California at this time was an enchanted land known for its "cattle on a thousand hills."[30]

John Rowland and William Workman rose quickly in Mexican society and secured ranchos of their own. Benjamin Wilson, another member of this famous group, went on to become a state senator and the first Indian agent of the southern California region.[31] In the future, Rowland, Workman, and Wilson would all be involved in political intrigue—they were jailed during the American conquest of California and then narrowly escape execution when John C. Frémont took Los Angeles from its Mexican defenders. Local hostilities ended with the signing of the Treaty of Cahuenga.

Even as various boosters continued to promote the Far West through publication of their memoirs, diaries, and journals, in 1842 Richard Henry Dana published *Two Years Before the Mast,* a colorful journal account of his experiences as a shipmate involved in the California coastal trade. Dana's vivid descriptions of the abundant trade in hides, the charms of

rancho life, and the natural beauty of California was widely read and captured the imagination of many Americans. Even so, it seems that the
gradual pace of the agrarian life of the *Californios* ran counter to Dana's
sense of pride and Puritan industry, for his work contains strong hints that
he felt the Mexicans may not have deserved the blessings the golden land
afforded them. For example, of the Santa Barbara rancheria, Dana observed:

> Day after day, the sun shone clear and bright upon the wide bay and the red
> roofs of the houses; everything being still as death, the people really hardly seem-
> ing to earn their sunlight. Daylight actually seemed thrown away upon them.[32]

Simultaneously, on the national scene, James K. Polk secured victory
in the 1844 presidential election based largely on a campaign that highlighted his optimistic view of American westward expansion and support
of the annexation of Texas. A year later, John O. Sullivan put a handy and
inspiring label on the expansionist visions of many Americans when he
coined the phrase "Manifest Destiny" in an article published in the *Democratic Review*. Even then, American families were streaming west in wagon
trains over the long Oregon Trail in hopes of reaching Oregon's Willamette
Valley, increasing the number of settlers there from 400 in 1842 to more
than 5,000 by 1845.[33]

In 1843, one Lansford W. Hastings, a brash and idealistic man, had
followed the California Trail into the Sacramento Valley. His exuberance
over the abundant land and temperate climate soon led him to write an
account of his trip west, *The Emigrants Guide to Oregon and California*.
Hastings's enthusiasm might be understood as a product of the national
excitement over continental expansion, but in extolling the riches of the
Far West and the ease of the trip along the Oregon Trail, Hastings proposed
a new short-cut, one that severely understated the difficulty of the trip. He
touted a cutoff from the Oregon Trail through the rugged Wastach Mountains, across the Salt Lake Basin, and over the imposing Sierra range at
Truckee Lake. And once over the Sierra, the trip to Sacramento was easy.
The only problem was that Hastings had not personally traveled the cutoff prior to the publication of his guidebook; the route was far more ominous than he had realized. In the wake of the publication of his guidelines,
in the summer of 1846, Hastings assisted an overland party south of the
Great Salt Lake through his purported "cutoff." Only then did he realize
the magnitude of his underestimation of the difficulty of the precarious
Sierra Nevada crossing. This egregious lapse in judgment turned out to be
one that held dire consequences for one group that took his advice.[34]

John Charles Frémont also crossed the Sierra Range in 1843, but he,
unlike Hastings, was left with a healthy respect for the rugged terrain. While
leading a geological survey for the United States military over the Oregon

Trail, Frémont and his men undertook a winter crossing of the Sierra Nevada. The group traveled a route similar to the one Jedediah Smith had covered, except that Smith had been travelling east from California. Heavy snows and dwindling rations soon reduced the Frémont expedition to eating horses, mules, dogs, even raw frogs, in order to survive. In February 1844, Frémont and eight other men descended the snow-packed mountains into the Sacramento Valley, taking several weeks to recuperate at Sutter's Fort. Historian Andrew Rolle noted that "the men resembled a band of skeletons, but their misery seemed temporarily over."[35]

Frémont was fortunate. He and his men survived this reckless winter crossing of the Sierra Nevada only because of the experience and adroit skills of veteran guide Kit Carson, a man who understood well the challenges of survival in snow and freezing temperatures. No such guide accompanied the ill-fated Donner Party, an 1846–1847 overland migration of families anxious to start life anew in California.

In the spring of 1846, Jacob and George Donner led a group of seventy-nine men, women, and children out of Missouri bound for California. Using Hastings's *Emigrant's Guide* for a reference, the leaders of the Donner party, eager to save time, decided to take the suggested cutoff over the Sierra Nevada. Quarreling among themselves and short on food, the haggard group was surprised to find the going so rough once they started on this route. These surprises led to delays that were to prove fatal. Along the trail, they began to find ominous notes warning of the harshness of the terrain that lay ahead. The notes had been left by none other than Lansford Hastings, who had realized from his recent experience that it would be nearly impossible for a wagon train to climb the Wastach Mountains, cross the barren Salt Lake, and climb the Sierra over his proposed cutoff, even in the best of weather.

In November, only one day's travel from the Sierra summit, the Donner Party neared Truckee Lake. Suddenly it started to snow; and it snowed, and snowed, and snowed—what well may have been the worst winter storm in the Sierra during the entire nineteenth century. Trapped in the deep snowdrifts and out of food, nearly half of the group members perished over the next four months from exposure and starvation. A few members of the Donner Party straggled out of the Sierra in January 1847, just as the United States was defeating Mexico for control of California. Word of the trapped emigrants spread throughout Sacramento and volunteers were enlisted to help rescue anyone still alive. Rescue missions did not bring out the last of the survivors until the following May, well after the nightmarish winter had ended. Coverage of the tragic ordeal received national attention, challenging the human imagination regarding the limits of courage and fear. At the same time, sensational accounts of the events began to circulate throughout the territory, replete with ghastly tales of suffering and resorts to cannibalism punctuated by accounts of superhuman bravery played out by larger-than-life heroes and villains.[36]

The Donner tragedy may well have severely retarded the rate of migration to California if not for outbreak of the war with Mexico and the subsequent discovery of gold by James Marshall at Sutter's Mill. Indeed, patriotism, expansionist fever, and plain and simple greed quickly erased any anxiety inspired by the Donner calamity. With Mexico defeated in 1847 and excitement accelerating over the Gold Rush, argonauts from all parts of the United States streamed across the overland trails in search of fertile land and easy money. And like every emigrant wave before them, the newcomers traversed the same dirt trails forged by traders, trappers, and a handful of pathfinders who first pointed the nation west to California.

Notes

Acknowledgment: Maps are by Jane Domier based on renditions by artist Catherine Wilson and author's estimates and interpretive material derived from Warren A. Beck and Ynez D. Haase, *Historical Atlas of California* (Norman: University of Oklahoma Press, 1974).

1   On the fur trade in the West, see Robert Glass Cleland, *This Reckless Breed of Men* (New York: Alfred A. Knopf Publisher, 1950); Ray Allen Billington, *The Far Western Frontier* (New York: Harper & Brothers, Publishers, 1956); and John Walton Caughey, *The American West Frontier & Region* (Los Angeles: Ward Richie Press, 1969).

2   For excerpts and narrative accounts of the Lewis and Clark expedition see Stephen E. Ambrose, *Lewis and Clark: Voyage of Discovery* (Washington, D.C.: National Geographic Society, 1998); David Freeman Hawke, *Those Tremendous Mountains: The Story of the Lewis and Clark Expedition* (New York: Norton, 1980); Donald Dean Jackson ed., *Letters of the Lewis and Clark Expedition, with related documents, 1785–1854* (Urbana: University of Illinois Press, 1978); and Paul Russell Cutright, *A History of the Lewis and Clark Journals* (Norman: University of Oklahoma Press, 1976). For a definitive analysis of the Lewis and Clark expedition, see Stephen E. Ambrose, *Undaunted Courage, Meriwether Lewis, Thomas Jefferson, and the Opening of the American West* (New York, Simon & Schuster, 1996).

3   Ronald C. Woolsey, "The West Becomes a Problem: The Missouri Controversy and Slavery Expansion as the Southern Dilemma," *Missouri Historical Review* 77 (July 1983): 409–432.

4   D. W. Garber, *Jedediah Strong Smith: Fur Trader From Ohio* (Stockton, CA.: University of the Pacific, 1973), 1–6.

5   Dale L. Morgan, *Jedediah Smith and the Opening of the West* (Indianapolis: The Bobbs-Merrill Company, Inc., 1953), pp. 175–192.

6   Ibid., pp. 193–201.

7   George Harwood Phillips, *Chiefs and Challengers, Indian Resistance and Cooperation in Southern California* (Berkeley: University of California Press, 1975), 35.

8   Thomas R. Tefft, "Jedediah Smith's Story" *The Californians* 8 (Sept./Oct 1990): 48–51.

9   Morgan, *Jedediah Smith*, pp. 208–215, 227.

10 Siegfroed G. Demke, "The Hudson's Bay Company in the San Francisco Bay Area" *Los Angeles Westerners Corral, The Branding Iron*, 198 (Winter 1994): 1, 12–18.

11 David J. Weber, *The Californio vs. Jedediah Smith, 1826–1827* (Spokane, WA.: Arthur Clark Company, 1990), pp. 39–47.

12 Publications of Smith's journals and letters can be found in George R. Brooks, *The Southwest Expedition of Jedediah S. Smith* (Glendale: Arthur Clark Company, 1977).

13 On the life and times of James Pattie, see Richard Batman, *American Ecclesiastes: The Stories of James Pattie* (San Diego: Harcourt Brace Jovanovich, 1984), and Stanton A. Coblentz, *The Swallowing Wilderness: The Life of a Frontiersman: James Ohio Pattie* (New York: T. Yoseloff,

1961). Also see Timothy Flint ed., *The Personal Narrative of James O. Pattie of Kentucky* (Chicago: R.R. Donnelley & Sons C., 1930), and Reuben Gold Thwaites ed., *The Personal Narrative of James O. Pattie of Kentucky* (Cleveland, OH: Arthur H. Clark Co., 1905).

14 Kenneth L. Holmes, *Ewing Young, Master Trapper* (Portland: OR: Binfords, and Mort, Publishers, 1967), p. VII.

15 Ibid., pp. 46–60.

16 John Walton Caughey, *California* (New York: Prentice Hall, 1940), 234–236.

17 On the life and times of William Wolfskill, see Iris W. Engstrand, *William Wolfskill, 1798–1866; Frontier Trapper to California Ranchero* (Glendale: A. H. Clark Co., 1965). Early Spanish explorers like Silvestre Veliez de Escalante and Father Francisco Garces had traveled a portion of this trail in their adventures across the Southwest. See Charles E. Chapman, *A History of California: The Spanish Period* (New York: The Macmillan Company, 1930), pp. 316–319.

18 For an overview of Walker's accomplishments see, Bill Gilbert, *Westering Man: The Life of Joseph Walker* (New York: Atheneum, 1983).

19 Life in Mexican California is vividly described in the memoirs and correspondence of traders and settlers such as Alfred Robinson and William Heath Davis. See Doyce B. Nunis, Jr., *A Commentary on Alfred Robinson and his life in California* (Los Angeles: R. Hoffman, 1970); Charles B. Churchill, "Alfred Robinson: A Yankee Parses Paradise" *The Californians* 9 (March/April 1992): 42–48; Maynard Geiger, ed., *Letters of Alfred Robinson to the De La Guerra Family of Santa Barbara, 1834–1873* (Los Angeles: Zamorano Club, 1973); William Heath Davis, *Sixty Years in California* (San Francisco: A. J. Leary, 1889, and Charles B. Churchill, "Hawaiian, American, *Californio*: The Acculturation of William Heath Davis," *Southern California Quarterly* 76 (Winter 1994): 341–376. For a biographical overview of these and other early travelers to California, see Charles B. Churchill, *Adventurers and Prophets, American Autobiographies in Mexican California, 1828–1847* (Spokane, WA: Arthur H. Clark Co., 1995).

20 For a biographical look at Abel Stearns, see Doris Marion Wright, *A Yankee in Mexican California, Abel Stearns 1798–1848* (Santa Barbara: Wallace Hebbard, 1977); John Cushing Hough, "Abel Stearns, 1848–1871," Ph.D. diss., University of California at Los Angeles, 1961; Ronald C. Woolsey, "A Capitalist in a Foreign Land: Abel Stearns in Southern California Before the Conquest," *Southern California Quarterly* 75 (Summer 1993): 101–118; and Woolsey, "The Rancho In Two Worlds: Don Abel Stearns and the Los Alamitos Rancho," in Kenneth Pauley, ed., *Brand Book Twenty, Rancho Days in Southern California* (Studio City, CA: The Westerners, Los Angeles Corral, 1997).

21 On Hugo Reid's life and times, see Susanna Bryant Dakin, *A Scotch Paisano* (Berkeley: University of California Press, 1939); and Ronald C. Woolsey, *Migrants West: Toward the Southern California Frontier* (Claremont, CA.: Grizzly Bear Publishing Company, 1996), 16–28.

22 Richard Dillon, *Captain John Sutter: Sacramento Valley's Sainted Sinner* (Santa Cruz: Western Tanager, 1967), p. 15.

23 Sutter's life was significant and problematic. For diverse views on Sutter and his significance in the West, see Richard H. Dillon, *Fool's Gold: The Decline and Fall of Captain John Sutter of California* (Santa Cruz: Western Tanager, 1987); Kenneth N. Owens ed., *John Sutter and a Wider West* (Lincoln, Nebraska: University of Nebraska Press, 1994); Blaise Cendrars, *Gold: Being the Marvellous History of General John Augustus Sutter* (New York: M. Kesend Publishers, 1982); and Oscar Lewis, *Sutter's Fort: Gateway to the Gold Fields* (Englewood Cliffs, N.J.: Prentice-Hall, 1966).

24 Harlan Hague and David J. Langum, *Thomas O. Larkin: A Life of Patriotism and Profit in Old California* (Norman: University of Oklahoma Press, 1990), p. 8.

25 On the Larkin correspondence, see Oscar Lewis, ed., *California in 1846: Described in Letters from Thomas O. Larkin* (San Francisco, CA.: Grabhorn Press, 1934).

26 John Bidwell, "The First Emigrant Train to California" found in Doyce B. Nunis, Jr., ed., *The Bidwell-Bartleson Party, 1841 California Emigrant Adventure* (Santa Cruz: Western Tanager Press, 1991), 101

27 Ibid., 49, October 18, 1841 entry.

28 Ibid., pp. 8–9.

29 Donald E. Rowland, John Rowland and William Workman, *Southern California Pioneers of 1841* (Spokane, Washington: Arthur H. Clark Company, 1999).

30 Robert Glass Cleland, *Cattle on a Thousand Hills* (San Marino, CA.: Huntington Library, 1941).

31 Benjamin Davis Wilson, "Reflections," 1853 notes, Wilson Collection, Box 3 Henry E. Huntington Library, San Marino, CA. On Wilson, see Midge Sherwood, *Days of Vintage, Years of Vision* v.1 (San Marino, CA: Orizaba Publications, 1982); and Charles B. Churchill, "Benjamin Davis Wilson, Man in the Middle" *The Californians* 10 (Nov./Dec. 1992): 30–35.

32 Richard Henry Dana, *Two Years Before the Mast, A Personal Narrative of Life at Sea* (New York: A. L. Burt Company Publishers, 1845), 181. For an analysis of Dana's impressions of California, see Charles B. Churchill, "The Limits of Empathy: Richard Henry Dana" *The Californians* 9 (Jan./Feb. 1992): 34–39.

33 Gary B. Nash, Julie Roy Jeffrey, eds., *The American People: Creating a Nation and a Society* (New York: Harper Collins, 1994), 436.

34 On Hasting's cutoff, see Charles Kelly Salf, *Desert Trails: A History of the Hastings Cutoff and Other Early Trails which Crossed the Great Salt Lake Desert Seeking a Shorter Road to California* (Salt Lake City, Utah: Western Printing Co., 1930); and Lansford Warren Hastings, *The Emigrants Guide to Oregon and California* (Cincinnati: G. Conklin, 1845).

35 Andrew Rolle, *John Charles Frémont, Character as Destiny* (Norman, OK: University of Oklahoma Press, 1991), 61.

36 Joseph A. King, *Winter of Entrapment: A New Look at the Donner Party* (P. D. Meany Publishers, Toronto, 1992). For a brief historiographical overview of Donner Party literature, see King "The Breens v. Persistent Donner Party Myth: Critiquing the Chroniclers," *The Californians* 10 (July/August 1992): 8–27.

CHAPTER THREE

L.A. behind Bars, 1847 to 1886: Establishing a Secure Institution

John Joseph Stanley

The light of review shines very brightly on Los Angeles County jails at the beginning of the twenty-first century. The Los Angeles County jail system is the largest in the country. On any given day more than 20,000 inmates are housed within the ten jails it comprises. The Los Angeles County jail system is sophisticated. Inmates are carefully screened at intake and are housed according to their various needs. Various state and federal court decisions and mandates dictate how inmates are classified. One court decision mandates that all male inmates claiming to be homosexual are interviewed to determine whether this is true and are then segregated from the general inmate population.[1] The United States Department of Justice also regulates where and how mentally disturbed inmates are housed due to past allegations of poor treatment of these persons. The number of inmates taking psychiatric medication in Los Angeles jails is in the thousands and rivals even the largest psychiatric hospitals in the nation. More than

This photograph of Los Angeles taken in 1869 shows the old brick jail (arrow) built in 1853 and completed in 1854 as well as the stockade subsequently built around it.

4,000 sworn deputy sheriffs and civilians are employed to monitor these inmates, and almost one-third of the Los Angeles Sheriff's $1 billion annual budget is spent administering the jail system. The most recently opened jails, the Twin Towers Correctional Facility and the Inmate Reception Center, opened in 1997 at a cost of more than $330 million. Between them, at any given time they are housing or processing more than 6,000 inmates. These buildings are physically connected via a secure bridge to the Central Jail. This, the main jail, houses an additional 4,000 inmates, although it can hold many more if necessary.

One hundred and fifty years ago a young L.A. County had nothing resembling a jail system. There was simply the County Jail and perhaps a series of one-room holding cells spread out in various communities throughout the county. Managing these early jails lacked the sophistication that more than a century and a half of experiment and design have produced today. Still, it would be wrong to say that officials of the young county gave little thought to the design and construction of these jails and the supervision of the inmates they held. Indeed, the establishment of a secure jail was an important first step for any community in its fight to establish legitimacy and viability. The absence of one could contribute to a host of problems, not the least of which was vigilante activity.

With the discovery of gold at Sutter's Mill in 1848, the world seemingly rushed into northern California. Virtually everything in early San Francisco was makeshift and hastily assembled, from county government to city buildings. The general respect for the rule of law and human dignity that marked the conduct of travelers on the Overland Trail often gave way to "gold fever" once those persons reached the diggings. In addition, the glittering ore attracted an entirely different type of emigrant to California than those who had arrived with family in tow in search of a better life. To the new wave of fortune seekers, California was a means, not an end. As such, those who wished to establish local governments had to anchor themselves quickly, like rows of mussels against a relentless surf. To protect legitimate citizens against those who would exploit them, familiar institutions such as courts, law enforcement agencies, and jails needed to be put in place quickly. In short, a viable criminal justice system was essential. The most visible centerpiece of this system was a secure jail.

The belief in California in the early 1850s was that a secure jail would prevent prisoners from escaping in order to continue their criminal activities. This in turn would prevent frustrated citizens from taking the law into their own hands. This was certainly the case in San Francisco during the 1851 vigilante action.[2] Early San Franciscans were not at all satisfied with their jails. The failure to complete the construction of San Francisco's first legitimate jail rested with a town council motivated more by self-interest than civic responsibility. The insecurity of San Francisco's early makeshift jails was listed by the 1851 vigilance committee as a reason for its formation. Between 1846 and 1851, San Francisco's criminals were detained in a number of locations including the decrepit Mexican calaboose, a makeshift military blockhouse, a warship, a schoolhouse, an area on the ground floor of city hall, a commercial ship, and even rented rooms in a hotel. San Francisco's first significant jail only received sufficient funds to complete its construction after the 1851 vigilance committee began its activity.

While considerably smaller than San Francisco at the time, Los Angeles faced similar problems, even if they did not manifest themselves in the same high-profile manner. And while the construction of a secure jail in Los Angeles was not by itself an effective deterrent to popular justice, it was, nevertheless, an important initial step toward legitimizing local government.

FIRST ATTEMPTS AT JAILING

There were three successive jails in Los Angeles between 1847 and 1853: the first was made of wood, the second of adobe, and the third of brick. The county faced no specific big bad wolf in this period, but the mood of the state's populace itself was ravenous. The old *Californio* order was threatened by the sudden influx of opportunists looking to get rich quick. Los Angeles learned quickly that solid institutions with walls of brick spoke of permanence and, hopefully, ultimate victory over assaults on the established order. If a community was to hold the line and maintain its foundation against assault, it needed a secure jail.

The sheriff has always been the chief law enforcement officer of Los Angeles County, and the sheriff's chief mandate remains the same today as it did in 1850: supervise and maintain the security of the county jail. George Thompson Burrill was elected as the first sheriff of Los Angeles County in April 1850. The Rhode Island born Burrill was forty years old and a veteran of the recent war with Mexico.[3] Overseeing the county jail was not the only function the fledgling county asked of him, however. Sheriff Burrill and his two deputies *were* the law for an area that within a year of formation of the state had grown to comprise 34,520 square miles. This included the present counties of Orange, Riverside, and San Bernardino, as well as parts of Kern and Ventura Counties.[4] In addition to being the county's top lawman, the sheriff was to act as bailiff for the County Courthouse and was ex-officio tax-Collector until 1875.[5] These enormous duties, coupled with the administration of the jail, were time consuming enough, but much of Burrill's time was devoted to a decidedly more mundane task.

From 1850 to 1852, Los Angeles was governed by the Court of Sessions. This body consisted of the county judge and two justices of the peace. County Judge Augustín Olvera spoke no English. At least one of the justices spoke no Spanish. So, for an additional payment of $50.00 a month,

Burrill served as the official court interpreter. Burrill had come to Los Angeles via Chihuahua, Mexico, where his wife Refugio was born; he undoubtedly learned his Spanish there.[6] While Burrill surely welcomed this supplemental income, being sheriff could be a lucrative occupation in 1850. Sheriffs worked under a fee system that paid them for each arrest they made and each legal task they performed. Most early California sheriffs were so industrious they nearly bankrupted their county treasuries. To prevent this from happening in Los Angeles, the Court of Sessions reduced such fees in 1851. Nevertheless, Burrill was still well paid. Although Los Angeles County in 1850 was not the hotbed of crime it would become in subsequent years, there was enough criminal activity, combined with his other duties, to keep Burrill busy.

Although Burrill was, as mentioned, responsible for the operation of the jail, his presence there was not required. The Court of Sessions hired a jailer to act as live-in babysitter for the prisoners. The first such appointee was Samuel Whiting, who was made jailer on June 25, 1850, and served in that capacity until January 1851.

The Mexican *calabazo* Los Angeles inherited from occupying American forces in 1847 was little more than a guardhouse. A replacement was quickly erected after troops took control of the pueblo. F. W. Emerson described this structure as:

> . . . one long room, built of logs, and without cells. This jail was erected on a part of the site of the present Federal Building. A log ran through the center of the room, in which were bolted a number of heavy rings. Prisoners were chained to the log, and because of its size and weight it was not possible for them to walk out with it. It thus served to anchor them securly [sic] until decision had been made concerning their disposition.[7]

This wooden structure did not last long. One night a sentry on guard duty challenged what he believed was a would-be intruder outside the jail. When the alleged aggressor failed to respond to the sentry's query, the alert guard raised his weapon and fired. The shot was true and the offending party, a local cow, fell dead. A nearby artilleryman, called to action at the sound of the sentry's shot, lighted a fuse and prepared to touch off his cannon should the intruder have a herd of accomplices. When the sentry's error was recognized, the artilleryman reportedly tossed his lighted fuse away in disgust. Unfortunately, it landed in an ammunition chest. The resulting explosion knocked down the walls of the jail and raised its roof. Four men were killed; twelve others were injured. The jail was rebuilt using the same floor plan as the previous structure, but this second jail was constructed with adobe instead of logs.[8]

This adobe jail was the one Whiting took charge of in 1850. The building was adequate as a guardhouse, but it was a failure as a county jail. One of the first Documents the Court of Sessions received on June 26 was a report from the jailer to Sheriff Burrill on the condition of the jail.[9] This act reaffirms that the jailer was clearly subordinate to the sheriff on matters of the jail. The county also entered into an agreement at that time with Dr. A. P. Hodges as "physician to the jail."[10] Recognizing the inadequacy of the existing jail, the Court of Sessions on July 12 "appointed Abel Stearns, Francisco Figueroa and B. D. Wilson to recommend a site for a county jail and the Mayor and Council of Los Angles were requested to confer with the court on the subject of a site at the next session."[11] All three men were prominent rancheros and town fathers. The rancho owners were a close-knit group. Most such men married within one another's families. Both Stearns and Wilson had been residents of Los Angeles well before the annexation of California by the United States, and they were as comfortable speaking Spanish as they were English. The names of all three men adorn landmarks today, although Mount Wilson is the most prominent of these. The review by this impressive triumvirate was swift. Four days later, the committee recommended, "that the city donate for a jail site Lots 1, 2, 3, 7, 8, and 9 of Square 34 of Ord's Survey."[12] The city was requested to donate the site and loan the county $2,000 to fund the construction of the new jail. The city would be allowed to house their prisoners in the structure free of charge until the loan was repaid. Rather than leading to the swift construction of a new jail, however, this mandate proved to be the first of three failed attempts in successive years to build a new facility. Meanwhile, Whiting was left with the difficult task of making due with the adobe jail.

JAIL COSTS

A one-room jail, even if subdivided as this one must have been, presents many problems. For example, only marginal provisions can be made for different types of inmates. (No doubt, some impromptu arrangements were made, especially when a female was arrested.) For its part, the Court of Sessions attempted to ease Whiting's burden by fixing his salary at a generous $7.50 a day. From this sum, however, Whiting was expected to do more than meet his own needs. The money was to serve, "as compensation for his services, as jailer, he furnishing a competent assistant, at least one of whom to be at the jail at all times."[13] Whiting also had to find and hire his assistants. There was no mention of the standards to which these assistants need adhere. The Court of Sessions and sheriff apparently left this to the discretion of the jailer. The term *assistant* may have referred to a single individual. There were numerous minute book entries listing payment to individuals for their services as night guards. The going rate was $3 a night. The first part-time guards listed were David Brown and George Searls, whose compensation was recorded on September 17, 1850. Brown received $15 for having worked five nights while Searls received $10 for three and a half nights.[14] Three dollars a night remained the going rate for guard duty well into the decade, and it was not increased or decreased based on the number of nights served. Thomas Gordon received $126 for "guarding the jail at night 42 nights" on January 3, 1855.[15] Obviously the same $3 rate remained in place. What had decreased significantly by this time, however, was the salary for the jailer himself. It was down to $4 a day from the lofty $7.50 that the Court of Sessions originally authorized.[16] Whether a sudden increase in the inmate population had triggered the need to higher overnight guards, or some other reason, was not stated.

One historian asserted that, "In local jails, confusion was king, along with plain dirt and humiliation. These were the sewers and toilets of humanity."[17] There is some evidence to support this assertion at the adobe jail, but there is also evidence that implies that earnest efforts were made to provide for the welfare of the prisoners. The Court of Sessions created an allowance of fifty cents a day for feeding inmates. "Each prisoner shall have per day an amount of bread to the value of twelve and a half cents, or its equivalent in rice and beans, and the balance of the amount first mentioned [fifty cents] in good meat."[18] This sum would constantly be modified as the strain on the county coffers demanded, but this was the last time that the county specified the type and amount of food each inmate was to receive. In the future, officials would focus their attention on the amount of money allotted for the care of each prisoner. Unfortunately, the significant change in how this money was allocated in the future had nothing to do with the type of food served and a great deal to do with the type of inmate receiving it.

On September 18, 1850, there is a curious entry in the Court of Sessions Minutes. Usually the money to cover jail expenditures was drawn from the general fund, or in later years, the jail fund. On this occasion, money for seven inmates was taken from the Indian Fund. At least two of these prisoners appear to have been juveniles, but all their names have one thing in common, Spanish roots: "Francisco, boy Andres, boy Bartelo, Estephen, two Indian Joses and one Indian Pablo."[19] In 1853, the Court of Sessions was replaced by the Board of Supervisors. This body consisted of five elected officials. The Board of Supervisors ran county government. The city of Los Angeles had its own city council and mayor. Often these two groups worked together to solve their common problems, problems such as housing criminals. On July 9, 1853, the new Board of Supervisors made an interesting modification to the cost of daily maintenance of prisoners. The jailer's maintenance fees "for each white man 50 cents per day and each Indian 25 cents per day."[20] An extra 25 cents was to be allotted for sick prisoners, but it is unclear whether this would have raised the compensation for a sick Indian to 75 cents or just to the 50 cent rate for a healthy white man. The vast majority of criminals listed in the Court of Sessions records had Spanish surnames; the 1850 entry suggests that at least a number of such inmates were regarded as Indians. Just how an inmate's ethnicity was determined was unclear, but it certainly made a difference in the amount of money allotted toward his care. The daily expenditure per inmate was increased by 25 cents on October 10, 1854,[21] and this increase was reiterated on August 5, 1857.[22] Each time, however, the 25-cent gap between whites and Indians persisted. This situation was no doubt one more source of tension between Hispanics and Anglos in early Los Angeles. That animosity reached an early zenith with the ambush and murder of Sheriff Barton in early 1857 by the Joaquin Murrieta gang.[23] James Barton was Los Angeles County's second sheriff. He succeeded George Burrill in September 1851 and served until January 1856. His successor, David W. Alexander, left office unexpectedly in August of that year. Barton defeated E. C. Hale, who had been appointed by the Board of Supervisors, and became sheriff again in January 1857. Within weeks of his return to office he was killed. Barton had a reputation as being especially hard on Hispanics. Joaquin Murrieta and his men, on the other hand, despite being thieves and murderers, had developed almost a Robin Hood status in the Hispanic community as they defied Anglo authority. In pursuit of Murrieta, Barton followed a good lead on the gang's whereabouts into southern Los Angeles County, present-day Orange County, but his pride got the better of him and he and his men were lured into a trap. Four out of six of them, including Barton, were killed. Murrieta and most of his men would subsequently be run to ground. Tension between the sheriff's office and the Hispanic community eased after Barton's death. The election of Tomas Sanchez to Sheriff in 1860, and his eight years in office, seemed to have ended it.

The amount of money allocated for jail prisoners continued to decline over the years, however. In years to come, the amount of money spent on inmates would drop precipitously, but at least distinctions of dollar amounts allotted to different ethnic groups would disappear. The only other cost distinction made for a particular type of inmate was for what were described as "lunatics." On August 6, 1852, Jailer George Robinson submitted a separate bill for $40 for guarding and feeding lunatic Julian Ingrentez [sic].[24] The time and attention needed to segregate and care for an inmate of this type no doubt justified the expense. Unfortunately, it was not stated just how this segregation was done. By 1894 the amount of money allotted for inmates was only 30 cents a day for meals.[25] By 1905 that amount dropped to 11 cents a day.[26]

Beyond the costs for the care and feeding of the inmates, jailers incurred incidental costs for "articles and provisions." Often these items were not described, but most of those in the records are mundane things such as candles, wood, water, blankets, rawhides, and lanterns. There was certainly nothing exotic or unusual here. Still, a new county tight on resources wanted a tighter reign on the jailer's spending habits. On May 19, 1851, the Court of Sessions "Ordered that hereafter the jailer purchase nothing for the jail without order of court or order of sheriff."[27] The county would go back and forth with jailers over the next several years regarding their costs. In August 1857, the Board of Supervisors fixed the jailer's income at $1,600 a year, which was to be paid quarterly. From this sum, "lights, water and wood [were] to come out jailer's 'own proper cost.'"[28] This was repealed three months later and the old per diem, per head rates were reinstituted, albeit at a lower rate than before the August change. This rate change may have led to the first departure of Jailer Francis Carpenter. He first served as jailer from October 1854 until February 1858. In 1860, after two other men served as jailer, Carpenter returned to the task, but by then, the accounting and compensation system was a bit more streamlined.

JAIL RECORDS

Just how jailers kept their personal records prior to the 1880s is unknown. Given later practices it is safe to assume that a jail register of some sort was kept to record the comings and goings of inmates. The Court of Sessions criminal proceedings indicate that business was sent to the jail from the earliest days of the county. Jail stays were often the result of a defendant's inability to pay a fine, so most stays must have been short ones. Just how long inmates actually spent in jail on average is impossible to calculate absent a ledger, however. The first surviving jail register begins with the recording of the movement of the jail population in August 1884.[29] Whiting and his early successors must have kept a similar document in order to keep track of their inmate populations and document the costs they incurred for the care of prisoners.

The first official action of the Court of Sessions added another burden to Jailer Whiting's task. The first three articles passed by that body concerned the use of inmate labor to work off their fines.[30] The sheriff was apparently assigned the task of administering this policy. On August 22, 1850, the Court of Sessions ordered the authorization of the sheriff, "To hire out the following named prisoners for the payment of their cost and for the period of their confinement."[31] Inmates Henry Huntz and Leanuta Saliza were selected for this program. The details of how this worked and whether the two returned to the jail at night to sleep are unknown.

JAIL STAFFING PROBLEMS AND ESCAPES

Whiting served as a member of a grand jury in October 1850 and was compensated for his time in this capacity. Six different men put in claims in November for duty as guards; it seems likely they were filling in for

Whiting while he was serving as a grand juror.[32] That it took six men to perform Whiting's job in his absence clearly suggests that the jail was understaffed. It was ironic that in November, the grand jury on which Whiting served brought an indictment against the county entitled, "The People of the State of California vs. the County Jail."[33] Despite Whiting's efforts, living conditions in the adobe structure were clearly substandard.

Moreover, the weakness of this jail was demonstrated during October when felon Matias Cortaza escaped. The grand jury's first review noted that "the building could be pierced with a knife or a sharpened stick at any point and escapes were occurring daily."[34] This may have been true, but Cortaza's escape from the jail was the first one recorded. The problem of escapes was temporarily addressed by reintroducing the notion of chaining inmates to a huge log in the middle of the room by affixing their wrists to "iron staples." Overcrowding necessitated that at times some of the worst offenders be chained in the yard outside the jail.[35] For his part, Cortaza was still at large in January 1852, when the Court of Sessions set a $100 reward for his capture.

It was only after Cortza's escape that Whiting finally received adequate assistance. C. H. Brownfield, county clerk B. D. Wilson, I. S. Mallard, and H. Bromfield all put in claims for compensation as jail guards on November 21. Casimiro Lara and Samuel Stowers put in similar claims on November 23. This was in addition to Whiting's usual claim on that same day.[36] That a man of the stature of Don Benito Wilson was putting in time as a jail guard suggests the importance to which even the more powerful citizens of the community attached to the jail. Little else is known about the other men who served with him.

The combination of the grand jury's indictment and Cortaza's escape may have cost Whiting his job. The next claim for compensation by the county jailer was made on January 23, 1851, by George Robinson, not Whiting. Robinson also filed the next claim on March 9 and would file claims as the jailer until November 1852.

The sudden employment of extra jail guards immediately following Cortaza's escape ended abruptly. Whiting's extra staff were gone almost as quickly as they appeared. Clearly, the Cortaza escape was embarrassing and had raised considerable local ire. To calm the populace—one that demonstrated during the next twenty years little patience for breakdowns in the criminal justice system—extra guards were hastily hired to show that the jail was secure. A few weeks later, when the public awareness had subsided, the guards were let go and the jailer was once again left to fend for himself. The inconsistency with which guards filed claims over the next several years suggests that this extra help filled in when the jailer was absent, or during some unusual peak in the jail population. For the most part, however, the jailer seems to have run the jail alone.

In short order, escapes became a recurrent problem in the adobe jail, adding powerful ammunition to the argument, made by many established members of the community, that vigilante activity was necessary to deal with crime. In June 1851, merchants in San Francisco formed their ad hoc vigilance tribunal to handle criminals. The rate of escape from San Francisco's inadequate jail was listed by the committee as one of the principal reasons for its formation. San Francisco's vigilante example was copied statewide, but nowhere was the extra-legal body more frequently employed than in Los Angeles.

In July 1852, Doroteo Zaveleta, Jesus Rivas, and a third unnamed inmate escaped from the Los Angeles County Jail. Zaveleta and Rivas fled south to San Juan Capistrano, where they robbed and murdered two American cattle buyers. The pair then fled to Santa Barbara, where they were arrested along with a third man, not the other man who escaped with them, for stealing horses. A detachment of "volunteers" was dispatched from Los Angeles to collect and transport Zaveleta and Rivas back to the county to face justice for the murders. The detachment's arrival in Santa Barbara apparently spared the pair from being lynched there. Upon reaching Los Angeles, however, they were not returned to the adobe jail. Instead, "they were placed in the custody of a citizens' committee." After a trial by a jury of seven Americans and five *Californios* the pair was found guilty and executed.[37] The details of the trial and execution were reported in the *Los Angeles Star* on July 21.

The fact that Zaveleta and Rivas were not returned to the county jail was an indictment of the adobe structure. Recognizing the gross inadequacy of the adobe jail, the Board of Supervisors once again ordered publication for bids for the building of a new jail two days before Zaveleta and Rivas were executed.[38] The deadline for the submission of bids was August 4 at 10 A.M. Interestingly, this is the same day on which the reduction in compensation for the jailer was announced. Perhaps this was meant as a punishment by the board for the escape, or perhaps the previous arrangement was not being kept by the county and they were attempting to establish a new one to better provide for the jailer's needs. The record is not clear on which view is the correct one.

One thing is certain, the jail and jailer received a great deal of the board's attention over the next several days. On August 6, the board squared its accounts with Jailer George Robinson for the past several months. There are four separate entries in the minutes for that day regarding his account. He was owed $86.50 for work performed before July 1, another $66.66 for the month of July, and a separate amount of $280 for his services from April 25 to July 6. Subsequent entries into the minutes did a better job at distinguishing between salary payments and compensation for provisions and inmate care. The last entry is probably not salary but compensation, as it itemizes costs. Robinson was paid $40 for candles purchased prior to July 16 and another $32.50 for wood.[39]

TOWARD THE CONSTRUCTION OF A SECURE JAIL

With the accounts of its jailer in order and the memory of two failed attempts to fund and construct a new jail in the previous two years fresh in everybody's mind, the Board of Supervisors attempted to succeed where the Court of Sessions had failed. On August 14, the board announced that Captain J. D. Hunter had submitted the winning "Bond" and it was the board's intention to enter into a contract with him for the construction of the new jail. The *Los Angeles Star* printed a description of the proposed jail. It was to be a two-story building, thirty feet long and fifteen feet high. The lower floor would house the jail and would have a stone floor and stone walls three feet thick. The jailer would live on the top floor, which would have adobe walls.[40]

Now a jail fund was created, from which $3,000 was to be paid to Captain Hunter.[41] Problems with this arrangement began immediately. On August 30, the previous agreement was declared "entered erroneously" and new terms were announced. Now the county was to pay Hunter $3,000 up front and an additional $4,000 upon delivery of the jail, which was to be completed no later than nine months from August 30.[42] For his part, Hunter offered "to give security in the sum of $14,000 for the faithful performance of his contract with B. D. Wilson and J. Floyd Jones."[43] Having Wilson's support especially must have boosted Hunter's credibility. At this time (in 1852) Benjamin Wilson was the region's Indian agent, the mayor of Los Angeles, and heir, through marriage, to huge tracts of land including parts of Rancho Santa Ana. The following year, he would be elected to the Board of Supervisors. Despite Wilson's backing, however, Hunter quickly ran into trouble that no one could have anticipated.

On January 5, 1853, the board met and noted that, "Hunter commenced the work and by an act of providence is now prevented from proceeding with it and the board being satisfied that the locality of said jail is unsuitable and the land on which it was to be built not conforming to the requirement of the law, desire to discontinue said contract and therefore it was mutually agreed between the said Hunter and the board. . . ."[44] Apparently, the location selected for the jail was in an area where it was likely to be damaged by rain runoff. The county allowed Hunter to keep the $3,000 advanced to him, and he released them from any further obligation to him. The board also noted that on the previous day, the County Treasurer and Auditor also submitted their report stating that county indebtedness was $47,017. Coupling this deficit with the loss to Hunter, the board now found itself hard pressed to find some way to raise the necessary funds to build a new jail. To this end, the board proposed that "the Legislature of this State be respectfully petitioned hereby on behalf of this Board, that a law may be passed immediately authorizing said Board to levy a tax upon all real and personal property in this County not to exceed one dollar upon every one hundred dollars worth of such property for the purposes of building a Jail . . ."[45] There is no evidence that this proposal was successful, however.

By July of that year, the new jail was no nearer construction, but the current jail arrangements were officially deemed inadequate by the Board. It now ordered that, "In view of the expenses of the Rent of the building as present occupied as the Jail of Los Angeles County . . . ordered that the proprietor of said building be warned that the County will not continue to Rent said Building from him after the last day of this month."[46] The mandate went on to direct the county clerk to draw an order from the treasury for $70 for Sheriff Barton to pay to F. A. Alvarado "for the Rent of a building for the County Jail and to repair the same so as to make it suitable for that purpose." This rented property was to serve as the jail until the completion of a proper facility.

On August 11, serious movement was finally made toward the construction of an adequate jail. A contract was entered into between the county, city, and John Temple for the acquisition of a property of his known as the Roche House. The existing building was to be renovated for use as county offices and a new jail was to be constructed on the adjacent lot. The agreed upon price for the entire property was $3,160. Temple, a prominent town father, was a Massachusetts trader who had come to Los Angeles in 1827. By 1848 he owned an estimated 14,000 head of cattle, 5,000 sheep, and 1,000 horses, as well as an extensive rancho.[47] J. B. Sanford and Supervisor Stephen C. Foster were appointed as the building committee. This committee was given authority by the Board of Supervisors and Los Angeles town council to prepare and conclude construction contracts, but was told that it "shall make no contract that in the aggregate will make the whole cost of the jail when completed . . . more than six thousand dollars."[48] Unlike the arrangement with Hunter, the new agreement made no provision for a cash advance. The county's financial situation precluded any such arrangement. The contractor was to have a lien on the property for the value of materials and labor until such time as the county treasurer issued payment. The County's target date for payment was November 30, 1853. The contractor was not obliged to "deliver the said jail to the Sheriff of said County until every claim thereon is satisfied." This placed a burden on the county to make its payment. The City of Los Angeles was a joint partner in this venture and held a one-quarter interest in the property. For its $1,500 (up front) contribution toward the construction of the jail, and a subsequent $1,000 to be paid on or before August 1, 1854, the city received the use of certain rooms in the existing Roche House and new jail, in the latter case in partnership with the county jailer, "forever." To pay for the balance of the construction costs, the county would draw from a tax imposed on real property in fiscal year 1853–1854 of 10 cents on each $100 worth of property. While this clearly fell far short of the $1 per $100 on real property that the county had hoped the state legislature would authorize, the amount would have to do. A further order placed a cap of $7,000 on the total building fund. Monies received in excess of this amount would be placed in the Jail Contingent Fund. The county probably took possession of the completed jail and began housing prisoners there some time after November 1853.

Supervisor and building committee member Stephen C. Foster submitted the jail's architectural plans to the entire board of supervisors. He would be the jail's builder. The supervisors apparently saw no conflict of interest with this. Foster would serve as mayor of Los Angeles from 1854 to 1855, and then returned as mayor in 1856. He resigned from his first term as mayor to lead a lynch mob, which says a great deal about the criminal justice system in Los Angeles in the 1850s. In 1880, an early history of Los Angeles County was published by the Thompson and West Company. This history records a description of Foster's jail from an account written on January 30, 1858.

> The jail is a two-story brick building. The first floor is occupied as city prison or lock-up, and is divided into two apartments, for males and females. The upper story is the county prison. The joists which support this floor are traversed with strong iron bars throughout, about six inches apart. Over these is laid down thick planking, then a covering of sheet iron, and over all planks again, forming a floor which it would be impossible to cut through without detection. The prison comprises a large room, well ventilated, and six cells, deficient in that respect. The partitions are made of heavy timber, well secured by iron clamps. The doors are massive iron gratings.[49]

As of the publication of the Thompson and West history, no one had ever escaped from the jail. Mr. Foster reported this fact to the compilers of the jail's history with some satisfaction.

The layout of the brick jail suggests that careful thought went into its construction. Such matters as classification of inmates (sentenced and unsentenced, male and female) were addressed. Clearly, the beginnings of a *system* of incarceration were in evidence. A brick pavement was laid from the street to the jail entrance to make the structure more appealing from the outside. The 1858 account recorded in Thompson and West indicated that the pavement was kept "neat and clean." The jailers clearly took pride in the structure. Part of the first floor was no doubt used by the jailer as an office, but, as mentioned, the city was entitled to "occupy forever the rooms in the ground floor of the Jail. . . ."[50] The city must have maintained an office here, presumably for city law enforcement personnel who were processing prisoners, although this is not certain.

The evidence does not suggest what type of plumbing the building had. Obviously, inmates as well as jail personnel needed to clean up and relieve themselves. There probably was an outhouse. Perhaps there might have been some type of washroom on the first floor, or else a washbasin was provided in each cell. Undoubtedly, the job of escorting inmates to the lavatory was one of the more tedious tasks jailers and their assistants faced daily. It was probably done on a scheduled rather than on an as needed basis. The only alternative to an outdoor latrine would have been providing a bucket in each cell. If this method was employed, the smell may well have been nearly unbearable, especially on a warm summer day. Anyone who has spent any time in a jail can attest that it harbors some of the foulest odors imaginable.

The 1858 description of the brick jail describes the second-story prison as "well ventilated." This tends to support the notion that the building had some kind of lavatory arrangements. This description of the jail as "well ventilated" notwithstanding, other evidence attests that it was not always so. In November 1855, Jailer Francis Carpenter submitted a request to better "ventilate the apartments used by himself and family." Carpenter supported this request with the testimony of jail physician J. S. Griffin, who noted that sicknesses in the Carpenter family could be attributed to poor ventilation.[51] Any modifications made to the jail to accommodate Carpenter's concern were no doubt completed by Supervisor Stephen C. Foster, who maintained the condition of the jail. In May of 1855 Foster was appointed to make all repairs to the jail by the building committee.[52] Foster was not a supervisor at the time of this appointment, but he would be one again in 1856. It is doubtful that the board's actions were unbiased in awarding this contract to Foster, but questionable relationships between members of county government as they pertained to the construction of the county jail were not unique to Los Angeles County.[53]

An entire array of questions, besides that concerning plumbing, arise about the jail. Did the inmates wear uniforms or their own clothing? If they wore uniforms, who provided them and cleaned them, and where were the clothes the inmates wore into jail stored? One of the sheriff's stated duties was to escort inmates to court, but how were releases handled? How, for example, were fees collected? By the 1880s, jailers filled out release receipts, which were cosigned by a senior deputy sheriff.[54] No doubt some similar arrangement existed in the 1850s, but what about other mundane activities? Did inmates receive mail or regular visits? Did they receive religious services?

A SECURE JAIL IN LOS ANGELES
COUNTY AND COMMUNITY STABILITY

In some new communities, the presence of a secure jail tended to have a stabilizing effect. As noted, this happened in San Francisco in 1851, but a secure jail cannot be the only secure institution. San Francisco's population swelled rapidly and its institutions grew with it. Recent historians have shown that the formation of the vigilance committee five years later had everything to do with politics and little to do with crime.[55] The 1856 committee did not reflect a breakdown of the legal system but a housecleaning of its rivals by the dominant political group. By the mid-1850s, San Francisco's criminal justice system; its courts, police force and jails, were secure. The knowledge that its prisoners were securely inside the jail was merely one leg of the stool upon which the peace of mind of the community rested.

The problem in Los Angeles was that its crime rate simply overwhelmed its legitimate institutions. The vastness of the county was noted above. This was cattle country, widespread ranchos and sparse local law enforcement attracted criminals. San Francisco's inhospitable climate combined with the waning of the Gold Rush encouraged many drifters to venture into the southern half of the state. The clash between criminals and ranchers resulted in a period of vigilante justice in Los Angeles that far surpassed the better-known activities of the San Francisco committees of 1851 and 1856. Los Angeles witnessed at least 40 legal hangings, 38 lynchings and 32 executions by vigilance committees between 1851 and 1874.[56] The existence of a jail was little deterrent once a mob decided to act. One man accused of stealing horses was removed from the adobe jail in early February 1853 by a hastily formed committee and given 78 lashes on his bare back.[57]

The completion of the solid brick jail in 1854 did not stop the occasional visits by irate citizens. Despite Stephen C. Foster's proud claim to the Thompson and West authors that no prisoner ever escaped from his jail, he made no mention of the "early releases" granted by mob activity.[58] In November 1854, five men overpowered the jailer and dragged one David Brown from his cell. Brown had been sentenced to death for planning the robbery of town patriarch John Temple. There are three different versions of what happened next, but all of them end the same way: with Brown dancing at the end of a rope.[59] Juan Flores, one of the alleged murderers of Sheriff James Barton, was similarly liberated from the jail on February 14, 1857, and swung from a makeshift gallows.[60] Flores's partner, Pancho Daniel, met a similar end in November 1858. In this case the sheriff, deputy, and city marshal were called out of town on a ruse, then an armed and angry mob confronted the jailer on the street and demanded his keys. The mob then proceeded to the jail, where they seized Daniel and strung him up from the crosspiece of the building.[61]

Though lynchings in Los Angeles County continued to occur after 1857, it was six years before a mob called upon the jail again. In the interim, however, prisoners were taken from out of the sheriff's custody as he tried to escort them between the jail and court. Such was the case of Francisco Cota, the murderer of grocery store owner Lawrence Leck, on October 17, 1861. Cota was seized from custody by an angry crowd and hanged in the high gateway of a tannery on the corner of Aliso and Alameda Streets.[62] Manuel Cerradel also was forcibly liberated from Sheriff Tomas Sanchez's custody on December 9, 1863, this while the sheriff was escorting the convicted felon from a tugboat to the steamer *Senator*, en route to the Bay Area and San Quentin. Cerradel had been sentenced to ten years in prison for his involvement in a murder. Locals felt the punishment was not severe enough. After taking Cerradel they hung him from the tugboat's rigging. Charles Wilkins, a convicted murderer, was similarly taken from the sheriff while on the way back to jail from court on December 17, 1863. Like the others, he became acquainted with the end of a rope.[63]

These lynchings from out of the sheriff's custody in 1863 had followed a violent incident that occurred outside the jail. Sheriff Sanchez arrested four loathsome characters earlier in the fall. The band was led by Boston Daimwood, an ex-lawman. He and his cronies had recently arrived in Los Angeles from the Colorado mines, carrying money they reportedly had stolen from a miner they killed. The four were carousing about the city loudly threatening local citizens when Sheriff Sanchez saw fit to arrest them. During the arrest, local ruffians who were probably trying to hit Daimwood and his men fired shots at Sanchez and his deputies. On the morning of November 21, a mob of nearly 200 hundred men broke down the walls of the jail, removed Daimwood and his followers from their cells, and delivered the type of summary justice to which the community had grown so accustomed. This action, topped off with those of the following month, proved more than Sanchez could stand. Everyone knew that the same cadre of disgruntled citizens had been behind all these incidents. Unlike previous sheriffs, Sanchez threatened to arrest the group's ringleaders. He demanded the immediate end to the vigilance committee and insisted that citizens return to their customary civic duties as jurors. Sanchez's action worked. The committee disbanded, although none of the ringleaders who had led the lynching were tried.[64] Four years previously, in December 1859, the sheriff won permission from the board of supervisors to use inmate labor to construct a ten-foot fence around the jail yard to help with its security.[65] This did little to hold back the mob in 1863, however. Only Sanchez's bold determination finally forced them to back down.

One last mob assault was made on the jail in 1870. Another vigilance committee was the source of the mob and another murderer was the target. Michael Lacenais, a man with a long and violent history, had murdered one Joseph Bell over the use of some water. When Sheriff James Burns attempted to take Lacenais to court, a mob began to form and Burns retreated to the brick jail, whence he put out a call for a posse to form to protect the prisoner. Only two men responded. Meanwhile, the mob was joined by approximately 400 others, all of whom demanded Lacenais. Without a posse to support him, the sheriff surrendered his prisoner. Lacenais was marched to a corral a short distance away and hanged.[66] He had escaped justice nine years earlier when he fled the city after murdering Henry Deleval. The citizens were determined that this not happen again. This final lynching in Los Angeles was no doubt encouraged by sentiments expressed by the *Los Angeles Star* only two weeks earlier. In an article titled "Crime and No Punishment," the paper ridiculed the courts and bemoaned the fact that "the people are absolutely taxed to support the man who commits crime, as long as he thinks proper to remain in their boarding-house—for that is all the jails are now."[67] The paper issued the obligatory disclaimer against popular justice, but the level of contempt expressed toward the criminal justice system was plain. Lacenais's return was no doubt a reminder of those perceived failures.

THE JAIL AS PART OF THE CRIMINAL JUSTICE SYSTEM

The county jail was not the only pillar of the criminal justice system to come under attack during Los Angeles's early years. Indeed, the entire matrix was suspect between 1850 and 1870. Some of the most prominent members of the community took part in vigilante activity. And while sheriffs and jailers did their best to maintain the integrity of the jail, it was often a fight they waged alone. Only Sheriff Sanchez was willing to take on a committee, and this only after three frustrating lynchings of prisoners from out of his custody in less than a month.

The brick jail of 1854 served the county well, but by the late 1870s the facility was beginning to show its age. An escape attempt was thwarted in 1878. The most interesting result of this attempted escape was the scrutiny given to the brick jail after it. It was discovered that "division walls of four cells had been penetrated, admitting the occupants to the common apartment, where they had in turn begun to dig through the outer wall."[68] By the mid-1880s another condition began to plague the jail—overcrowding. Nowhere was the increased population in southern California more evident than in the brick jail. The average monthly prisoner count for August through December 1884 was 38.4. By the end of 1885, this increased to 54.7, and by the end of 1886, it reached 60.2. The average number of prisoners who remained in custody from one month to the next also increased over the period, from 21.6 in 1884 to 24.4 in 1885 and 26.7 in 1886.[69] With population figures within the county skyrocketing and given the age of the brick jail, a new facility was a necessity.

The 1885 grand jury's inspection found the, "County Jail [in] as good a condition as it is possible for its age, the sewerage is very imperfect and it is crowded with 62 prisoners. We hope for sake of humanity the Board of Supervisor will soon build a modern jail where each prisoner will be confined by himself."[70] The grand jury went on to offer its opinion of the purpose and function of jails:

> This Grand Jury believe that jails are built for the repression of crime. The great evil of our present jail is the indiscriminate intercourse. We believe the prisoners should be worked as their health would be greatly improved.[71]

The 1886 grand jury offered a similar opinion on the jail, but included a caveat, "The accommodations are entirely insufficient, but this will soon be remedied by the new building now in course of construction."[72]

The jail to which this grand jury was referring had been authorized for construction earlier that spring. The Board of Supervisors put out bids for the new structure at the end of 1885. Only two were returned. One anonymous contractor, who obviously failed to submit his own bid in a timely fashion, bemoaned this fact and suggested that the board reject the two bids that were returned and begin the process again.[73] This idea was ignored and on April 14, 1886, W. O. Burr submitted a written promise to build the new jail as per plan and specifications already on file in the County Clerk's office. The proposed price of the new structure was $22,000.[74] This did not include the cell work. That contract went to the Pauly Brothers of St. Louis, Missouri, for an additional $15,959.[75]

Overcrowding and other problems with the brick jail compelled Sheriff Gard and the county to move inmates into the new building on December 1, 1886, before it was completely finished. This move was accomplished without much public notice or fanfare, and the first chapter in the history of Los Angles County's jails came to a close. Perhaps this was as it should be. Jails are an unfortunate necessity in our society, and when they function smoothly they do so without drawing too much attention. Still, it is the responsibility of county leaders to recognize the importance of jails as legitimizers of our society. All early civic leaders in California recognized the importance of establishing a secure jail, and those in young Los Angeles County were no different. Maintaining the fragile balance between fledgling economies and jail costs was a test that lawmakers faced. Maintenance of the existing jail was not ignored, even as it was recognized that a new and improved structure was necessary. It took three years and three false starts before this happened, however. And it only happened when significant county fathers stepped forward and made sacrifices.

Still, the erection of a secure jail in Los Angeles did not effect a secure community. In some of its practices, namely allotting less money for Indian/Hispanic prisoners than white ones, the early criminal justice system fueled the very tensions that existed between the poor Hispanic majority and the wealthy, land-owning whites and *Californios*. Having a secure jail in Los Angeles did not contribute to the end of vigilante activity as it did in San Francisco because the other institutions were not solid. A secure jail is but one leg of a three-legged stool. If the courts and the law enforcement agencies cannot guarantee impartiality and security, a secure jail cannot hold back the tide of popular sentiment. When these other institutions caught up with the jail, namely when Sheriff Sanchez stood up to the mob and crime began to drop in the 1860s, the presence of a secure jail had more meaning in the community.

Even the 1850 jail, with all its problems, was more than a place where "confusion was king, along with plain dirt and humiliation."[76] Earnest efforts were made to provide inmates with decent housing and provisions and medical care despite the circumstances. County fathers were far from indifferent to the jail and attempted to deal with the problem of the old jail every year until they could construct a better facility. The lesson of incarceration in Los Angeles in the 1850s was that a secure jail alone could not resolve society's crime problems.

Notes

1   *Robinson* vs. *Block*, 1982.
2   For a good description of the condition of San Francisco's early jails and their effect on the vigilance committee of 1851 see, Kevin J. Mullen, *Let Justice Be Done—Crime and Politics in Early San Francisco* (Reno, University of Nevada Press, 1989.)
3   F. W. Emerson, *History of the Los Angeles Sheriff's Department, 1850–1940* (Pasadena: Federal Writer's Project, 1940), p. 73. (Hereafter cited as Emerson.)
4   Leonard Pitt and Dale Pitt, *Los Angeles, A to Z: An Encyclopedia of the City and County* (Berkeley: University of California Press, 1997), 277–278.
5   Emerson, *supra* note 1 at 81.
6   Ibid. p. 82.
7   Emerson, *supra* note 1, at 22.
8   Ibid. p. 24.
9   Minutes of the Los Angeles County Court of Sessions, Bk 1, p. 2.
10 Ibid. p. 3. The health of prisoners was a concern that was not overlooked. Dr. Hodges was "required to attend sick prisoners confined herein when called on by the sheriff or jailer presenting his bill for attendance at proper times to this court." At various times over the years a number of physicians were paid for services rendered to inmates. Finally, on November 10, 1859, the minutes record that a one-year contract was entered into with Dr. J. S. Griffin to serve as the jail physician. Dr. Griffin was to receive $25 a month for his services in this capacity, thus ending the piecemeal billing practices of his predecessors.
11 Ibid. p. 16.
12 Ibid. p. 17.
13 Thompson and West, *History of Los Angeles County, California* (Berkeley, reprinted from 1880 original), 127. (Hereafter cited as Thompson and West.)
14 Minutes of the Los Angeles County Court of Sessions, Bk. 1, p. 55.
15 Minutes of the Los Angeles County Board of Supervisors, Bk. 1, p. 186.
16 Ibid. p. 64. On July 9, 1853 the Board of Supervisors set the jailer's salary at $4 a day, which was actually an increase from the $3 a day it had originally lowered it to in August 1852.
17 Lawrence Friedman, *Crime and Punishment in American History* (New York, HarperCollins, 1993), 166. (Hereafter cited as Friedman.)
18 Thompson and West, supra note 12, at 127.
19 Minutes of the Los Angeles County Court of Sessions, Bk 1, p. 58.

20 Minutes of the Los Angeles County Board of Supervisors, Bk 1, p. 64.

21 Ibid. p. 177.

22 Ibid., Bk. 2, p. 120.

23 For a good recent overview of the early mistrust of the Anglo legal system in Los Angeles by Hispanics see Ronald C. Woolsey, *Migrants West: Toward the Southern California Frontier* (Claremont, CA, Grizzly Bear Publishing, 1996), 72–84. Perhaps the best work on this subject is still Leonard Pitt's *The Decline of the Californios* (Berkeley, CA, University of California Press, 1966).

24 It is difficult to follow the clear line of succession from one jailer to the next. Unlike sheriffs, who were elected, jailers were appointed and often left office suddenly. The only way to tell that a new jailer was in place was when a new name appeared filing a claim for services in the index to the Board of Supervisors documents on the county jail. Unfortunately, the documents themselves were destroyed several decades ago.

25 Los Angeles County Jail Register —July 1894–August 1897.

26 Walter R. Bacon, "Pioneer Courts and Lawyers of Los Angeles," *Southern California Historical Quarterly*, VI, No. III (1905), p. 215. (Hereafter cited as Bacon.)

27 Minutes of the Los Angeles County Court of Sessions, Bk 1, p. 95.

28 Minutes of the Los Angeles County Board of Supervisors, Bk 2, pp. 120–121.

29 Los Angeles County Jail Register—August 1884–December 1886.

30 Eunice Crittenden, "David W. Alexander, Third Sheriff of Los Angeles," *The Sheriff's Star News*, 20, Num. 4 (July 1957), p. 4.

31 Minutes of the Los Angeles County Court of Sessions, Bk 1, p. 41.

32 Ibid, pp. 67–68.

33 Bacon, *supra* note 25 at 219.

34 Eunice Crittenden, "The Story of Sheriff George Burrill," *The Sheriff's Star News*, 19, Num. 6 (September 1957), p. 3.

35 Ibid.

36 Ibid.

37 Robert W. Blew, "Vigilantism in Los Angeles, 1835–1874," *Southern California Historical Quarterly* LIV, Num. 1 (Spring 1972), p.16. (Hereafter cited as Blew.)

38 On September 18 the *Los Angeles Star* reported the escape of yet another inmate. Francisco Carmillo broke through the walls of the jail while chained at the neck and heels and hand-cuffed. The paper noted "in return for the affectionate care thus bestowed upon him by the jailer, the wretch exhibited only the basest ingratitude; and upon vacating Mr. Robinson's mansion actually stole and carried away his patron's irons." This escape and the paper's slaps at both Robinson and the jail demonstrate the paper's contempt with the structure and further highlighted the need for an adequate replacement.

39 Minutes of the Los Angeles County Board of Supervisors, Bk 1, p. 15.

40 *Los Angeles Star*, August 7, 1852.

41 Minutes of the Los Angeles County Board of Supervisors, Bk 1, p. 16–17.

42 Ibid. p. 19.

43 Ibid.

44 Ibid. p. 40.

45 Ibid. p. 41.

46 Ibid. p. 63.

47 Ibid. p. 80.

48 Ibid. p. 81.

49 Ibid.

50 Granville Arthur Waldron, "Courthouses of Los Angeles County," *Southern California Historical Quarterly*, XLI, Num. 4, December 1959, p. 360.

51 Minutes of the Los Angeles County Board of Supervisors, Bk 2, p. 18

52 Ibid, Bk 1, p. 206.

53 For example, in San Diego County Sheriff Agoston Haraszthy submitted the winning $5,000 bid to construct that county's first jail in 1850. His bid won despite being $2,000 higher than the lowest bidder at a time when San Diego County had only $10,600 in its treasury. See Theodor W. Fuller, *San Diego Originals* (Pleasant Hill, CA, California Profiles Publications, 1987), p. 161.

54 Los Angeles County Jail Register, November 1888–December 1889. Ten receipts were attached

in the back of this ledger from Jailer George Mannon. They were dated from July 28, through August 21, 1889. The first was signed by Sheriff James Kays. The remainder were signed by Deputy Juan Murrietta.

55 See especially, Arthur Quinn, *The Rivals—William Gwin, David Broderick and the Birth of California* (New York, Crown Publishers, 1994), p. 191–193.

56 Blew, *supra* note 23 at 13.

57 Ibid. p.17.

58 Thompson and West, *supra* note 9, at 127.

59 Blew, *supra* note 23, at 20–21.

60 Book 2, page 91 of the supervisor's minute book makes the following entry on March 25, 1857. "The sum of $400 allowed on said acct. for the maintenance of prisoners confined in the county jail and arrested during the excitement consequent upon the assassination of Jas R. Barton, Sheriff and his posse payable out of the fund for Suppression of Bands of Armed Banditti in LA County." Whether this is payment for the unpleasantness of February 14 in addition to the housing of future inmates who were involved in the Barton assassination is unclear.

61 Thompson and West, *supra* note 9, at 82.

62 Ibid. 83.

63 Ibid.

64 Blew, *supra* note 23, at 23–24.

65 Minutes of the Los Angeles County Board of Supervisors, Bk 2, p. 315.

66 Blew, *supra* note 23, at 25.

67 *Los Angeles Star*, December 3, 1870.

68 Thompson and West, *supra* note 9, at 127.

69 A recapitulation of the count was done on the first day of each month. All jail count tables were assembled using the first day of the month totals. The average number of new bookings was also tabulated for this date. This latter area demonstrated no consistent pattern over the years of the study. Gambling raids, and other mass arrests, could skew the figures for any given month.

70 B of S Document, 275G, October 3, 1885.

71 Ibid. This call to "work" the prisoners suggests that despite authorizing inmate labor that extended as far back as 1850 this was not being done, probably because of the size of the sheriff's staff and the design of the brick jail.

72 B of S Document, 278G, September 21, 1886.

73 *Los Angeles Times*, February 20, 1886.

74 B of S Document, 1J, April 14, 1886. The jail actually cost $23,000 to construct, a reasonable overage.

75 *Los Angeles Times*, April 14, 1886.

76 Friedman, *supra*, Note 16, at 166.

CHAPTER FOUR

Weather and History: The Climate of Nineteenth-Century Southern California

Wayne N. Engstrom

INTRODUCTION

In sharp contrast to a five-season-long drought that ended in 1991–1992, heavy precipitation drenched southern California during much of the rest of the 1990s. Indeed, a severe El Niño generated conditions that made the winter of 1997–1998 the sixth wettest winter since 1877–1878, with more than 31 inches of precipitation falling in Los Angeles, more than double the annual average of 14.77 inches for 1961–1990. El Niño is the name given to episodes of important sea surface temperature increases that occur off the equatorial coast of Peru and Ecuador. Typically, these events ultimately lead to the presence of warmer sea surface temperatures off the Pacific coast of North America and a strengthening and southward shift of the northern hemisphere jet stream. This brings increased storminess and wetter winters to southern California. Precipitation peaked in February 1998, the third wettest single month on record at Los Angeles, as 13.68 inches fell.[1] Accompanied by wind gusts of up to 70 miles per hour, four separate storms made landfall in southern California that February, bringing heavy rain at lower elevations and snow in the mountains. Highway closures, flooded homes, and storm-related deaths occurred: a robbery suspect drowned in the swollen Los Angeles River; a snowboarder perished from the effects of exposure in the local mountains; and falling trees and washed–out roads claimed the lives of three travelers.[2]

On the positive side, in some ways the exceptionally wet winter of 1997–1998 benefited California. Statewide, roofing companies and home-repair firms reported additional income in excess of $100 million and ski areas reported doing a much better than average business. Another positive outcome was that meteorologists had made highly accurate predictions of that winter's weather events, forecasts that state officials used to embark on a sweeping program to prepare for the coming bad winter. Consequently, the state suffered roughly half the losses ($1.1 billion in 1998

Waves during a severe El Niño event in early February, 1998, crashing into the southern California shoreline at San Clemente. *Photograph by Wayne Engstrom*

dollars) it had realized as a consequence of the equally severe El Niño winter of 1982–1983.[3] Clearly, accurate forecasts of climatic variation are of great value to society, particularly as they impact water flow and supplies. In California, where both dry climates and steep slopes capable of generating much runoff during storms are prevalent, agencies engaged in planning, designing, and operating water-supply and flood-control facilities are keenly interested in precipitation prediction.[4] Temperature forecasts are also important, as temperature influences evaporation rates and determines the percentage of precipitation falling as either snow or rain. But accurate precipitation and temperature forecasts require an understanding of the causes of previous climatic change, providing a stimulus for the study of past climates.[5]

Knowledge of past climates is useful for the student of history as well, for it can provide insight into the environmental conditions prevailing during significant historical events, perhaps even helping one to understand why those events took place at all. It may be argued that the effects of weather events in the past were much more dramatic, as engineering structures such as aqueducts and flood-control dams were not yet in place to mitigate the consequences of severe weather. Furthermore, relatively primitive living conditions made people more vulnerable to "bad" weather, heightening the awareness of meteorological phenomena. A nineteenth-century observer, for example, suggested that the circumstances of San Francisco settlers living in tents or beneath partly open roofs during the wet winter of 1849–1850 served to have "magnified and multiplied the falling drops, and penetrated sufferers with indelible hydropathic impressions."[6] These observations should not be construed as a call for a "revival of environmental determinism," nor do they mean to suggest that all changes in the environment are a result of climate, or that linkages between climate history and human history are clear and easy to detect.[7] Climate is simply one of the numerous factors that can influence historical events and as such is deserving of careful consideration.

This essay outlines the climate of southern California in the nineteenth century with particular emphasis on the latter half of the century, a time during which the area was experiencing rapid settlement and, coincidentally, one in which people began to record weather observations. Concern here is primarily with the Los Angeles Basin and adjacent mountains, although relevant information on weather events in San Diego, Santa Barbara, and beyond is included.

The sources of climatic information include the instrumental record of temperature and precipitation, systematically recorded in Los Angeles beginning in 1877. Climatic proxies, defined as "historical, geological, and biological substitutes for meteorological records" complement and extend the man-made instrumental record.[8] This distinction is sometimes blurred as information on biological substitutes, for example, appears in the historical record. The instrumental record obviously provides the least ambiguous source of climatic information, but for nineteenth-century Los Angeles it spans less than a quarter-century. Conversely, biological and geological proxies, such as tree-rings and undisturbed layers of sediment resting on the ocean bottom called varves, contain climatic information that extends far back in time. Finally, historical proxies, often in the form of private letters, journals, and the logs of sea captains, overlap both the instrumental and the biological and geological proxy records and also can shed light on specific weather events. Like all human creations, historical proxies can be biased, as people are more inclined to mention extreme events and their observations can be influenced by non-climatic considerations. Nevertheless, through careful evaluation and cross-checking, all of these forms of climatic information can be used to generate an overview of the climate of nineteenth-century California into which one can place reasonable confidence.

Climatically, the final half of the nineteenth century witnessed the end of the Little Ice Age, a time of cooling over much of the Earth during which glaciers advanced in some areas.[9] An increase in north-south air flow, periods of increased precipitation variability, greater storminess, and cooler ocean temperatures occurred in central and southern California during this climatic interval.[10] The Little Ice Age lasted several centuries, beginning about A.D. 1250, with the main phase from 1550 to 1700. It ended sometime between 1850 and 1900. Climatic instability developed in southern California as both the Little Ice Age and the nineteenth century came to an end. During this cool-to-warm transition, record-setting rainfall was recorded at Los Angeles during the 1880s. Meanwhile, the Santa Ana River experienced three floods between 1862 and 1891, the estimated peak discharge of which equaled or exceeded the largest twentieth-century flood.[11] This period was also marked by one of the worst droughts ever to afflict southern California, extending from the summer of 1862 to the fall of 1864 and responsible for the deaths of hundreds of thousands of cattle.[12] Shortly thereafter the cattle industry collapsed and was replaced by irrigated agriculture, the expansion of which was spurred by a number of social and natural factors combined with technological advances.[13] As the population of southern California swelled, settlers arriving from eastern states had to adjust to an unfamiliar Mediterranean climate characterized by wet winters and dry summers. At the same time, the climate of southern of California was experiencing a period of substantial instability.

THE CLIMATE OF SOUTHERN CALIFORNIA

Located at 34° N. latitude on the west coast of North America, coastal southern California has had a Mediterranean climate extending back to glacial times.[14] Found in similar locations around the world, the Mediterranean climate takes its name from the Mediterranean Sea, the region wherein this climate is the most extensive. Mediterranean climates typically feature dry summers and wet winters; virtually everywhere else in the world the opposite is the case. In California, the summer drought is brought on by the northward migration of the North Pacific High Pressure Cell. The vertical movement of air in a high pressure cell is always downward, reducing the likelihood of precipitation. The descending air is compressed as the atmospheric pressure increases. The compression leads in turn to an increase in the temperature of the air that lowers the relative humidity, preventing the formation of clouds and precipitation. Also contributing to the summer drought in California is the nearshore presence of the California Current and associated upwelling.

At least tens of miles in width, the California Current is a slow flow of cold water moving south along the coast of California. Driven by wind, it originates as water moving eastward across the central North Pacific Ocean is deflected southward by the Pacific coastline of North America. The California Current ends as the flow turns westward near the end of the Baja California peninsula. This same wind/current system was used by the Manila galleons during their trips from the Philippines to Mexico for over two centuries.[15] Dominating between July and November, the California Current is driven southward by northwesterly winds coming from the North Pacific High Pressure Cell. These winds also cause spring and early summer upwelling as the southward moving surface water tends to move off-shore, allowing even colder water to move upward.[16] Cold surface water discourages precipitation as evaporation, which otherwise adds water vapor to the air. Also, the cold water generates a strong temperature inversion in which cold, denser air, chilled by contact with the cold surface water, lies beneath air that has been warmed by compression as described above. Clearly, temperature inversions discourage uplift of the air as buoyant lift of the cold, dense surface air is not possible.

Winter, conversely, is the wet season in California as the North Pacific High Pressure Cell shifts southward along with the westerly wind belt. Embedded in the "Westerlies" are eastward-moving surface low pressure cells. Because they develop roughly between 30° and 60° of latitude, these are called middle latitude cyclones. Upon landfall in California, these middle latitude cyclones bring precipitation. In contrast to the downward movement of air in a high pressure cell, the vertical movement of air is upward in a low pressure cell. The rising air in a low pressure cell cools as the air expands, increasing the relative humidity to as much as 100 percent. Cooling above this point results in condensation, the formation of clouds and possibly precipitation. In a middle latitude cyclone, warm air meets cold air along a boundary known as a front. Because it is less dense, the warm air is forced upward. Precipitation produced this way is called frontal precipitation. Uplift is also achieved when the air in a middle latitude cyclone is forced upward by a mountain range, guaranteeing continued cooling as the air is forced to rise and resulting in what is called orographic precipitation. Also helping to encourage winter precipitation is the brief appearance in midwinter of the north-flowing Davidson Current along the coast. This brings warm water northward as the main stream of the California current moves farther off the coast.[17]

Although they arrived from the northwest or west, the middle-latitude cyclones were known as "southeasters" in the nineteenth century, as their arrival was heralded by southeasterly winds.[18] In an 1854 letter to the Superintendent of the U.S. Coast Survey [now U.S. Coast and Geodetic Survey] concerning navigational hazards on the Pacific Coast, Assistant W. P. Trowbridge provides a vivid description of the weather events associated with such storms:

> The meteorological phenomena attending a South Easter, or more properly, a South Wester, are very interesting—until these storms become so frequent, that one passes into another, thus making a continual storm for a week or two; their approach can be observed for many hours beforehand. The atmosphere becomes beautifully transparent, so that objects twenty or thirty miles distant appear to be no more than ten or fifteen; the usual hazy appearance disappears, and everything in nature assumes a pleasant aspect. Cirrus clouds then gradually ap-

pear to the Southward and finally spread entirely over the sky; the wind usually commences to blow lightly from the South East, gradually increasing in force
and shifting to the Southward. Heavy dark clouds accompany the Southerly
wind, and it soon becomes a gale, while the clouds discharge torrents of rain.
During the early part of the winter, November and December, the storms last
but a few hours, the wind works around to the Westward, and finally the re-
appearance of a steady N. W. trade is a sure indication that a vessel may safely
return to her anchorage.[19]

Middle-latitude cyclones are the primary source of precipitation in
southern California. The frequency and intensity of such storm systems
vary from winter to winter and so, accordingly, does the annual precipitation. In the nineteenth century, some wet winters have been linked with El
Niño conditions while others in non-El Niño years are associated with
periods when the north-south flow of air has been unusually strong, causing very cold and warm moist air to collide, bringing intense frontal
precipitation. Nevertheless, the final decades of the nineteenth century witnessed an overall decline in the intensity and frequency of "southeasters"
as the Little Ice Age drew to a close.[20]

SOURCES OF CLIMATIC INFORMATION

A. The Instrumental Record

Instrumental weather observations were not made by the Spaniards or
Mexicans in California; the first to do so was an English sea captain in
1826.[21] For the Los Angeles area, seasonal (July 1-June 30) precipitation
data is first complete for the 1860s; Drum Barracks, in present-day
Wilmington, recorded 7.62 inches in 1864–1865.[22] Dating back to July 1,
1877, when U.S. Army Signal Service Sergeant C. E. Howgate made the
first observation, the "official" instrumental record for Los Angeles (Civic
Center) maintained by the Signal Service and subsequently by the Weather
Bureau was kept at three different locations in downtown Los Angeles in
the nineteenth century.[23] Instrumental records go back farther at San Diego and Santa Barbara.[24] In all cases, changes in station location and the
type, exposure, and height of the instruments affect the measurement of
weather phenomena, the degree to which is difficult to evaluate, even if
documented. The movement of weather stations to the roofs of progres-
sively higher buildings over time is believed to have led to a decrease in the
precipitation amounts recorded and an increase in the temperatures recorded as windiness and the flow of anthropogenic heat from a building
both affect readings. In addition, human error can occur when values are
recorded.[25] Indeed, precipitation amounts recorded at Los Angeles in the
1990s were believed to be under-reported, as the rain gauge was sited on
a rooftop three stories above ground-level. Subsequent comparisons with

ground-level instruments and other gauges suggest that the official Los Angeles readings were only 90 percent of the "true" total during the last decade of the twentieth century. Therefore, one might easily surmise that similar under-reporting of rainfall may have occurred in the nineteenth century at Los Angeles, as three different rooftop locations were utilized: July 1877 to January 1881 (37 feet above ground-level); January 1881 to November 1888 (roof of a five-story building); and November 1888 to the end of the century (roof of a seven-story building).[26]

Several unusual precipitation episodes appear in southern California instrumental records for the late nineteenth century, indicating that this was a time of considerable hydrologic instability. The decade beginning in July 1883 and ending in June 1893 was especially wet in Los Angeles, as the average seasonal precipitation was 135 percent of normal. Rainfall in 1883–1884 set a seasonal record of 38.18 inches that has yet to be surpassed and was followed six years later by the second wettest season ever in 1889–1890, when 34.84 inches was recorded. Monthly precipitation totals were recorded in March (1884), June (1884), July (1886), October (1889), and December (1889) that have never been exceeded. Moreover, December 1889 has the distinction of being the wettest month ever in Los Angeles, with 15.8 inches of precipitation recorded. Instrumental records for San Diego exist from 1850 onward, capturing the severe drought of 1862–1864 that afflicted southern California. A mere 3.87 inches of precipitation fell in 1862–1863, and only 5.14 inches of precipitation fell in 1863–1864 at that station. Surprisingly, this drought immediately followed what was probably the wettest winter ever experienced in southern California, culminating in the storm of January 1862.[27]

B. Biological Proxies

As mentioned earlier, it is possible to turn to certain "proxies" to study the climate of years preceding the advent of the instrumental record. One widely used biological proxy is the width of tree rings because wide rings are produced in years favorable for tree growth, while narrow rings are produced in unfavorable years. Older trees growing on sites where climatic factors influence ring width are selected for such studies, and the rings are analyzed after adjustments are made for the age of the tree and for lagging climatic effects. The growth of buds, roots, and leaves in a favorable year also encourage growth in the next year and vice-versa, generally causing wide and narrow rings to occur in groups.[28]

Tree growth and tree ring width are both dependent upon a number of climatic variables depending upon the species of the tree and the region in which it grew. A number of tree ring records, series of which are known as chronologies, have been developed for sites in southern California. The bigcone spruce (*Psuedotsuga macrocarpa*) is frequently selected for tree ring analysis, as the species is long-lived and produces distinct annual rings.

Early work at a number of sites in the mountains of southern California emphasized this species, and later work at a single site in the Santa Ana Mountains in eastern Orange County considered bigcone spruce exclusively.[29] A study of the response of bigcone spruce growth to climate in the Transverse Ranges north of Santa Barbara and in the San Bernadino Mountains indicates that wider rings are largely indicative of greater winter and spring precipitation and cooler early spring and early summer temperatures, after the effects of age and prior growth are removed.[30] Moreover, a strong positive relationship exists between bigcone spruce growth and the annual runoff for the San Gabriel River at Azusa. Similar results emerged from a second study, in which the average annual discharge of five rivers in southern California were related to bigcone spruce tree ring widths in the San Jacinto Mountains.[31] Other species of trees native to southern California have been subject to tree ring analysis, including the Torrey pine (*Pinus torreyana*). Mostly influenced by winter and spring precipitation, Torrey pine growth is also stimulated, interestingly, by relatively foggy summers.[32] Several observers have remarked, however, that dry years are more faithfully recorded by tree rings than are wet years. This is especially true if heavy rains or the melting of deep snows occur in a short period of time. Under such conditions, the soils become quickly saturated with water, causing water arriving later to run off hillslopes and into stream channels, contributing to flooding rather than the growth of trees. Wet years during which numerous small storms are separated by drier periods are ones in which the soil absorbs more water, encouraging tree growth and the development of wide tree rings.

The early southern California tree ring study identified wet and dry intervals of varying length during the nineteenth century. Tree ring widths are dated to a particular year; the amount of growth in that year principally occurs in the spring and early summer and so is strongly influenced by the amount of precipitation received in the preceding winter that includes the latter part of the previous calendar year. A dry winter in 1840–1841 would produce a narrow ring in 1841, for example. Wet intervals in the early chronology, when bigcone spruce growth was 21 to 52 percent above normal include: 1797–1806; 1816–1819; 1825–1840; 1852–1855; 1865–1869; and 1884–1893. Dry intervals when growth was 21 to 34 percent below normal, include: 1807–1815; 1820–1824; 1841–1851; 1856–1864; 1870–1883; and 1894–1904. To varying degrees, some of these same intervals appear in the Santa Ana Mountains chronology developed later.[33]

Nineteenth-century temperature variations in southern California may be inferred from ring-width variation among bristlecone pines (*Pinus longaeva*) examined at the upper treeline in the White Mountains along the California-Nevada border.[34] Although precipitation and growth in the previous year influence tree ring width, temperature in the growing season is the primary factor limiting growth in this high-altitude location. Wide bristlecone pine rings record warmer temperatures in the previous autumn and the current summer while warm late winters and springs tend to retard growth in the following summer. It can be inferred from the bristlecone pine chronologies that the first half of the nineteenth century, particularly the late 1830s and early 1840s, generally was cold and that temperatures warmed steadily from the 1860s onward as the Little Ice Age and the nineteenth century were both coming to a close.[35]

Another biological indicator of climate is the extent of Giant Kelp (*Macrosystis pyrifera*) forests off the coast of southern California. Kelp forest expansion is encouraged by the presence of cold, nutrient-rich water along the coast that is produced by the combination of strong northwesterly winds, strong California Current flow, and vigorous upwelling. Dry and foggy weather prevails during these episodes. Winters free of intense storms and large waves also help the kelp forest thrive, as large waves tend to destroy the plants. Conversely, winter storms accompanied by large waves capable of kelp destruction often occur during El Niño periods; these periods are also times when warm water arrives from the south, both factors contributing to the loss of kelp. After such a compound event, recovery of the kelp forest may take quite a number of years. Historical sources have yielded information on variations in kelp forest extent at Santa Barbara that have been used by climatologists to infer the strength of preceding storms. Their work indicates, for example, that kelp was abundant in 1827–1828 and yet absent in 1835–1836.[36]

C. *Geological Proxies*

Observations on the presence or absence of kelp at Santa Barbara by nineteenth-century individuals is supplemented by the analysis of varves that have formed in the offshore Santa Barbara Basin. Accumulating at the rate of less than one-half inch per year, varves are soft, undisturbed layers of organic and inorganic material resting on the bottom of an ocean or lake. Yielding much paleoclimatic evidence for southern California are the varves of the Santa Barbara Basin. The basin is located on the floor of the Santa Barbara Channel between the mainland and the Channel Islands. Because oxygen levels are very low in the basin, burrowing organisms are absent, leaving the layers undisturbed and suitable for study; in fact they have been referred to as the most extensively studied varves in the world.[37] Kelp abundance is inferred from certain characteristics of the varves, including the chemistry of the organic matter, some of which is very quickly incorporated into the thickening sediment layer. Analysis of the varve record suggests that there were no El Niños between 1841 and 1870 and that over the course of the next twenty years there was a group of five El Niños: 1870, 1873, 1879, 1883, and 1891.[38] It would also be logical to infer that flood years on the mainland would help produce thicker varves, as more sediment would have settled out of the water column. However, certain lagging effects exist, as it takes longer than a single year for sediment washed into the ocean during floods to reach the floor of the ocean basin.[39]

D. Hydrological Proxies

Providing another type of proxy, the level of Lake Elsinore has varied greatly over the course of the nineteenth century. The lake was virtually dry in 1810, was very high and most likely overflowed in 1862, receded rapidly in 1866 and 1867, and was full once again in 1872. The 1862 and 1872 high-water periods were brief, for parts of the lake floor were exposed for an interval sufficiently long for willow trees to become established and grow to a large size. These willows were drowned by the exceptional rains of 1883–1884, which filled the lake basin to overflowing in three weeks. Water levels remained high for the next decade.[40]

E. Historical Proxies

Historical proxies include written sources of information such as letters, diaries, newspaper accounts, records, almanacs, and ship's logs, all of which can shed light on climatic conditions and weather events providing they are carefully evaluated. Reports of freezing water and the occurrence of lightning are the least ambiguous accounts. It is important, however, to realize that compound factors might have produced a single notable event.[41] For example, wharf destruction is often inferred to signify the arrival of large waves during a storm, but a serious infestation of the wharf by wood-boring organisms such as the common ship worm (*Teredo navalis*), may have substantially weakened the structure to the point that the arrival of waves of any size could have led to its destruction. In another case, the yields of crops grown at California missions were used uncritically in an early study. In that study, the author divided the amount harvested (yield) by the amount planted to make inferences about seasonal rainfall (large values were inferred to indicate wet seasons and low values dry seasons.) The work was widely cited.[42] A subsequent re-evaluation of this work, taking into account other factors that influence yields such as irrigation and social conditions (including size and skill of the labor force), has helped to produce revised rainfall indices.[43]

In addition to flawed research techniques, personal bias or distortion can lead to faulty interpretations of evidence. For example, an analysis of Franciscan documents from the California missions of the early nineteenth century led to the conclusion that the authors of the documents "may have, unknowingly or by design, erroneously attributed agricultural problems to drought."[44] Moreover, translations, compilations, almanacs, and newspaper accounts all represent at least one departure from the original source to the printed page, always allowing for the possibility of error or distortion.

Finally, there is a natural human tendency to emphasize extreme events, one that continues today. Extremes are relative to the experience of the observer, and many observers in southern California were recent arrivals from the mideastern or eastern United States and were therefore mystified by the nature of California rivers. The newcomers were unfamiliar with a hydrologic regime that left channels bone-dry much of the year only to fill them later with rapidly moving water. As an apparently newly arrived author of a county history wrote:

A "River" in the Californian sense means something very different to what that term implies in the Eastern States, . . . But to the Californian such mighty streams [Mississippi, Hudson, etc.] as these are unknown, and the value of the commodity being governed by its scarcity, creeks rank here as rivers, and brooklets are dignified as creeks. Even worse than this—a shadow, a memory, are at times compelled to do duty for the reality, and the thirsty traveler, crossing a dry bed of bleaching sand—guileless of even the suspicion of moisture is gravely informed by the native—that *"this is a river."* At some time within the scope of far-reaching tradition, this sand had been moistened by a tiny stream. That is enough, the memory of those blessed drops defies the centuries, and like Tantalus, the wayfarer may perish of thirst, lying prone in the main bed of *"a river."*[45]

Any relatively large flow may, then, have been labeled a "flood." This may account for the poorer agreement, compared to dry years, between historically documented floods and annual average stream flows reconstructed from tree ring evidence in southern California.[46] Written in ornate prose, newspaper accounts from the period show some tendency to exaggerate the description of "extreme" events such as floods during initial editions, only to be moderated in subsequent editions. This practice may have been an effort to boost newspaper sales.

Reliable accounts of events were most often provided when the observer had personally witnessed or experienced it and soon thereafter recorded the information. In many cases, the most informative accounts are those made by individuals "deeply involved in activities to which the weather was vital."[47] Ship captains' logs and the personal letters of cattle ranchers with a long California experience are especially useful: navigation is strongly influenced by the weather; and stock rearing is dependent upon grass growth, which in turn is almost entirely dependent upon rainfall.

CASE STUDIES OF CLIMATIC INTERVALS

Using a variety of available sources, we now will consider two very wet and two very dry nineteenth-century climatic intervals. Doing so will not only provide details of the nature of these exceptional periods, but also provide a fuller appreciation of the character of the evidence that can be assembled. Rainfall, rather than temperature, is emphasized, as the former is more critical to many types of human activity in southern California. The two dry periods are 1840–1841 to 1844–1845 and 1862–1864, and the two wet periods are the winter of 1861–1862 and the interval from 1883–1884 to 1892–1893.[48]

A. Dry Periods

Biological proxies indicate that the five-year period beginning in 1841 and ending in 1845 was very dry. The width of bigcone spruce tree rings for those years are quite narrow. Indeed, in the Transverse Ranges north of Santa Barbara, 1841 seems to be the driest single year and 1841 to 1845 the driest five-year span in a record that is 400 years long.[49] Farther south, data collected from several locations indicate that average tree growth for the same five-year period was 36 percent below normal. Similarly, work in the Santa Ana Mountains indicates that average growth there was 46 percent below normal.[50] Narrow rings also occur in the early 1840s in the Torrey pine chronology.[51] Consistent with the tree ring record, kelp was abundant off the coast of Santa Barbara during this interval. William Parker, on board the U. S. Sloop *Cyane*, recorded in the logbook that vast beds of kelp slowed the ship's progress as it neared the port in late October 1842.[52] Several months later, in April of 1843, Philo White, the purser on the U.S. sloop *Dale*, encountered much the same situation at the port, commenting "there is so much *kelp* in the water for a half mile off shore that we found some difficulty in working the Boat through it."[53]

Southern California flood histories, chronological lists of early flood events, compiled by U.S. Geological Survey personnel from available records and interviews with long-term residents, are in agreement with the biological proxies. One flood history does not mention floods during this period, while notations in a second flood history describe 1840–1841 as "dryest (sic) year ever known," 1842–1843 as "very open and dry," 1843–1844 as "very dry," and 1844–1845 as a "drought." The wettest season in this five-year period, 1841–1842, saw roughly average bigcone spruce growth. Paradoxically it was described in the second flood history as the "wettest year ever known."[54]

Accounts relating directly to the climate of this interval from observers who were in California at this time are compelling. William Dane Phelps, master of the ship *Alert*, on which he sailed along the coast while engaging in hide and tallow trading, recorded in his journal on 10 April 1841 while at port in San Pedro that "there has been very little rain on this part of the coast, and the ground which is usually at this time clothed with verdure, is now parched and dry; not the least green to be seen." While in San Diego on 4 June he noted "the season has been without rain."[55] California pioneer General John Bidwell arrived in the San Francisco Bay Area in November 1841. He remarked, "it had been one of the driest years ever known in California," leaving the countryside "brown and parched." Bidwell also noted that his host was reduced to using some of his seed wheat to make tortillas to serve his visitors.[56] Later in this dry interval, U. S. Navy Commodore Thomas Jones arrived in Los Angeles in January 1843 and found that little moisture had fallen that rainy season, producing an "arid and parched" landscape.[57]

Eugene Duflot de Mofras, a French diplomat, and Charles Wilkes, a Commodore in the U. S. Navy, traveled independently along the coast of California in 1841 and 1842 and made a number of useful observations. Large masses of "seaweed" (presumably kelp) were mentioned by Duflot de Mofras as growing at the Santa Barbara anchorage in about 45 feet of water in early 1842. Summarizing the climate of the California coast, he described the summer as a time of persistent fog, dense enough to make the sky appear "almost black during the daytime," making travel hazardous. Strong northwesterly winds at this season, described as "violent" but "steady" also posed navigational problems, reducing the amount of sail his ship could carry on two occasions in May and July 1841, finally forcing the vessel to anchor in a sheltered location. The northwest winds were sufficiently cold along the coast that "even in the month of August heat is required in homes exposed to their full force."[58]

Wilkes, who arrived in San Francisco in August of 1841, made similar observations, finding conditions there comparable to Cape Horn on the southern tip of South America. Wilkes cited the persistent northwest winds as very cold, moist, and uncomfortable, making summer the coldest time of the year.[59] The climatic conditions reported by Duflot de Mofras and Wilkes clearly indicate a much-strengthened North Pacific High Pressure Cell, a strong California Current, vigorous upwelling, and cold sea surface temperatures during the warmer part of 1841. All these conditions combine to reduce precipitation to a minimum. If this situation had prevailed through much of the previous winter as well, it might account for the severe drought of the winter of 1840–1841.

The second dry episode that, surprisingly, followed perhaps the wettest winter in the last two centuries, spanned two years, 1862–1863 and 1863–1864. Rainfall in Los Angeles was reportedly four inches or less for both years and, as mentioned earlier, San Diego recorded 3.87 inches in the 1862–1863 and 5.14 inches in 1863–1864.[60] This drought clearly appears in the southern California tree ring record. Bigcone spruce growth was 25 percent below normal in 1863, the situation perhaps mitigated by moisture in the soil still available from the previous (very wet) winter, but growth had fallen to 66 percent below normal in 1864.[61] Another tree ring chronology developed for southern California extending back to 1700, but including trees in the White Mountains and in northern Baja

California, also indicates that both 1863 and 1864 were years of extreme drought.[62]

This drought was one that contributed to the demise of the cattle industry in southern California, leading to major land use changes as the vast ranchos began to break up. The drought was statewide in extent and killed hundreds of thousands of cattle.[63]

The declining pasturage in late winter 1863 is vividly described in the correspondence of southern California ranchers. Writing from Los Angeles, Charles Robinson Johnson, apparently an employee of rancho owner Abel Stearns, lamented "There is absolutely no Grass, and it is the opinion of the Rancho men, the Cattle will commence dying within a month. Everything is dried up."[64] The news in early March from Cave Couts, owner of Rancho Guajome in northern San Diego County, was equally bleak: "What are cattle raisers going to do? No rain, no grass—nearly as dry as in the month of August."[65] A grasshopper plague made conditions worse by June of 1863, as Johnson reported "the Cattle have commenced dying; If the Cattle are not moved from the 'Laguna' you will lose at least one half."[66] Mounted men were needed both day and night to prevent starving cattle from breaking through the willow hedge surrounding the vineyards of the Anaheim Colony in their search for food.[67] Meanwhile, the carcasses of cattle already dead created a powerful stench. It was said that one could walk for miles on the carcasses without stepping foot on the ground. Buried accumulations of cattle bones were thick enough to interfere in later years with post-hole and well digging in the Alamitos area.[68]

B. Wet Periods

Historical proxies and instrumental records indicate that the winter of 1861–1862 may have been the wettest winter in the past two centuries. The convergence of two branches of the jet stream is inferred to have caused a vigorous collision of cold and warm air, generating intense frontal precipitation in the region from a steady progression of "southeasters." In northern California, precipitation was especially heavy in January 1862, with several stations recording four to five times the normal amount. A large lake of ice-cold muddy water covered the floor of the Sacramento Valley and fresh water poured seaward through the Golden Gate for nearly two weeks without tidal fluctuation. Fresh water covered the bays around San Francisco for at least two months, enabling local fisherman to land freshwater species.[69]

Similar events occurred in southern California. Starting on Christmas Eve, 1861, rain fell nearly continuously for some forty-five days and then sporadically in every month through June of 1862 in Los Angeles. Unofficial rainfall figures range up to 64 inches for the 1861–1862 season. The January concentration of precipitation is exceptional and culminated in the largest flood on the Santa Ana River in the last 140 years. This deluge is estimated to have had a peak discharge at Riverside Narrows gaging station three times larger than the largest twentieth-century flood. Flooding was widespread in the Los Angeles Basin and extended both south and east. The streams draining to the Pacific Ocean between Los Angeles and San Diego carried much water through June. In that month it was reported that a good-sized vessel might have traveled a mile up the normally tiny San Luis Rey River near its mouth. Lakes formed at a number of locations in the Mojave Desert, and water levels eighteen feet above normal were recorded along the Mojave River at present-day Oro Grande.[70] Meanwhile, Lake Elsinore was very high and most likely overflowed. Interestingly, the tree ring record for 1862 is mixed. Bigcone spruce growth was 150 percent of normal in the Santa Ana Mountains, and the Torrey pine tree ring is the widest in the 168-year chronology. Yet, strangely, 1862 does not appear in the list of the ten wettest years in the 400-year precipitation reconstruction developed from the tree rings of bigcone spruce growing in the Transverse Ranges north of Santa Barbara.[71]

The record-setting precipitation of 1883–1884 in Los Angeles and elsewhere ushered in a very wet interval that ended with the 1892–1893 season. In this decade, as mentioned earlier, five monthly maximum precipitation records were set (March, June, July, October, and December) in addition to the recording of the highest seasonal total ever in 1883–1884. Several second-wettest-ever records also occurred in the months of February (1884) and March (1893) and for the season of 1889–1890. Our knowledge of this interval is much more detailed, as the historical record is much richer, reflecting the larger population. This especially stormy period was accompanied by large waves that helped to cause 600 feet of blufftop retreat at Encinitas between 1883 and 1891 (according to available subdivision maps). Analysis of San Diego County Tax Assessor Records reveal that the loss of seaward parcels was accompanied by an increase in assessed value for tracts immediately inland, which had now become oceanfront parcels by default.[72] U.S. Signal Service weather maps and publications became available in the 1870s, and they have been used to make inferences about the meteorology of some exceptional rainfall events in late 1889. Encinitas experienced 7.5 inches of rain in eight hours on October 12–13 during the passage of a tropical cyclone that may have made landfall near Monterey. December of 1889 has proved to be the wettest month of any year for a number of localities in southern California, including Los Angeles, where nearly 16 inches of rain fell, an amount exceeding the annual precipitation for that station. Twenty days of moderate rainfall occurred during that December as a consequence of a deep trough of low pressure, at the surface and aloft, just off the West Coast. The continuous rainfall also was encouraged by warm local sea-surface temperatures.[73]

By any measure, precipitation during the season of 1883–1884 in southern California was exceptional, not only in downtown Los Angeles but elsewhere as well. Unofficial record keeping at higher elevations produced totals for that season that, if accurate, are staggering. Sixty inches of precipitation reportedly fell at Kinneloa Ranch at an elevation of 1,500 feet above Pasadena and over 93 inches fell at Bear Valley at an elevation of 6,000 feet in the San Bernadino Mountains, now the site of Big Bear Lake.[74] San Diego recorded 25.97 inches and elsewhere in San Diego County amounts ranged up to 80 inches.[75] There is substantial agreement that 1884 was a strong El Niño year.[76] There is also much speculation that the August 1883 explosion of Krakatoa volcano in Indonesia intensified that year's El Niño, as tremendous quantities of material were injected into the atmosphere of a region that plays a significant role in the whole El Niño phenomenon.[77]

Newspapers of the time provide much detail about the effects of the heavy precipitation falling at Los Angeles in February and March 1884. Steady rains lasting for three weeks coupled with warm southeast breezes melted snow fifteen feet deep in the San Gabriel Mountains and led to severe flooding in Los Angeles in mid-February. Large sections of bridges across the Los Angeles River were washed out and drifted downstream to slam into and pile up against lower bridges, creating an obstruction to the river's flow that caused massive flooding, inundating streets, gardens, and orchards. Buildings in low-lying areas were particularly vulnerable, according to a newspaper article in the *Los Angeles Herald*:

> All at once, great waves began to roll in a terrific manner in front of the Evergreen Laundry, a large two-story building, and the current changing still more towards the interior of the city, it became clear that the building was doomed. The waves, though muddy and without the sparkling foam of the sea, were in no wise less violent and their onset was kept up in such quick successions that the foundations of the building, barely sufficient to resist a mild stream, gave way. Then a trembling motion was perceived in the house. Next the roof slid off, the walls toppled to pieces as they reeled from one side to the other, and all at once with a deafening noise, overpowering the roar of the water, the building flew apart, as if exploded from within.[78]

By February 20, 1884, forty houses had been destroyed and about ninety lots were eroded away in the city of Los Angeles.[79] The "great waves" are inferred to be what are called standing waves or breaking antidune waves, which occur only during extreme flow conditions when the water velocity/water depth ratio is very high. Very turbulent flow and very high rates of sediment transport are achieved under such conditions. Such waves, described as "foaming billows" at least two feet higher than the channel banks, were reported on the Santa Ana River during this period.[80]

The heavy precipitation had other hydrologic consequences. Lake Elsinore filled to overflowing in a short time. The San Gabriel River reached the sea, an event that occurred only about once a decade at that time, as did the Santa Ana River.[81] At Daggett in the Mojave Desert, it was reported that the usually shallow and presumably relatively easy to cross Mojave River was higher than it had been for some time and ferries had to be used to carry passengers across the river so they could continue on to Calico.[82] Of lasting benefit was the rise of the water table as detected in wells. According to the *Anaheim Weekly Gazette*, the water was fifteen feet closer to the surface in early May than it had been before the rains.[83]

CONCLUSIONS

Reconstructed from a large mix of instrumental records and proxy information, the climate of nineteenth-century southern California was marked by much instability as the Little Ice Age came to an end. The evidence assembled varies in quality and is occasionally contradictory or remains to be supported by other independent sources. Nevertheless, it is clear that the nineteenth century was a time of much hydrologic variance during this cool-to-warm climatic transition.[84] Extremely wet periods occurred during which seasonal and monthly precipitation records were set, many of which still stand over a century later. Yet evidence for severe droughts also exists. Since that time, the urban landscape of southern California has spread over extensive floodplains, climbed up steep slopes, and crept to the very faces of coastal bluffs. In the process, as one contemporary observer of the Los Angeles scene comments, "market-driven urbanization has transgressed environmental common-sense."[85] Is another climatic interval as dramatic as that of the late nineteenth century possible? No one knows for certain, especially as global warming looms. Should those climatic conditions return, however, they would undoubtedly provide a severe test of existing flood and erosion-control systems, as well as the ability of government agencies to continue to supply millions of southern California residents with safe drinking water.[86] The lessons learned through a consideration of historical climate change may be more than interesting, they may prove vital.

Notes

1   See William F. Ruddiman, *Earth's Climate: Past and Future*, (New York: W. H. Freeman and Company, 2001), 366–368 for an overview of the El Niño phenomenon and see David Bruno and Gary Ryan, *Climate of Los Angeles, California*, NOAA Technical Memorandum NWS WR-261, (Springfield, Virginia: U.S. Department of Commerce, National Technical Memorandum Service, 2000), 24, 38–39, 139–140 for Los Angeles weather records and a brief discussion of the impact of El Niño events on winter precipitation.

2   National Climatic Data Center, "Los Angeles WBO—Miscellaneous Storm Events in Los Angeles County—Flood," [database on-line]; available from: http:www4.ncdc.noaa.gov/; Internet accessed 4 October 2000.

3   Stanley A. Changnon, "Impacts of 1997–98 El Niño-Generated Weather in the United States," *Bulletin of the American Meteorological Society* 80 (1999): 1819–1827.

4   Laura Haston and Joel Michaelsen, "Long-Term Central Coastal California Precipitation Variability and Relationships to El Niño-Southern Oscillation," *Journal of Climate* 7 (1994): 1373.

5   Raymond S. Bradley, *Paleoclimatology: Reconstructing Climates of the Quaternary,* 2nd ed. (San Diego: Harcourt Academic Press, 1999), 1.

6   Dr. H. Gibbons, "The Climate of San Francisco," *Ninth Annual Report of the Board of Regents, Smithsonian Institution, Showing the Operations, Expenditures, and Conditions of the Institution up to January 1, 1855, and the Proceedings of the Board up to February 24, 1855* (Washington: Beverley Tucker, Senate Printer, 1855), 246.

7   Reid A. Bryson and Christine Padoch, "On Climates of History," in Robert I. Rotberg and Theodore K. Rabb, eds., *Climate and History: Studies in Interdisciplinary History* (Princeton: Princeton University, Press, 1981), 3.

8   Harold C. Fritts, G. Robert Lofgren, and Geoffrey A. Gordon, "Past Climate Reconstructed from Tree Rings," in Robert I. Rotberg and Theodore K. Rabbs, eds., *Climate and History: Studies in Interdisciplinary History* (Princeton: Princeton University Press, 1981), 194.

9   See Jean M. Grove, The Little Ice Age, (New York: Methuen, 1988), Rhodes W. Fairbridge, "Little Ice Age," in John E. Oliver and Rhodes W. Fairbridge, eds., *The Encyclopedia of Climatology* (New York: Van Nostrand Reinhold Company, 1987), 547–551, and Ruddiman, 355–381 for overviews.

10 Laura Haston and Joel Michaelsen, "Spatial and Temporal Variability of Southern California Precipitation over the Last 400 Years and Relationships to Atmospheric Circulation Patterns," *Journal of Climate* 10 (1997): 1836–1852; Haston and Michaelsen, "Long–Term Central Coastal," 1385; Wayne N. Engstrom, "Nineteenth-Century Coastal Gales of Southern California," *Geographical Review* 84 (1994): 306–315; Arndt Schimmelmann and Carina B. Lange, "Tales of 1001 Varves: A Review of Santa Barbara Basin Sediment Studies," in A. E. S. Kemp, ed., *Paleoclimatology and Paleoceanography from Laminated Sediments,* Special Publication no. 116 (London: Geological Society, 1996), 131.

11 W. A. Sidler, *Agua Mansa and the Flood of January 22, 1862 Santa Ana River* (n. p.: San Bernadino Flood Control District California, 1968); Wayne N. Engstrom, "The California Storm of January 1862," *Quaternary Research* 46 (1996): 141–148.

12 L. T. Burcham, *California Range Land: An Historico-Ecological Study of the Range Resource of California* (Sacramento: State of California, Division of Forestry, Department of Natural Resources, 1957), 152.

13 H. F. Raup, "Transformation of Southern California to a Cultivated Land," *Annals of the Association of American Geographers* (Supplement) 49, no. 3 Part 2 (1959): 58–78.

14 Donald Lee Johnson, "The Late Quaternary Climate of Coastal California: Evidence for an Ice Age Refugium," *Quaternary Research* 8 (1977): 154.

15 Theodore M. Oberlander and Robert A. Muller, *Case Studies in Physical Geography* (New York: Random House, 1987), 24–25.

16 Douglas M. Pirie, Michael J. Murphy, and J. Robert Edmisten, "California Nearshore Surface Currents," *Shore and Beach* 43, No. 2 (1975): 23–34.

17 Pirie, Murphy, and Edmisten, 28.

18 Engstrom, "Nineteenth-Century Coastal Gales," 306–307.

19 W. P. Trowbridge, to A. D. Bache, 10 July 1854, Correspondence of A. D. Bache, 1843-1865, Record Group 23, Microfilm Roll 107, National Archives, Southwest Region, Laguna Niguel, California, 348.

20 More information on precipitation/El Niño relationships is provided by Haston and Michaelsen, "Long-Term Central Coastal," 1374–1375; Engstrom, "Nineteenth-Century Coastal Gales," 311–313.

21 Gunnar I. Roden, "A Modern Statistical Analysis and Documentation of Historical Temperature Records in California, Oregon, and Washington, 1821–1864," *Journal of Applied Meteorology* 5 (1966): 3-24.

22 H. B. Lynch, *Rainfall and Stream Run-off in Southern California Since 1769* (Los Angeles: Metropolitan Water District of Southern California, 1931), 22.

23 The U.S. Army was the first agency to collect long-term weather observations in the western United States as there was interest in the impact of climate on Army soldiers and on possible climate change. See Kenneth G. Hubbard, "The History of Weather Observations in the West-

ern United States," *Journal of the West* 40, No. 3 (2001): 26–30; Bruno and Ryan, 9. All subsequent references to "Los Angeles" refer to data collected at the Los Angeles Civic Center.

24 See Ford A. Carpenter, *The Climate and Weather of San Diego, California* (San Diego: San Diego Chamber of Commerce, 1913). The Santa Barbara record for rainfall dates back to July 1867 and for temperature back to January 1871 and appears in Jesse D. Mason, Reproduction of Thompson and West's History of Santa Barbara & Ventura Counties California with Illustrations and Biographical Sketches of Its Prominent Men and Pioneers, (Berkeley: Howell-North, 1961), 457, 459.

25 These issues are addressed by James P. McGuirk, "A Century of Precipitation Variability Along the Pacific Coast of North America and Its Impact," *Climatic Change* 4 (1982): 43, by Harold C. Fritts and Geoffrey A. Gordon, *Annual Precipitation for California Since 1600 Reconstructed from Western North American Tree Rings* (n. p.: California Department of Water Resources Agreement No. B53367, 1980), 5–13, and by Ronald U. Cooke and Richard W. Reeves, Arroyos and Environmental Change in the American South-West, (Oxford: Clarendon Press, 1976), 142.

26 Bruno and Ryan, 24, 9.

27 See Bruno and Ryan and Carpenter for precipitation amounts and Engstrom, "The California Storm" for details on this episode.

28 A thorough review is provided by H. C. Fritts, Tree Rings and Climate, (New York: Academic Press, 1976).

29 Edmund Schulman, "Tree-Ring Hydrology in Southern California," *Laboratory of Tree-Ring Research Bulletin* no. 4, (Tucson: University of Arizona, 1947) and Arthur Vern Douglas, "Past Air-Sea Interactions off Southern California as Revealed by Coastal Tree-Ring Chronologies," (M.S. Thesis, University of Arizona, 1973).

30 Laura Haston, Frank W. Davis, and Joel Michaelsen, "Climate Response Functions for Bigcone Spruce: A Mediterranean Climate Conifer," *Physical Geography* 9 (1988): 81–97.

31 Schulman, 23–25 and Daniel O. Larson, "California Climatic Reconstructions," *The Journal of Interdisciplinary History* 25 (1994): 225–253.

32 Franco Biondi, Daniel R. Cayan, and Wolfgang H. Berger, "Dendroclimatology of Torrey Pines (Pinus torreyana Parry ex Carr.)," *American Midland Naturalist* 138 (1997): 243–244.

33 Schulman, 30–31; Douglas, 81.

34 Valmore C. LaMarche, Jr. and Charles W. Stockton, "Chronologies from Temperature-Sensitive Bristlecone Pines at Upper Treeline in Western United States," Tree-Ring Bulletin 34 (1974): 21–45. See also Gordon C. Jacoby, Jr. and Rosanne D'Arrigo, "Reconstructed Northern Hemisphere Annual Temperature Since 1671 Based on High-Latitude Tree-Ring Data from North America," *Climatic Change* 14 (1989): 35–59 for a useful review.

35 LaMarche and Stockton, 32–36.

36 Arndt Schimmelmann and Mia J. Tegner, "Historical Evidence of Abrupt Coastal Climatic Change in Southern California, 1790–1880," in K. T. Redmond, ed., *Proceedings of the Eighth Annual Pacific Climate (PACLIM) Workshop, March 10–13, 1991,* Interagency Ecological Studies Program Technical Report no. 31 (n.p.: California Department of Water Resources, 1992), 49–51.

37 Schimmelmann and Lange, 121.

38 Schimmelmann and Lange, 126; Arndt Schimmelmann et al.,"Sea Surface Temperature and Paleo-El Niño Events in the Santa Barbara Basin, AD 1841–1941," in C. M. Issacs and V. L. Tharp, eds., *Proceedings of the Eleventh Annual Pacific Climate (PACLIM) Workshop, April 19–22, 1994,* Interagency Ecological Program Technical Report no. 40 (n. p.: California Department of Resources, 1995), 99.

39 Andrew Soutar and Peter A. Crill, "Sedimentation and Climatic Patterns in the Santa Barbara Basin during the 19th and 20th Centuries," *Geological Society of America Bulletin* 88 (1977): 1168.

40 Francis R. Schanck, "Elsinore Lake at Elsinore, Calif." In H. D. McGlashan, *Surface Water Supply of the Pacific Slope of Southern California,* United States Geological Survey Water-Supply Paper 447, (Washington: Government Printing Office, 1921), 321–322.

41 Bryson and Padoch, 5.

42 Lynch, 7–9.

43 Lester B. Rowntree, "A Crop-Based Rainfall Chronology for Pre-Instrumental Record Southern California," *Climatic Change* 7 (1985): 333–340.

44 Lester B. Rowntree, "Drought During California's Mission Period, 1769–1834," *Journal of California and Great Basin Anthropology* 7 (1985): 11.

45 J. Albert Wilson, *History of Los Angeles County California with Illustrations Descriptive of Its Scenery, Residences, Fine Blocks and Manufactories* (Oakland: Thompson & West, 1880), 56.

46 Larson, 248.

47 M. J. Ingram, D. J. Underhill, and G. Farmer, "The Use of Documentary Sources for the Study of Past Climates," in T. M. L. Wigley, M. J. Ingram, and G. Farmer, eds., *Climate and History: Studies in Past Climates and Their Impact on Man* (Cambridge: Cambridge University Press, 1981), 187. This is a particularly valuable source.

48 Larson also provides a discussion of the first dry episode, 245–247.

49 Joel Michaelsen, Laura Haston, and Frank W. Davis, "400 years of Central California Precipitation Variability Reconstructed from Tree-Rings," *Water Resources Bulletin* 23 (1987): 813.

50 Schulman, 18; Douglas, 81.

51 Biondi, Cayan, and Berger, 247.

52 William A. Parker, *Logbook of the U. S. Ship* Cyane *Jan. 1842–Oct. 1844,* Manuscript, Bancroft Library, University of California-Berkeley.

53 Philo White, *Philo White's Narrative of a Cruize in the Pacific to South America and California on the U. S. Sloop-of-War "Dale" 1841–1843* Charles L. Camp, ed., (Denver: Old West Publishing Company, 1965), 72.

54 Harold C. Troxell et al., *Floods of March 1938 in Southern California,* U. S. Geological Survey Water-Supply Paper 844, (Washington: United States Government Printing Office, 1942), 388–389 and H. D. McGlashan and F. C. Ebert, *Southern California Floods of January 1916,* U. S. Geological Survey Water-Supply Paper 426, (Washington: Government Printing Office, 1918), 35.

55 William Dane Phelps, *Alta California 1840–1842: The Journal and Observations of William Dane Phelps Master of the Ship "Alert,"* Briton Cooper Busch, ed., (Glendale: The Arthur H. Clark Company, 1983), 154–155, 175.

56 General John Bidwell, *Echoes of the Past* (New York: The Citadel Press, 1962), 67–68.

57 Commodore Thomas ap Catesby Jones, "A Visit to Los Angeles in 1843: Commodore Thomas ap Catesby Jones' Narrative of his Visit to Governor Micheltorena," *Quarterly Publication of the Historical Society of Southern California* 17 (1935): 131–132.

58 Eugene Duflot de Mofras, *Duflot de Mofras' Travels on the Pacific Coast,* trans. and ed. Marguerite Eyer Wilbur (Santa Ana: The Fine Arts Press, 1937), Vol. 1, 193; Vol. 2, 22–23, 25.

59 Charles Wilkes, *Narrative of the United States Exploring Expedition During the Years 1838, 1839, 1840, 1841, 1842* (Philadelphia: Lea & Blanchard, 1845), Vol. 5, 154–155.

60 J. M. Guinn, "Exceptional Years: A History of California Floods and Drought," *Publications, Historical Society of Southern California* 1 (1890): 36–37; Carpenter, 36.

61 Schulman, 18; Douglas 81.

62 David M. Meko, Charles W. Stockton, and William R. Boggess, "A Tree-Ring Reconstruction of Drought in Southern California," *Water Resources Bulletin* 16 (1980): 599.

63 Burcham, 152–153 provides information on the number of cattle lost; see also Robert G. Cleland, *The Cattle on a Thousand Hills: Southern California, 1850–80* (San Marino: The Huntington Library, 1941), 130–137 for more information.

64 Charles Robinson Johnson, to Abel Stearns, 14 March 1863, Abel Stearns Collection, Huntington Library, San Marino, California.

65 Cave J. Couts, to Abel Stearns, 8 March 1863, Abel Stearns Collection, Huntington Library, San Marino, California.

66 Charles Robinson Johnson, to Abel Stearns, 13 June 1863, Abel Stearns Collection, Huntington Library, San Marino, California.

67 Guinn, 37.

68 J. W. Reagan, *J. W. Reagan's Report on Flood and Flood Control Necessity in Los Angeles County* (n. p., 1914–1915, typewritten), 6, 499.

69 Engstrom, "The California Storm," 141–143.

70 Ibid., 143–146.

71 Douglas, 81; Biondi, Cayan, and Berger, 246; Michaelsen, Haston, and Davis, 815.

72 Gerald G. Kuhn and Francis P. Shepard, *Sea Cliffs, Beaches, and Coastal Valleys of San Diego County: Some Amazing Histories and Some Horrifying Implications* (Berkeley: University of California Press, 1984), 34–35.

73 Charles B. Pyke, *Some Aspects of the Influence of Abnormal Eastern Equatorial Pacific Ocean Surface Temperatures Upon Weather Patterns in the Southwestern United States,* Report no. NR 083–287, vol. II (Arlington, Virginia: Office of Naval Research, 1975 (updated in 1984 and 1988), 53–54, 60, 64, 69.

74 Abbot Kinney, *Forest and Water* (Los Angeles, The Post Publishing Company, 1900), 79; William H. Hall, Irrigation in California: Southern, (Sacramento: State Office, J. D. Young, Superintendent, State Printing, 1888), 116, map in pocket.

75 Carpenter, 37; Kuhn and Shepard, 34.

76 Luc Ortlieb and Jose Machare, "Former El Niño Events: Records from Western South America," *Global and Planetary Change* 7 (1993): 185.

77 Pyke, 27–27a; Kuhn and Shepard, 13–28.

78 "Fury of the Flood," *Los Angeles Herald,* 19 February, 1884.

79 "The Great Flood of 1884," *Los Angeles Herald,* 20 February, 1884.

80 "The Flood at Santa Ana," *Los Angeles Herald,* 23 February, 1884.

81 "Storm Notes," *Los Angeles Herald,* 16 February, 1884; "Local Brevities," *Los Angeles Herald,* 13 February, 1884.

82 "Great Desert Storm," *Los Angeles Herald,* 14 February, 1884.

83 "Kleinigkeiten" (Little Comments), *Anaheim Weekly Gazette,* 10 May, 1884.

84 Similar associations occur in a long flood record from Arizona and Utah described by Lisa L. Ely et al., "A 5000-Year Record of Extreme Floods and Climate Change in the Southwestern United States," *Science* 262 (1993): 410–412.

85 Mike Davis, "Los Angeles After the Storm: The Dialectic of Ordinary Disaster," *Antipode* 27 (1995): 223.

86 Similar concerns are expressed by Kuhn and Shepard, 167.

CHAPTER FIVE

The Limits of Patriarchy: The "Unwritten Law" in California Legal History *

Gordon Morris Bakken

In 1995, Americans watched perhaps the best television drama ever aired: the trial of Orenthal James "O. J." Simpson for the June 1994 murders of his ex-wife, Nicole Brown Simpson, and Ronald Goldman in the upscale Brentwood neighborhood of Los Angeles. The prior spring, Simpson, the 1968 Heisman Trophy winner out of the University of Southern California, former star running back for the Buffalo Bills, and erstwhile television commentator and advertising pitchman, riveted the nation's attention as he led police on a slow-speed chase in a white sport utility vehicle—a scene captured by remote cameras, some of them on helicopters—immediately prior to his arrest for the crimes.

The trial that commenced the following January united sports and Court TV fans with the rest of a nation of spectators eager to see the California criminal justice system in action. Before and throughout the 133-day trial, television reporters, some of whom trumpeted the event as the "trial of the century," jammed downtown Los Angeles (site of the trial court) as well as the city's more-fashionable districts with camera equipment and remote broadcasting trucks, creating a three-ring media circus.

---

* A short version of this chapter was published as "The Limits of Patriarchy" in *The Historian*, vol. 60 (Summer, 1998), pp. 703–16. The portions reprinted here are with the permission of Phi Alpha Theta and Michigan State University Press. Hendrik Hartog, "Lawyering, Husbands' Rights, and "the Unwritten Law" in Nineteenth-Century America," 84 *Journal of American History* (June, 1997), pp. 67–96. Also see for recent work on the same type of issue James D. Rice, "The Criminal Trial Before and After the Lawyers: Authority, Law, and Culture in Maryland Jury Trials, 1681–1837," 40 *The American Journal of Legal History* (October, 1996), pp. 455–75. Contrary to Hartog, Rice found that defense attorneys "exerted little or no control" over "the more fundamental changes in cultural perceptions of men, women, and African-Americans." Ibid, p. 475. Earlier work on the subject includes Robert M. Ireland, "Frenzied and Fallen Females: Women and Sexual Dishonor in the Nineteenth-Century United States," 3 *Journal of Women's History* (Winter, 1992), pp. 95–117. Also see Elizabeth Pleck, "Feminist Responses to 'Crimes Against Women,' 1868–1896," 8 *Signs: Journal of Women in Culture and Society* (Spring, 1983), pp. 451–70. Robert M. Ireland, "The Libertine Must Die: Sexual Dishonor and the Unwritten Law in the Nineteenth-Century United States," 23 *Journal of Social History* (Fall, 1989), pp. 27–44.

Top: California Supreme Court, 1890. Front row, L-R: Charles N. Fox, Chief Justice William H. Beatty, Thomas B. ['the thinker"] McFarland; Back row, L-R: John R. Sharpstein, John D. Works, James D. Thornton, A. Van R. Patterson.

Bottom: California Supreme Court, 2002. L-R: Janice R. Brown, Joyce L. Kernard, Kathryn M. Werdeger, Chief Justice Ronald M. George, Ming W. Chin, Marvin R. Baxter, and Carlos R. Moreno.

For months, television viewers, radio listeners, and newspaper readers followed the colorful proceedings of the trial—the media with their invitation to tour the crime scene and O.J.'s home with jurors, meet the wealthy defendant's "dream team" of lawyers, even take in and make their own commentary on the fashion sense of lead prosecutor Marcia Clark. In short order, persons once familiar only to the bar became household personalities, as defenders Johnny Cochran, Carl Douglas, F. Lee Bailey, Barry Scheck, and Alan Dershowitz jousted with Clark, Christopher Darden, and the rest of the prosecution. Witnesses, such as L.A.P.D. detective Mark Fuhrman had to suffer their testimony being replayed on the nightly news and in special-report segments. Memorable quotes such as Cochran's "if it [the glove] doesn't fit, you must acquit" became schoolyard palaver.

Ultimately, it took the jury only three hours to reach a verdict on a case that had taken more than one hundred days to present, included the testimony of more than one hundred witnesses—among them medical and forensic experts—and cost the taxpayers of California millions of dollars. They found O.J. "not guilty of the crime of murder."

While the nation's reaction to the verdict seemingly divided over racial lines, many Americans wondered how the solemn criminal courtroom had become a plaything of the media. Indeed, persons throughout the nation threw up their hands, declaring that only in the present day could the media have such free rein to report the salacious details of people's personal lives and be so obtrusive as to affect the courtroom proceedings, making instant celebrities out of all the courtroom players.[1]

But historians know that such phenomena are hardly new, that many of the "modern" features of, and surrounding, the California criminal justice system have deep roots in the past. California's criminal justice system has always reflected middle-class values.[2] Jury verdicts of "not guilty" sometimes were declarations that justice must protect society against the libertine.[3]

THE TRIAL OF THE CENTURY: WHAT CONSTITUTES MARRIAGE?

In the 1880s, the California Supreme Court gained state and national notoriety for the most sensational divorce case of the century: *Sharon* v. *Sharon*.[4] The case involved United States Senator William Sharon of Nevada and his alleged wife, Sarah Althea Hill.[5] Other prominent figures in the case included Jeremiah Sullivan, San Francisco Superior Court Judge and a nominee for the Democratic Chief Justiceship at the 1888 Los Angeles Convention, David Smith Terry, former Justice of the California Supreme Court, Stephen J. Field, former Chief Justice of the California Supreme Court and Justice of the United States Supreme Court, and David Neagle, who not many years later would gain notoriety for shooting David Smith Terry dead. The case had it all: sex, violence, politics, dream teams of lawyers, and the pull to make front-page headlines for years. The case also found the State Supreme Court in transition and the law of marriage and divorce in flux.[6] The 1879 California Constitution created a trial court system with superior courts replacing district courts and an elected single appellate court, the State Supreme Court. Furthermore, the Supreme Court could rehear cases and render final decisions.

The chronicle of events was lengthy. Sara Althea Hill met William Sharon, a mining millionaire known as the "King of the Comstock" and United States Senator from Nevada, after moving to California in 1871. The two signed a written declaration of marriage on August 25, 1880. Per that contract, Hill agreed not to make the marriage public for two years from date and Sharon agreed to pay her $500 (the 2001 equivalent of $8,668.57) per month.[7] While they did not cohabit, they did meet periodically to consummate their relationship. Sharon later testified at trial that he never signed the document and had never promised to marry Hill, who had filed for divorce in superior court. In September 1883 she made the marriage public and promptly accused Sharon of adultery. Sharon was arrested on the charge, but his attorneys went to federal court to claim that the document certifying the union between their client and Hill was a forgery. Meanwhile, Hill's attorneys, George Washington Tyler, a San Francisco criminal lawyer, and David Terry, went to state court and filed for divorce and division of community property. The resulting legal battle spawned six years of litigation and twenty printed judicial decisions, including three from the United States Supreme Court. Hill marshaled a dream team of six attorneys while Sharon put ten lawyers onto the field of battle, including William Morris Stewart, former U.S. senator from Nevada, William F. Herrin of the Southern Pacific Railroad Company, Francis G. Newlands, a future senator from Nevada and father of the Newlands Reclamation Act, Samuel M. Wilson, a leader of the San Francisco Bar, and J. P. Hoge, president of the 1878–79 California Constitutional Convention.

At this time in California and the rest of the nation, the law of marriage and divorce was part of a broad public and judicial discourse. The legal standing of common-law marriage had won recognition in an 1809 New York decision, *Fenton* v. *Reed*, and gained national notice in James Kent's *Commentaries*, one of the most influential treatises in American law, in 1826.[8] With treatise and judicial precedent growing in favor of recognizing common-law marriage, judges increasingly considered cohabitation based upon personal acknowledgment, eye-witness accounts, and personal reputations central to determining common-law status.[9] In 1869, a Pennsylvania decision, *De Armaell's Estate*, 2 Brew. 239, brought together the strands of antebellum thought regarding legal marriage. In this case, the Pennsylvania Supreme Court upheld the secret marriage between a University of Pennsylvania professor of aristocratic Italian birth and an Irish servant girl. The Court held that secrecy did not void the union, declaring that "mystery may surround its origins, suspicion may linger in its circumstances, and light doubt may disturb its clearness, but the policy of the state demands that this relation should not be lightly discredited and the issue bastardized."[10] This judicial support for marriage based upon contract or course of conduct did not go unchallenged. By the 1870s, an organized reform campaign motivated by moral panic attacked secret unions in the name of public interest.[11] Regardless, Michigan Justice Thomas M. Cooley, author of *Constitutional Limitations* (1868), declared in *Hutchins* v. *Kimmell* (1875) that "the settled doctrine of American courts, the few cases of dissent, or apparent dissent, being borne down by the great weight of authority in favor of the rule" favored the recognition of common-law marriage.[12] However, reformers in the 1880s wanted legal certainty, and they gained legislative favor with solons who passed statutes requiring that couples obtain marriage licenses, that public officials conduct wedding ceremonies, and that all such unions be officially recorded. Judges, however, found these statutes directory rather than compulsory. As Michael Grossberg, a prominent historian of family law, has observed, "the common-law presumptions of matrimony were elaborate and ambiguous legal tools. Their continued existence left nuptial law in a state of flux despite the new codes."[12] And so it was in 1884 when the parties in *Sharon* v. *Sharon* entered Judge Sullivan's trial court.

The trial opened on March 10, but the media already had reported every legal maneuver and document the parties had generated before they officially entered the lists.[14] The prior October, one William M. Neilson hauled Sharon into the San Francisco Police Court on a misdemeanor adultery charge. The October 14, 1883, edition of the *San Francisco Chronicle* listed every argument of the counsel for both sides. General William H. L. Barnes, a New York emigrant to California after the Civil War, represented Sharon and George W. Tyler represented Neilson. Barnes was particularly disturbed because "the story of this accusation ha[d] traveled as far as the electric wires extend and the Associated Press teems with every fact and circumstance, real or imaginary, that belongs to it." Sharon's affidavit asserting that he had never signed any marriage document and demanding the production of said paper in court was reprinted in full in the November 6, 1883, edition of the *Chronicle*. Three days later, the *Chronicle* ran a story regarding pretrial discovery proceedings, this report included coverage of the dramatic delivery of a sealed envelope to the judge.

On November 9, 1883, the pretrial story continued, the reporters for the *Chronicle* apparently well-versed in the literary habits and imagination of their Victorian readership. It was thirty minutes short of high noon on November 8 and an unrelated trial was proceeding in Judge Finn's court when in walked Sarah Hill, Miss Brackett, a friend of Hill and former acquaintance of ex-Senator Sharon, William Neilson, and Frank Rodney. Shortly thereafter attorneys Barnes and Tyler, also for Hill, made an appearance. "A moment later William Sharon and Dick Dye, the Nevada mining expert" and experienced divorce investigator, "entered the courtroom." At this point, the counsel took their places at the bar with an air that, in the eyes of the *Chronicle* reporter, seemed like "Everybody must give way for us—this is a millionaire's case." Judge Finn quickly dismissed the jury in the pending case until two o'clock to allow the pretrial antics to play out.

Now the parties squared off. The *Chronicle* noted that William Sharon wore "a black dress-coat and black pantaloons," that his face was "blanched[,] and straight white hair completed the summary of his appearance." For her part, Sarah "was almost as faultlessly attired . . . though there was no lavish display of the elegance of dress or personal adornment which might be expected on the part of a millionaire's wife." Indeed, she "wore a neat black silk dress, well fitted to her slight figure, a long mantle and a rather high-crowned hat, with a rolling rim." Sadly, the anguish of the past three years had "left its blighting marks upon her features." And she appeared "neither a decided brunette nor a decided blonde, but her complexion [was] that happy medium described by poets and idealized by painters." Clearly, Sarah Hill constituted a fashion statement before the courtroom that the readership needed to hear. Finally, the proceeding, "one of the most exciting civil Court scenes which has transpired for a long time," commenced.

General Barnes opened with his old demand—one now backed by a court order—to see the alleged document of marriage. Speaking for Hill, Tyler informed the court that he was not aware that he had been expected to produce the document by high noon and was presently in court to argue a show cause order, a procedural phase designed to allow a party to appear and give the court reasons and considerations why proceedings should continue to trial. The Court informed Tyler that he was mistaken and that he was indeed expected to produce the agreement. Tyler responded to the Court that his client had refused to deliver the document of marriage to him, but that she personally was in court and wished to make a statement. Barnes objected, and the Court inquired whether or not Hill was present in order to deliver the document. Again, Tyler deferred, offering instead that his client wished to make a statement and that "she is here to speak for herself." He added, however, that Hill "has been subpoenaed before the Grand Jury, to appear in a matter in connection with this identical paper. I see one of the detectives in Court now. I understand she is charged with the forgery of this paper and I think this Court will not require her to produce the paper until that matter is settled." Judge Finn informed counsel that he would "not presume that it [the document] is a forgery. The question remained the production of the paper. The defendant is entitled to an inspection." At this point, Sarah swept forward with an envelope, saying "I have the paper here in a sealed envelope and will deliver it if I am ordered to do so." Barnes quickly objected to Sarah assuming the bench with the judge and demanded that she return to counsel's table. Sarah turned, and "in a hysterical voice and excited manner" told the judge that "the paper is in the envelope, I desire that neither Mr. Barnes nor Mr. Sharon shall handle it. I regard it as the only protection for my honor. I have held it and guarded it for three long years, and I do not want them to get it." The Judge took the letter, and Sarah declared that "Mr. Sharon knows all there is in the envelope as well as I do, so help me God." Now, William Sharon rose to declare "in a very loud voice . . . It's a ———lie; the ———lie ever uttered on earth."

The theater into which trials could evolve had begun. Order rapidly evaporated. The sheriff was forced to restrain Mr. Sharon. Sarah Hill "burst into tears" as she placed her plight before the public, asserting that "he has his millions against me. He has taken my money and driven me from my home and I have no money to defend myself." After some banter, the letter was delivered to the clerk, with William Sharon crying out "It's a forgery; the whole thing is a forgery." Now Tyler, Sarah's lawyer, sprang to his feet and "in a very violent manner and shaking with rage". . . objected to the "outrageous" comment. William Sharon fired back, "your threats don't alarm me." Tyler repeated Hill's theme, saying "you are not bigger than any one elsewhere, even if you have the money." Finally, the verbal sparring escalated to such a pitch that Judge Finn ordered Sharon out of the courtroom. The lawyers repaired to chambers and out of the public arena. The session and the fanfare ended, at least until the next headline.

Sarah and William Sharon were once again paraded before the public in the November 21, 1883, edition of the *Chronicle*, with their champions now jousting in Judge Toohy's Superior Court to determine whether the grand jury had overstepped its jurisdictional bounds in investigating the allegations of forgery. Colonel George Flournoy, yet another attorney for Hill, appeared for her, arguing that "Miss Hill could not be asked to furnish evidence against herself, and because the Grand Jury by that means might become acquainted with her proofs in the civil case, thereby giving the defendant every line of evidence by means of which there certainly had been no delay. The attempt of the Grand Jury to get possession of the evidence of this case must strike every man's sense of justice as an undue, indecent proceeding." Moreover, he said, "it was an attempt to blacken character by an indictment and to demoralize the plaintiff's side. . . ." Sharon's dream team was not present in Toohy's court, but D. J. Murphy, yet another attorney for Sharon, asked for and was granted a delay in the proceedings.

So the pretrial hearings went, and by the time of the actual trial, the public was primed and ready for grand theater.[15] In fact, the March 12, 1884, edition of the *Chronicle* so noted that "the spectators looked very similar to an audience which generally gains the first orchestra seat at the ballet, old, gray, bald-headed men being in the majority." But this was a trial for all of the people and the cast kept changing. In the same edition of the paper, it was noted that the illustrious David Smith Terry had "joined the plaintiff's array of lawyers." The fashion report, by the way, had not changed much. "Sarah Althea wore the same costume and smile, while

Sharon maintained the same questioning, sphinx-like face." However, the appearance of Nellie Brackett, a star witness for Sarah and a former William Sharon campanion, evidently demanded more print. Per the report, Nellie Brackett was "built by the Creator upon a model showing more strength than beauty." Yet, she was "a comely young woman, looking mature and sensible. Her face denotes more than firmness; it betrays obstinate determination, for her massive, prominent mouth, overhanging, a slightly receding chin, expresses nothing of womanly weakness." On that face was "her nose, likewise . . . well-defined, generous in size and separating two dark gray eyes. . . ." Her looks notwithstanding, Brackett was a formidable witness and gave the judge and the readership plenty to ponder.

According to Brackett, one fateful night Sarah hid her behind a bureau in her bedroom in order that she might witness and later be able to attest to the nocturnal sport between Sarah and William. When Nellie concluded her testimony, in which she described what she had seen that night in vivid detail, "she sat quiet and composedly, waiting for the next question. The stunned Attoney Barnes was not ready with it. He looked overwhelmed and astonished, only managing to blurt out: 'You did?' 'I did,' calmly replied the witness." The reporter noted that thereafter "the examination was . . . turned into more decent channels." Nevertheless, the *Chronicle* saw fit to devote three columns of print to the less-than-decent channels! From a legal point of view, Sarah had evidence of normal marital relations on the record in the testimony of an eyewitness.

The March 18, 1884, edition of the *Chronicle* had Sarah Althea Hill on the stand and in full style, the reporter noting that she wore "a new bonnet adorned with black feathers which shaded her expressive features much more becomingly than did the frown which sat upon General Barnes' brow." Also dutifully reported to the reading public was the observation that "all the actors in the great drama were promptly on hand" despite the Saint Patrick's Day festivities. The trial went on with "Judge Sullivan . . . resting his forehead on his hand, as if his brains were bothering him." Meanwhile, George Washington Tyler, Sarah's lead counsel, "was in his usual playful mood and more than once forgot that "Brother Barnes," as he liked to call the great soldier lawyer, "was not in a fit state of mind to relish his jokes." Judge Sullivan was forced to keep Tyler to his task. Again, three columns of trial coverage graced that day's *Chronicle*.

On August 5th, the *Chronicle* reported that "all the evidence" was before the court. W. B. Tyler, George Washington Tyler's son whom most called Junior another addition to the litigation team, "without further ceremony, stepped up to the table where he had piled a score or more lawbooks, and after unrolling a dozen or more rolls of notes, depositions and references, began the argument for the plaintiff." The younger Tyler confined "himself exclusively to the law in the case . . . [particularly] the law of marriage, tracing it from the Hebrew custom through the Greek and Roman forms down to the Scotch law, which, he said, was the same as that of California." On the arguments went, and they generated plenty of newsprint. Eventually, the parties absented themselves from the courtroom. When General Barnes finally argued the defendant's cause, only David Smith Terry was in court for Sarah. Judge Sullivan, of course, had no choice but to sit and listen to the arguments.[16]

When the trial finally concluded, it was declared that Sarah had indeed been legally married to William and was now legally divorced. But what, you well may ask, was the bottom line? On February 16, 1885, the *Chronicle* reported that Judge Sullivan rendered his decision of alimony and counsel fees to a packed gallery and anxious lawyers. Sarah's lawyers present were George W. Tyler "whose face wreathed with smiles," W. W. Foote, another seasoned barrister now on the Hill team, Walter H. Levy, and George Flournoy. Sharon's team now included Barnes, O. P. Evans, William Morris Stewart, Francis G. Newlands, and Henry I. Kowalski, another recent recruit nimble enough to thwart an assassination attempt by two women in the Baldwin Hotel. Judge Sullivan awarded Sarah $2,500 per month in alimony and counsel $55,000. William Sharon responded by telling a reporter, "I shall neither pay promptly, nor shall I pay at all." Rather, his lawyers were taking "the matter before the Supreme Court." He branded the whole thing "an infamous conspiracy." Furthermore, he said "We were not unprepared for something like this, and papers were drawn up ready to take the case before the higher courts at once." And appeal he did.[17] He wasted no time in getting his this lawyers busy in federal court.[18]

The California Supreme Court opinion on *Sharon* v. *Sharon* opened volume seventy-five of the *California Reports* (1888) and consumed more than 10 percent of its expanse. By the time of the final appellate decision, William Sharon was dead, but the case and his lawyers waged on. By the end it took three entire lines of newsprint to list the Sharon dream team, including William Morris Stewart, Francis G. Newlands, Samuel M. Wilson, William F. Herrin, and Joseph P. Hoge. Now David Smith Terry led Sarah's corps.[19] Elisha Williams McKinstry authored the majority opinion for the California Supreme Court.

First, McKinstry analyzed the law of marriage. The facts found at trial were revived in print to sharpen the lens for legal dissection. Section 55 of the California Civil Code provided that marriage was a personal relation arising out of a civil contract requiring consent to marriage. But consent alone was not enough. The code also required "solemnization" or a "mutual assumption of marital rights, duties, or obligations." Terry posited that the assumption of marital rights, duties, and obligations were necessarily private matters and that an agreement to keep a marriage secret was not contrary to code or public policy. Sharon's dream team thought otherwise. In the end, McKinstry wrote that the agreement to keep the marriage secret "was a collateral agreement, and not a condition to marriage contract taking effect. The agreement to become husband and wife was complete."[20] But was the secret agreement an illegal promise? McKinstry ruled it was not.

The second issue on appeal was a matter of money, namely alimony and attorney fees. The trial court had awarded Sarah an initial alimony payment of $7,500 and $2,500 a month thereafter. Attorney fees were, as mentioned, in the amount of $55,000: the Tylers won $20,000. Col. George Flournoy, Walter Levy, and David Smith Terry obtained judgment for $10,000 [$187,058.60 in 2001 dollars] each. So had said the trial judge, but not the majority of the California Supreme Court. After a review of case law, the majority of the Justices on the state's highest court, all of whom were male, deemed the amount excessive and also exhibited their Victorian class and gender bias in telling Sarah "to live in the discreet and quiet manner appropriate to one whose domestic relations are being made the subject of public investigation, and without expenditures for mere display or the gratification of personal vanity."[21] They proceeded to slash her alimony to $500 per month. In light of the fact that Sarah's attorneys had a contingent fee contract, the majority of the high court reversed the whole of that portion of the award.

Associate Justice Jackson Temple filed a concurring opinion, sustaining the validity of the marriage and placing the law on a broader footing. Apparently, he found Christian church teachings and the Justinian code of the sixth century relevant. He noted that "there have always been secret marriages. They have always been condemned by the church and by the courts. And yet they have always been held legal."[22] Secrecy was only one aspect of evidence rather than a condition voiding the contract at public policy.

Associate Justice James Dabney Thornton, joined by John Randolph Sharpstein, were the only dissenters. In their view, the text of the code was the foundation of the law and the statute changed the common law. Sexual intercourse by mutual consent did not constitute marriage; the parties must live together. William Sharon and Sarah Hill had not. Nevertheless, the decision recognizing the marriage, albeit with reduced alimony, was five to two.

Fully aware that the case would have one more hearing by the State Supreme Court, the adverse decision hardly gave the Sharon side pause, as William mocked the press "with a smile." Now the reporters tried to run down Sharon's counsel, Newlands. Instead they found his law partner, who told them that the case established "rather a bad precedent to allow the validity of secret marriages. Suppose a man should have formed a secret alliance and marries again? After his death, the first wife can now come in and throw out the other wife and her children. She then is no more to a man than his mistress, and her children are of course illegitimate," he asserted.[23]

The rehearing of the appeal, on motion, took place, but this time before a new group of California Supreme Court Justices, these just elected by the people. Now the Court, with three new justices and a new Chief Justice, William Henry Beatty, decided the case again. This time, John Downey Works, a new Associate Justice, wrote the majority opinion. Fittingly, as *Sharon* v. *Sharon* had opened volume 75 of the Reports, *Sharon* v. *Sharon* (1889) closed volume 79 of the *Reports*.

Justice Works opened by disposing of a procedural matter relating to exhibits, judicial authentication of exhibits, and omissions in the record coming up on appeal. Terry did not prevail on any of these points and Works then turned to the issues so much in the press and in the prior case.

Was the marriage contract valid? Samuel Wilson and William Herrin on behalf of Sharon wanted the recent federal court determination of the document as a forgery held determinative of the California Supreme Court's holding here. Works found that the federal court's judgment could not be offered for the first time on appeal.

With the forgery issue out of the way, Works next turned to the facts found below and whether the findings could be sustained by the evidence. Notably, Works asserted that the Court preferred "to meet and decide the question whether the doctrine that a decision once made in an action is forever after the law of the case is applicable to this case in its present status."[24] The status of the case now before the Court was different from the prior decision because California law permitted two appeals of the same case—one from the judgment and another from the order denying a new trial. The fact that the previous Court had decided the case one way did not prevent this "court from fully investigating and deciding the second appeal to the extent of modifying or wholly changing its former decision, if it be satisfied that an error has been committed."[25]

Works then went on to consider the merits, first reviewing the evidence offered at trial. After review, the Court found that Sarah Hill and William Sharon did not live and cohabit together "in the way usual with married people." They did not live or cohabit together at all. Hence, "their acts and conduct were entirely consistent with the meretricious relation of man and mistress."[26] Therefore, the only conclusion possible was "that the evidence was insufficient to sustain" the finding and this was a question of law for the Court to decide.[27] The case was finally over, but the saga continued. On August 14, 1889, Justice Field's body guard, Dave Neagle, shot and killed David Terry while defending Field from an alleged attack. For Terry, the saga ended. For California's print readership, the end was nowhere in sight.[28]

A Woman's Virtue:
Moral Justice Served?

On March 16, 1881, the *Los Angles Evening Express* announced the terrible news: Francisco "Chico" Forster, the forty-year-old son of Don Juan Forster, whose wife was of the royal Mexican Pico family and whose vast rancho is now the Camp Pendleton U.S. Marine Corps base, had been shot dead on the streets of Los Angeles by Lastencia Abarta, an eighteen-year-old beauty of Basque and Mexican descent.[29] Abarta had fired a single shot from a distance of ten feet, the ball entering Forster's head through his right eye. Disarmed by a bystander, Lastencia joined her sister, Hortensia, and walked "to Judge Trafford's old Court room, corner of Temple and New High streets, for the purpose of giving herself up. Throughout the terrible affair the woman who was chief actor in it seemed perfectly cool and collected." The deed was done at four o'clock in the afternoon and a coroner's inquest was held one hour later. Eyewitnesses described the scene of the crime adequately, but the testimony regarding Lastencia was far more descriptive.

Testimony painted Lastencia as the perfect picture of civic responsibility. One Louis Goodfriend testified that after the shooting, he told her "to go up to the Sheriff's office. She was cool. She said "No, I am going to Judge Trafford's." As she and her sister turned and started on their way, one of them said: "You are not going to fool another woman again." Frank H. Burke, the man who disarmed Lastencia, agreed that she willingly went to the law. He testified that "we got into Judge Trafford's office. I asked him if he was Judge Trafford and gave him the pistol that I took away from the tallest of the two women." Lastencia had made one remark to him as they marched to the judge's office: "Why didn't you let me have another shot at him?" She also "made the same remark, when she went into Judge Trafford's office." There was no struggle. There was no hiding of the obvious.

Another witness, Nick Covarrubias, put another spin on the affray. The evening before the homicide he had conversed with Chico, who told him of Lastencia's demand that he marry her but that he "had never promised to marry her." In fact, Covarrubias asserted that he had asked his friend directly: "Chico, have you promised this girl that you would marry her?" He replied, "No, Nick, I never did."

The trial of Lastencia Abarta occupied April 28–30, 1881.[30] The first morning was occupied with impaneling an all-male jury. The press reported that Lastencia was "neatly attired in black and with a modestly self-possessed manner." When trial opened, the crowd was mostly "young men whose speech betrayed their Mexican descent." The prosecution successfully got all the elements of the crime admitted into evidence. The prosecution even produced John Leiver, the gunsmith who had sold

Lastencia the pistol about one hour before the killing. On cross-examination, Leiver revealed that he had shown her how to load the weapon and how to fire it.

Then the defense had its turn. Col. John F. Godfrey, Lastencia's seasoned defense attorney, told the jury that "at the time of the shooting, the mind of the defendant was incapable of judging between right and wrong." It was the insanity defense, all right, but there was much more to it. Lastencia had been promised marriage by Chico, she had been seduced by him believing marriage to be certain; ruined, she had purchased the gun to kill herself, but, believing that they were going to Judge John Trafford's office to be married, she agreed to accompany Chico there. When they alighted from the carriage, the gun went off accidentally. "From that time until she found herself in Trafford's office she remembers nothing of what occurred. It will also be shown that the defendant is subject to hysteria at certain times of the month and is then subject to great physical and mental perturbation." What a hodgepodge of defenses, something for every juror. Or was this just good lawyering? Now the defense would have to provide evidence to back up this shotgun-load of excuses.

The defense opened by placing Lastencia herself on the stand. She told a love story with numerous promises of marriage and entreaties for sex prior to the ceremony. After resisting Chico's advances time and time again, finally she acquiesced. "I loved Mr. Forster," she testified, "and was afraid he would not marry me if I did not consent and went to bed with him." Furthermore, she had a note from Forster that read "Come quick, I am waiting for you, don't be afraid, I am going to marry you." She produced the note in open court. She also testified that prior to the seduction, Chico had assured her that "It would be just the same to-morrow, we are just the same as if we are married." Her sister had heard a similar commitment the day of the shooting: "My sister asked him if he was going to marry me; he said, 'Oh, yes, of course, I have promised her, I am going to marry her'."

This last statement to Hortensia was made in Lastencia's presence in the coach headed for the church. But when the three arrived there, Forster "told the driver to drive to Ducommon street." Lastencia blanked out at this time. "All I remember was seeing Mr. Forster standing on the sidewalk and hearing a shot. . . ." She concluded by telling the jury that "I have always suffered from hysteria at certain times of the month."

During cross-examination, Abarta "maintained her composure unruffled, even under the somewhat embarrassing questions put to her" by the prosecution. In this instance, her memory had sustained her.

Then came the battle of the medical experts. First, Dr. Joseph Kurtz "made a decided impression on the jury" and held firm during cross-examination in his opinion "that any virtuous woman when deprived of her virtue would go mad undoubtedly." This statement was greeted with "decided marks of applause" from "the concourse without the bar." Then Dr.

Henry Worthington testified that Lastencia had been treated by him for "dismenorrhea" and was "irrational and insane at that time" of the shooting. Dr. Worthington also testified "that uterine diseases tended to disease the mind." He asserted that "when a medical expert testified of his own personal knowledge his opinion was more entitled to weight than that of an equally capable physician who had not that personal knowledge." Asked whether he had seen a case like Lastencia's, Worthington testified that he even then had a different patient suffering from "homicidal mania produced by dismenorrhea." Next came the testimony of Dr. N. P. Richardson, who had treated Abarta for dismenorrhea "accompanied by hysterical spasms." Finally, Dr. K. D. Wise chimed in that he, too, had treated her for dismenorrhea, adding that "at times she suffered under mental aberration, due to the physical troubles from which she suffered; at the time of the shooting undoubtedly her nerves were entirely unstrung, and she was irresponsible for the act." Wise also defined an insane impulse for the jury; he concluded that she did not know that "her offense" was "against God and man at the time of her slaying Forster; at the time her brain was undoubtedly congested with blood."

Surprisingly, even back in 1881 this type of defense was not a new one. Sixteen years earlier, lawyers had produced experts on temporary insanity and what we now refer to as premenstrual syndrome in *People* v. *Harris*. On January 30, 1865, Mary Harris had pumped two .32 rounds from her four-barreled Sharps pistol into the back of Adoiram J. Burroughs on the second floor of the Treasury Building in Washington, D.C. Harris proclaimed that Burroughs had promised to marry her, ruined her, then married another. Her lawyer, Joseph H. Bradley, Sr., produced experts who told the jury that "severe congestive dysmenorrhea due to irritability of the uterus . . . always affects the nervous system."[31] The prosecution had countered with "common-sense medical" experts, but the jury bought the uterine connection and the judge spared Harris from prison, sending her instead her to a psychiatric hospital. Amazingly, even this early defense based on premenstrual syndrome or PMS hardly was precedent. Nevertheless, the Harris case did get the issue into the medical journals.[32]

Back at the trial of Lastencia Abarta, it was the prosecution's turn to roll out its experts. On to the stand came Dr. W. W. Ross, who testified on the difference between hysteria and mania. "A hysterical person is never afflicted by homicidal mania," Ross asserted, adding that he had "treated a great many cases of dismennorrhea" and "it may, in time, affect the mind, and in various ways," but "the period at which the patient suffers must differ . . . it lasts, sometimes, all week." He admitted that he thought that Lastencia did indeed suffer from the disease, but he added that "insanity might result, but not in one so young." In other words, "a person cannot be sane, then insane so as to commit homicide, then sane again, previously not, having manifested insane symptoms." On cross-examination, Dr. Ross defined "irresistible impulse" as "a disease of the mind;" and he drew "a distinction between mental and moral insanity," concluding that "the defendant" was not "insane or suffering from dementia of any kind" and she "knew right and wrong." In closing, Ross admitted that he had never personally treated a patient with such symptoms.

Next to testify was Dr. Joseph Hannon, the Los Angeles County Physician. He claimed to have seen one hundred persons "charged with insanity." He opined that "insanity in women does not generally depend on sexual diseases." He had "seen a few cases of insanity due to uterine trouble, almost all occurring at the change of life," but he had never seen "insanity arising from dismenorrhea." With this testimony, the court adjourned on April 29th at 10:50 P.M.[33]

All reassembled the next morning at 9:00 A.M. "The fair protagonist in the drama, of which it may be, to-day's proceedings form the last act, attended by her sister, gracefully sought her accustomed seat," the *Los Angeles Evening Express* reported. The first act of this day's drama was the cross-examination of Dr. Hannon.

And Dr. Hannon's testimony this day was most revealing. He admitted believing in the "same teaching as Drs. Kurtz, Wise, and Worthington." He differed with Worthington on some points, but not on others, "His principal difference with Dr. Worthington is as to transitory mania, emotional insanity." Hannon admitted that he personally did not "know that in Mexican families girls are brought up to never be alone with men" and that "such a girl would be more apt to be excited when alone with a man for the first time than a girl brought up in the American way would." He also admitted that "emotional insanity is recognized by medical writers all over the world," but he was "not prepared to say that a great proportion of them does." Defense counsel then pulled out a copy of *Rae on Insanity*, the most authoritative treatise of the times, and obtained Hannon's admission of the authority of that text recognizing emotional insanity. Now defense informed Judge Ygnacio Sepulveda that they were ready to address the jury with their closing.

Having called their last witness, the prosecution began its closing statements. Opening for the prosecution, Theodore Lynill reviewed the evidence and reminded the jury of their duty under the law. He also "elaborated the usual argument against transitory insanity."

Now attorney J. E. Stevenson strutted upon the stage and delivered the defense's first soliloquy. Lastencia, he opined, was a mere child who had been wronged. The *Evening Express* offered that "The orator detailed in an eloquent manner the steps by which Forster accomplished his purpose, and the gradual approaches of that despair that seized upon her in consequence . . . rapidly culminated in insanity." He closed with the assertion that "Forster met his just deserts and the jury should show by their verdict that it thinks so." When Stevenson finished speaking, "the speech was followed by applause, suppressed by the Sheriff."

Now, Col. John F. Godfrey, also for the defense, emphasized both the insanity of the accused at the time and that the shot was, after all, an accident, "a chance shot." Then, "the gentleman closed with an eloquent appeal to the sympathy of the jury, sympathy the outgrowth of a full and conscientious consideration of the evidence." He "painted a glowing picture of the woman wronged as the girl has been wronged, and the horror attending her future as contrasted with that of her seducer." This speech, too, "was followed by applause, and one passage was applauded by one of the jurymen."

Finally, G. Wiley Wells rose for the defense. He, too, reminded the jury of its duty to society but also asked them to remember how Chico had used his "arts" to ruin Lastencia, a young lady whom he would be happy to call his "sister." At this point, some members of the audience "burst into applause—which was not checked." Wells wrapped it up by saying Lastencia did no wrong in killing Forster. "Mr. Wells's speech throughout was delivered with evident feeling, and its close was the signal for great applause."

Prosecuting attorney Stephen Mallory White, later a United States senator, gave the final rebuttal oration, calling upon the jury to adhere to its oath and "carry out the will of the blind goddess whom it legally represents."

It took Judge Speulveda thirty minutes to relay his instructions to the jury, which then retired. "Their verdict might almost be read upon their faces," the *Evening Express* reported.

Fifty-four minutes later the jury reported back with a verdict of "NOT GUILTY on the ground of insanity." The crowd responded immediately. "A cheer, loud and long, went up from the assembled crowd, a demonstration which passed unreproved of justice." The defendant's "friends crowded about the lady and shook her hand." The jury "stood two for conviction to ten for acquittal" on the first ballot, but it is clear that the goddess they served was not entirely blind.

AN ABUSED WIFE

On December 18, 1899, the trial of Katie Cook opened in Santa Ana, California, for the murder of her husband, T. J. "Tom" Cook, shot through the brain while he slept. The December 19, 1899, edition of the *Los Angeles Times* reported that "Since the tragedy Mrs. Cook has been suffering greatly from nervous prostration, but has so far recovered now as to sit composedly in the prisoner's dock between her father and mother." She admitted killing her husband, but only because she could no longer stand his infidelity; without other recourse, "she took the law into her own hands, sending a bullet through his brain." The *Times* concluded that "public sympathy is strongly with Mrs. Cook."[34]

The trial began in earnest on December 19 with a jury seated by noon and the prosecution presenting its case. W. W. Baron, the Cooks' hired man, testified to hearing a shot, finding Katie with a smoking gun in her hand, and hearing her accuse Mabel Moody, the hired girl, "of taking her husband." Barton also testified that the night before he had heard "some one walk into Miss Moody's room, and afterward heard two voices, those of a man and woman." On the fatal day, he had looked into Ms. Moody's room and noticed "by the pillows and the appearance of the bed that it had been occupied by more than one person." Other witnesses testified regarding a few material facts, but when Katie's father, Henry Pope, testified about "an alleged deed to the valuable peatland farm of the deceased from Mrs. Cook to her husband," the ears of the packed crowd perked up. Pope said he could not find the paper. J. A. Turner's testimony as notary public was offered to prove that "such a deed had been acknowledged." The defense objected, "making a strong fight to not permit this evidence . . . as it will tend to strengthen the theory that Mrs. Cook had another motive than that of injured feeling for killing her husband."[35]

The next day, the overflow crowd appeared along with the players. The *Los Angeles Times* reported that "Mrs. Cook still retains that stolid indifference which has characterized her conduct since the beginning of her trial." She sat with her father, mother, and brother "calmly until adjournment." Only when Mabel Moody took the stand did "her face" assume "a crimson hue." Moody was a defense witness, the prosecution having rested with the admission of the testimony regarding the acknowledgment of the deed to the Cook ranch.

Mabel Moody was prepared to tell the jury about Katie's condition two weeks prior to the homicide. Mabel said that Katie "seemed depressed, absent-minded and weak, and the greater portion of her time was spent lying on a couch, crying hysterically." When Moody was asked whether she felt Katie knew right from wrong in such an agitated state, the district attorney rose to object, which resulted in a "heated debate" that lasted "more than an hour, during which many authorities were cited." The court chose to admit the testimony that Katie, in Mabel's opinion, did not know right from wrong. The day's last witness was J. H. Paty, a butcher, who also said he had seen Katie's "steady decline." According to Paty, "she had become daft for some reason." Experts on insanity would be heard later.

The defense's grand parade of twenty-six witnesses on December 21 would heavily varnish the acknowledged deed in the audience's mind. The *Los Angeles Times* noted that "for many years Tom Cook has been known here by many people as a very immoral man, but until today the full import of his hellish disposition was not realized." In fact, those who had criticized Katie "for taking the law into her own hands" were now treated to the shocking details of the depths of Tom's sin as well as Katie's suffering. One girl testified that Tom had forced her and Katie "to sit and listen while he read them over twenty pages of a vulgar poetical effusion, declaring he would kill them both if did not listen to it." Jailer Graham's wife testified that Katie's "mind seemed gone" the day after the killing. Furthermore, she was "very thin in flesh, extremely nervous and hysterical". . . and refusing "sufficient nourishment to keep her alive."

On December 22, Katie Cook took the stand, the *Los Angeles Times* noting that "the court, jury and the great crowd of spectators were apparently moved when. . . ." she did so. Her testimony was worth the wait. She told of "the unspeakable life led by her husband," who had "brought young girls to their home, and . . . accomplished their ruin." She had "entreated him to live different". . . and "begged him to send the girls away." He had "compelled one German servant girl to appear in the "all-together" before himself and Mrs. Cook," and he had, as mentioned, forced "another young girl and herself to sit and listen to the reading of page after page of the vilest poetry known to the tenderloin district." Finally, Tom had "openly boasted to her of his degradation, and what he would do with her if she betrayed him." If that was not bad enough, Mabel Moody entered the picture.

When Tom started talking dirty to Mabel and took to trimming her finger nails for her, it triggered more tears and pleas from his beleaguered wife, who one last time "implored him to come and live with her, be true to her, and to forsake his wicked ways," but "he pushed her away—and then she knew no more," that is, until she found herself in the Orange County Jail. In the interim, "her mind had been a blank." At this point, "she burst into tears, sobbing bitterly for some minutes, during which many handkerchiefs throughout the courtroom brushed away tears."

After cross-examination, the defense put four physicians on the stand to testify that Katie was insane at the time she killed Tom. Two other witnesses testified that three years ago she had taken a hard fall and hit her head.

The closing arguments were predictable. The defense's Jud Rush of Los Angeles made "one of the best addresses before a jury that has ever been heard in the county." Victor Montgomery of Santa Ana and Prosecuting Attorney Jackson added their two cents, but Lecomte Davis of Los Angeles painted a portrait of the "depravity of the murdered man . . . while . . . the misery of the trusting wife [was] pathetic. District Attorney Williams closed and the judge gave the jury "a brief but vigorous charge."

The jury stayed out fifteen minutes. When they filed back into the courtroom, Katie Cook rose and faced them. The foreman read the verdict of "not guilty," at which point the *Los Angeles Times* reported that "Mrs. Cook fell into the arms of her mother, and the great crowd of spectators arose as one person, filling the corridors with deafening applause. Such a scene probably never was witnessed in the courtroom before." Yet, two items of equal significance apparently need reporting. First, the verdict was *not guilty*, not *not guilty by reason of insanity*. Second, "one juryman remarked after the adjournment of court that he was sorry the jury could not have awarded a medal to Mrs. Cook."[36]

Why did these nineteenth-century California cases take a similar linguistic turn, and to exonerate women, not men?[37] Was it simply good lawyering? Lawyers do have a tendency to try as many arguments, rhetorical twists, and visual displays as possible to win. Or was it something else?

Perhaps the West has always been different and these California cases reflect that difference.[38] The concept that marriage is a partnership was deeply imbedded in California law since 1849.[39] Even in the Hispanic period, women had litigated their property rights to maintain their land and "ironically, despite legal obstructions, the tradition of married women independently owning land continued in this increasingly inhospitable environment" of the American era.[40] Community property and sole trader laws in California had allowed women to conduct business for many years, and feminists in the West "recognized the common-law badge of inferiority" and worked to eradicate it.[41] In fact, by 1890 the gender imbalance in California largely had been eliminated and women were expanding the reach of their reform campaigns.[42] Maybe all-male juries in California were less threatened by, or more accustomed to, women having rights than were their eastern counterparts.

Perhaps, historians are too enamored of journalistic flair. True, the *Sharon* trial contained fashion reports, cosmetic evaluation of complexion, courtroom antics worthy of *L.A. Law*, and bedroom adventures to rival any self-respecting soap opera, but when the trial was over and the appeal concluded, we are left with the law. Sarah lost. Yet we must distinguish her loss from the jury verdicts for Lastencia and Katie. There is no appeal from a verdict of *not guilty by reason of insanity* or just plain—*not guilty*. Even with the distinction, the construction of gender as well as the nature of unwritten law can be teased out of historic documents.[43] Chico Forster had violated his betrothed and abandoned her. In the eyes of a Victorian society, he had ruined her for all time for marriage to a "respectable" male. Tom Cook had managed to violate every fiber of the Victorian social tapestry.[44] He had ruined servant girls, local adolescents, and the minds of innocents. Who, then, could stop these violators of the unwritten law? The answer is women armed with the strong arm of the unwritten law, doing what they felt they had to do, even if they could not recall doing so later, and defended by lawyers willing to use every possible defense argument, however preposterous. Sometimes a jury will latch on to a slogan and give the rest of the evidence little weight.[45] In any event, the legal process is very much part of the history of any state, and the context of time and place plays a critical role.

These three trials demonstrate that historians of western criminal justice may be mistaken about women who found themselves caught up in the nineteenth-century courts. Some scholars have argued that women were the least prepared to deal with the realities of the legal system.[46] Furthermore, women were infrequently hauled into criminal courts.[47] A survey of the literature indicates that scholars have yet to look systematically at gender as an issue in western criminal trials.[48] Yet as these three trials indicate, women at the bar of justice were far from powerless. Rather, these women and their lawyers skillfully manipulated gender stereotypes as well as cultural values to gain advantage within the legal system.

Notes

1   Wayne K. Hobson, "Narratives in Black and White: The O.J. Simpson Trials as Social Drama," in John W. Johnson, ed., *Historic U.S. Court Cases: An Encyclopedia*, 2 vol., (New York: Routledge, 2001), vol. 1, pp. 139–45.

2   Lawrence M. Friedman and Robert V. Percival, *The Roots of Justice: Crime and Punishment in Alameda County, California, 1870–1910* (Chapel Hill: University of North Carolina Press, 1981), p. 218.

3   Mark Hickerson, "Everything's Up to Date in Contra Costa," 8 *The Californians* (May/June, 1990), p. 35.

4   Anne M. Butler, *Gendered Justice in the American West: Women Prisoners in Men's Penitentiaries* (Urbana: University of Illinois Press, 1997), p. 228. Also see Shelley Bookspan, *A Germ of Goodness* (Lincoln: University of Nebraska Press, 1991). Jane Totman, *The Murderess* (San Francisco: R & E Research Associates, Inc., 1978). Otto Pollak, *The Criminality of Women* (Philadelphia: University of Pennsylvania Press, 1950). Clarice Feinman, *Women in the Criminal Justice System* (New York: Praeger Publishers, 1980). JoAnn G. Gora, *The New Female Criminal: Empirical Reality or Social Myth?* (New York: Praeger Publishers, 1982). Keith Edgerton, "Power, Punishment, and the United States Penitentiary at Deer Lodge City, Montana Territory, 1871–1889," 28 *Western Historical Quarterly* (Summer, 1997), pp. 161–84. Of particular significance for social history is Mary Odem, *Delinquent Daughters* (Chapel Hill: University of North Carolina Press, 1995).

5   Clare V. McKenna, Jr., *Homicide, Race, and Justice in the American West, 1880–1920* (Tucson: University of Arizona Press, 1997), pp. 16–19, 29, 39, 60, 67, 104.

6   The issue of justice and the unwritten law is far from new. A good place to start is Alison Dendes Renteln and Alen Dundes, eds., *Folk Law: Essays in the theory and Practice of Lex Non Scripta*, two volumes (Madison: University of Wisconsin Press, 1994). For examples of the use of trial court records, see Lyle A. Dale, "Rough Justice: Felony Crime and the Superior Court in San Luis Obispo County, 1880–1910," 76 *Southern California Quarterly* (Summer, 1994), pp. 195–216; Linda S. Parker, "Superior Court Treatment of Ethnics Charged with Violent Crimes in Three California Counties, 1880–1910," 74 *Southern California Quarterly* (Fall, 1992), pp. 225–46; Robert H. Tillman, "The Prosectuion of Homicide in Sacramento County, California, 1853–1900," 68 *Southern California Quarterly* (Summer, 1986), pp. 167–82.

7   Donald W. Hamblin, "The Sharon Cases: A Legal Melodrama of the Eighties," 25 *Los Angeles Bar Bulletin* (Dec., 1949), pp. 103, 122–23, 125–28. Brooks W. MacCraken, "Althea and the Judges," 18 *American Heritage* (June, 1967), pp. 61–63, 75–79. Robert H. Kroninger, *Sarah and the Senator* (Berkeley: Howell-North, 1964). Judge Kroninger has the best account of the legal machinations in the cases. Also see Matthew J. Lindsay, "Reproducing a Fit Citizenry: Dependency, Eugenics, and the Law of Marriage in the United States, 1860–1920," 23 *Law and Social Inquiry* (Summer, 1998), pp. 541–85. The article is an example of the failure of eastern scholars to note legal developments in the West.

8   On Sharon and the political context see Gilman M. Ostrander, *Nevada: the Great Rotten Borough, 1859–1964* (New York: Alfred A. Knopf, 1966), pp. 70–118. On the trial and the involvement of William Morris Stewart also a Nevada Senator see Russell R. Elliot, *Servant of Power: A Political Biography of Senator William M. Stewart* (Reno: University of Nevada Press, 1983), pp. 88–91.

9   Glenda Riley, *Divorce, An American Tradition* (New York: Oxford University Press, 1991), pp. 62–129. Michael Grossberg, *Governing the Hearth: Law and the Family in Nineteenth–Century America* (Chapel Hill: University of North Carolina Press, 1985), pp. 64–152.

10 Computation based on John J. McCusker, *How Much is That in Real Money? A Historical Price Index for Use as a Deflator of Money Values in the Economy of the United States* (Worcester: American Antiquarian Society, 1992).

11 Grossberg, *Governing the Hearth*, pp. 70–78.

12 Ibid., p. 79.

13 Ibid., pp. 80–81. The Court also noted that this public policy arose from the facts of life in the state "in a country where marriage is a civil contract and often unattended by ceremony or performed by a single officiating witness."

14 Ibid., pp. 83–88. It was also in the 1870s that Laura D. Fair shot her married lover who failed to perform on his promises to divorce his wife and marry her. This California case had all the elements that Hartog's cases had except she was found guilty and sentenced to hang. See Kenneth Lamott, *Who Killed Mr. Crittenden?* (New York: David McKay Co., 1963). Andrew J. Marsh and Samuel Osborne, *Official Report of the Trial of Laura D. Fair for the Murder of Alex. P. Crittenden* (San Francisco: The San Francisco Co-Operative Printing Co., 1871). Laura Fair, *Wolves in the Fold*, printed as a pamphlet in San Francisco in 1873. The *San Francisco Chronicle, Bulletin, Alta* and *Examiner* all gave the trial extensive coverage as did the *Sacramento Union* and *Bee*.

15 Grossberg, *Governing the Hearth*, p. 88.

16 Ibid., p. 99. On the legislative and judicial reactions to reform see Ibid., pp. 92–98. For a more recent appraisal of the legislative and judicial record see Jana B. Singer, "The Privatization of Family Law," 1992 *Wisconsin Law Review* 1444–1567. Clearly, the events at the time of *Sharon* v. *Sharon* and the "reforms" of the past century have had significant impact on the law today. The California public was well aware of the state of the law. For example, the Dec. 8, 1882 issue of the *San Francisco Chronicle* carried a story about "Informal Unions: Idiosyncrasies of the Laws of Marriage." In the story a "leading lawyer" commented upon the problem of breach of promise suits being frequent and too often groundless. The story also quotes the attorney as saying "in 52d California Reports you will find the McCausland case. . . . This is a case where marriage was promised, followed by cohabitation. The woman was recognized as McCausland's wife only once, it is proved, and that was in the presence of Dr. Behrens, who was attending her in Sacramento, just previous to the birth of a son, in 1866. The Probate Court held this constituted a marriage, and she was allowed $100 a month. The decision of our Supreme Court is similar. It holds that the verbal promise of a marriage, followed by cohabitation, constitutes marriage. This is based on a New York decision, in the case of Cheny, where there was an engagement to marry, and the parties lived together, but did not pass in public as man and wife." The attorney goes on to argue against this law and condemns the practice of "criminal intercourse."

17 On the importance of following the newspaper coverage to understand the context of historical development see Philip J. Ethington, *The Public City: The Political Construction of Urban Life in San Francisco, 1850–1900* (New York: Cambridge University Press, 1994). Ethington's study is of William Randolph Hearst's *San Francisco Examiner* noting that the old-line *Alta California*, the non–partisan voice of the public interest, common ground, and republican order, was soon driven from the streets by Hearst's pandering to interest group interests and politics. For alternative views of the trial see *Daily Alta California*, Dec. 27, 1885 or the *Sacramento Bee*, Dec. 26, 1885. Most importantly, Ethington correctly establishes that the old republican world of a public interest was replaced by a media theatre of melodrama, burlesque, and victim's plight. So too, we find *Sharon* v. *Sharon* in the *Chronicle*.

18 The paper also kept track of the events in the federal court. See the *Chronicle*, Dec. 4, 1883, Jan. 22 and March 4, 1884 editions as examples.

19 For example, see the *Chronicle*, Aug. 20, Sept. 4, 1884.

20 The *Chronicle*, Feb. 26, 1885.

21 See the *Chronicle*, March 10, April 22, 1885. MacCracken, "Althea and the Judges," pp. 63, 75.

22 Terry was a former justice of the California Supreme Court and known for his dueling past. See A. Russel Buchanan, *David S. Terry of California: Dueling Judge* (San Marino: Huntington Library Press, 1956). Stewart as noted above was a U.S. Senator, Newlands would follow in his footsteps, Wilson was a prominent member of the San Francisco Bar Association, Herrin was a noted railroad trial lawyer, and Hoge was a prominent San Francisco attorney. Terry and Hoge were 1878–79 California Constitutional Convention delegates.

23 75 Cal. 1, 10 (1888).

24 75 Cal. 1, 47 (1888).

25 75 Cal. 1, 53 (1888).

26 The case also was in the federal courts during this period. See *Sharon* v. *Hill*, 24 Fed. 726 (1885). *Sharon* v. *Hill*, 36 Fed. 337(1888). Terry married Sarah on Jan. 7, 1886, shortly after Sharon's death on Nov. 13, 1885. William Morris Stewart had carried the case into federal court and Sarah had been cited for contempt after brandishing a pistol and threatening to shoot Stewart. Further, in federal court, the marriage contract had been declared a forgery on Dec. 26, 1885. Sarah was ordered to surrender the document, but refused to do so partially on the ground raised by David Smith Terry that the order died with Sharon. Stewart's place in federal court was taken by his law partner, William Herrin, and the attack in federal court was continued in 1888. On Sept. 3, 1888, the federal court ordered the document surrendered. In the proceedings, Stephen J. Field ordered Sarah to be seated, she refused, federal marshal Dave Neagle attempted to remove her, Terry jumped to her defense, and both were disarmed, she of a pistol and he of a bowie knife, and both were adjudged guilty of contempt. These events in federal court were very public due to press coverage. See Elliott, *Servant of Power*, pp. 88–91. *San Francisco Chronicle*, March 11, 15, 16, July 17, 1888, Feb. 1, 9, Sept. 5, 13, 1889, March 4, April 15, 1890 [Neagle case]. Again, Kroninger, *Sarah and the Senator* provides an excellent narrative of the events.

27 79 Cal. 633, 653 (1889). On the changing expectations in the marriage relationship see Karen Lystra, *Searching the Heart: Women, Men, and Romantic Love in Nineteenth-Century America* (New York: Oxford University Press, 1989).

28 79 Cal. 633, 654 (1889).

29 79 Cal. 633, 663–64 (1889).

30 79 Cal. 633, 671–72 (1889). On the secrecy issue, the Court held that secrecy alone or the contract agreement to keep the marriage secret, standing alone, was not sufficient to declare the marriage void so long as the other elements required by the statute were complied with by the parties. 79 Cal. 633, 680–81 (1889). The California legislature abolished common-law marriage in 1895. 1895 Cal. Stat., Chapter 129. Marriage then required a marriage license and solemnization. See *Norman* v. *Norman*, 121 Cal. 620 (1898).

31 On Terry see Buchanan, *David S. Terry of California, Dueling Judge*, pp. 210–30. *In re Neagle*, 135 U.S. 1 (1890). Also see Owen M. Fiss, *History of the Supreme Court of the United States: Troubled Beginnings of the Modern State, 1888–1910* (New York: Macmillan Publishing Co., 1993), pp. 29–30, *San Francisco Chronicle*, Sept. 5, 1889.

32 Also see *Los Angeles Herald*, March 16, 1881. Paul Bryan Gray, *Forster v. Pico: The Struggle for the Rancho Santa Margarita* (Spokane: Arthur H. Clark, 1997), pp. 228–29. Chico's mother was the sister of Pio Pico, one of the great Californios of the century. The *Los Angeles Express* reported her name as Lastania, others had it as Lastenia Abartachipi. Gray's research yielded Lastencia as the correct spelling of her name.

33 The following is taken on whole or in part from the *Los Angeles Evening Express*, April 28–30, 1881.

34 Allen D. Spiegel, "Temporary Insanity and premenstrual syndrome: Medical testimony in an 1865 murder trial," 88 *New York State Journal of Medicine* (September, 1988), pp. 482–92, 485.

35 Ibid., pp. 490–91. The question of moral insanity had been raised as early as 1863 and Dr. Isaac Ray popularized the concept. Robert M. Ireland has argued that this defense coupled with the unwritten law "that forgave men and women who killed to avenge sexual dishonor" resulted in acquittals. Ireland, "Frenzied and Fallen Females," 3 *Journal of Women's History*

(Winter, 1992), p. 95. Ireland saw the period 1843–1896 as the heyday of this unwritten law. He cites the Harris trial as well as the Laura Fair trial in California, the Fanny Hyde trial in New York, and the Theresa Sturla trial in Chicago as evidence of the trend.

36 The physical nature of woman and her mental condition were contested at this time. Alexander J. C. Skene in his *Education and Culture as Related to the Health and Diseases of Woman* (1888) argued that "deranged sexual organs often produced insanity, although how this occurred was still in many cases a mooted question." At the same time, physicians like Mary Dixon Jones were "gendering and reconstituting an older, more holistic approach to physician–patient relationships." Regina Morantz-Sanchez, *Conduct Unbecoming a Woman: Medicine on Trial in Turn-of-the-Century Brooklyn* (New York: Oxford University Press, 1999), pp. 123, 157, 195–210.

37 Unless otherwise noted, the narrative is taken in whole or in part from *Los Angeles Times*, Dec. 19–24, 1899. The microfilm of the case #207, *People* v. *Cook*, is in Microfilm Box #1248, Orange Count Clerk of Court Office, Santa Ana, CA.

38 The necessity of an acknowledgement on the transfer of property owned by a married woman was well established in California law. In *Rico* v. *Brandenstein*, 98 Cal. 465 (1893), the Court at 481 held that "the evident policy of our law-makers, to loosen the chains which bound married women at the common law, so far as their separate property is concerned, to confer upon them like power of alienation with that possessed by their husbands." Also see *Mathews* v. *Davis*, 102 Cal. 202 (1894). *Lamb* v. *Harbough*, 105 Cal. 680 (1895). *Loupe* v. *Smith*, 123 Cal. 491 (1899).

39 The *Orange News*, Dec. 28, 1899 edition noted that "the defense was insanity; and Mrs. Cook's testimony of the marital infidelity and the cruelty and threats of her husband, coupled with his bestiality, did much to bring about the speedy verdict." Further, "Cook communicated a loathsome disease to his wife, and his treatment of her was most shocking and bestial."

40 See Lawrence M. Friedman and Robert V. Percival, *The Roots of Justice: Crime and Punishment in Alameda County California, 1870–1910* (Chapel Hill: University of North Carolina Press), pp. 239–44. The authors analyze the trial of Clara Fallmer, a fifteen year old, pregnant, and refused marriage. She shot her lover to death when he refused to marry her. She was guilty on the facts, used the insanity defense, and made the trial about her plight and the dastardly deeds of her lover. The jury bought it. The authors also note an important book on this type of trial putting it into the context of a morality play, Mary Hartman's *Victorian Murderesses* (New York, 1977), p. 239n.

41 A case very close to the facts that Hartog recites is that of Eloise Rudiger of Omaha who, in 1893, killed Henry Reiser after he "seduced" her and then turned his back on her. She, like Lastencia, purchased a handgun on the day of the killing and shot him down on a public street. Her aim was not restrained and she shot him three times. When her husband arrived on the scene, she told him that it was his duty to do the killing. Her jury acquitted her. McKanna, *Homicide, Race and Justice*, pp. 59–60.

42 Donna C. Schuele, "Community Property Law and the Politics of Married Women's Rights in Nineteenth Century California," 7 *Western Legal History* (Summer/Fall, 1994), pp. 245–81.

43 Gloria Ricci Lothrop, "Rancheras and the Land: Women and Property Rights in Hispanic California," 76 *Southern California Quarterly* (Spring, 1994), p. 79.

44 Mari J. Matsuda, "The West and the Legal State of Women: Explanations of Frontier Feminism," 24 *Journal of the West* (Jan., 1985), p. 55.

45 Christine Fischer, "Women in California in the Early 1850s," 64 *Southern California Quarterly* (1978), pp. 231–53. Mental cruelty had been added to the list of grounds for divorce in California by 1890. *Waldron* v. *Waldron,* 85 Cal. 251 (1890). On these developments see Robert Griswold, "The Evolution of the Doctrine of Mental Cruelty in Victorian American Divorce, 1790–1900," 20 *Journal of Social History* (Fall, 1986), pp. 131–33. On another plane of analysis, deadly force had been applied and spousal abuse used as justification for homicide in the case of William Rubottom. On September 7, 1858, Rubottom shot and killed his son-in-law because of his abuse of Rubottom's daughter. He was not charged with the homicide because the killing was ruled justifiable. *Los Angeles Star*, September 11, 1858. The suffrage campaign, started in the 1870s, was in full swing in the 1890s. Robert J. Chandler, "In the Van: Spiritualists as Catalysts for the California Women's Suffrage Movement," 73 *California History* (Fall, 1994), pp. 188–201, 252–54. Donald G. Cooper, "California Suffrage

Campaign of 1896: Its Origin, Strategies, Defeat," 71 *Southern California Quarterly* (Winter, 1989), pp. 311–25. Also see Peggy Pascoe, *Relations of Rescue: The Search for Female Moral Authority in the American West, 1874–1939* (New York: Oxford University Press, 1990).

46 For some other attempts at this task see Sally Engle Merry, *Getting Justice and Getting Even: Legal Consciousness among Working-Class Americans* (Chicago: University of Chicago Press, 1990). Deborah A. Rosen, *Courts and Commerce: Gender, Law, and the Market Economy in Colonial New York* (Columbus: Ohio State University Press, 1997). Robert M. Ireland argues that "the ideology of [the trials he studied] argued that men constituted the stronger of the sexes and had a duty to protect weak women who were ready prey to slimy, snake-like libertines or, conversely, to punish the consorts of Eve-like women who too readily embraced those libertines. . . . The women defendants were depicted as either weak and hysterical, whose hysteria rendered them legally insane and therefore innocent of any criminal wrongdoing, or inherently licentious and the purveyors of social evil." Dysmenorrhea as temporary insantity was used in several trials. Ireland, "Frenzied and Fallen Females," 3 *Journal of Women's History* (winter, 1992), pp 99–100, 101, 105.

47 See Ireland, "The Libertine Must Die," 23 *Journal of Social History* (Fall, 1989), pp. 27–44.

48 For alternative theories of causation, particularly on twentieth century sentencing behavior and the images of female felons, see Barbara Ellen Bloom, "Triple Jeopardy: Race, Class and Gender as factors in Women's Imprisonment," Ph.D. dissertation: University of California, Riverside, 1996. Of particular interest for nineteenth century studies is her analysis of the "chivalry hypothesis" at pp. 57–58. Also see Louise Lander, *Images of Bleeding: Menstruation as Ideology* (New York: Orlando Press, 1988), p. 187 arguing that feminists should be working to make menstruation a "non-issue."

CHAPTER SIX

Educational Housekeepers: Female Reformers and the California Americanization Program, 1900–1927

Danelle Moon

Immigration long has been and remains a dominant issue in California. The large influx of new immigrants, primarily from Mexico, over the course of the last several decades combined with diminishing public resources, particularly in education and public assistance, has renewed political, legal, and social hostilities toward these new arrivals. The 1990s witnessed the revival of xenophobic anti-immigration sentiments with the enactment of Proposition 227, which abolished bilingual instruction in public schools, and Proposition 187, a host of measures designed to slow immigration by denying public assistance and education and health-care services to illegal aliens. Once enacted, both of these controversial laws faced a series of legal battles; 227 remains in effect, while 187 may well come before the U.S. Supreme Court.[1]

For students of California history, this conflicted issue is not a new one. During times of recession and unemployment, immigrants, who like all other residents consume resources, become easy targets for blame and racial hatred. The past holds numerous examples including the Chinese Exclusion Acts, racial covenants limiting housing and property ownership opportunities, segregation, labor strikes, and race riots. Yet, history can serve as a guidepost for the present if we can grasp its important lessons. By taking a step back in time, perhaps we can better understand, and hope to meet, today's economic, social, political, and legal challenges.

Between 1890 and 1920, the United States experienced cyclical economic downturns and massive immigration problems not unlike those we face today. These turbulent times saw the formation of "third" parties to challenge the political status quo and a wave of "progressive" reformism undertaken by politicians and private citizens alike. During what historians now refer to as the Progressive Era, a variety of different groups, sometimes singly, sometimes in alliance, set out to remedy the political and social ills of American society. In California, progressives shaped public opinion and played a central role in advancing educational reform through the

Mary Simons Gibson. *This item is reproduced by permission of The Huntington Library, San Marino, California, Margaret C. Graham Collection, Box 37 (2).*

formation, adoption, and implementation of a set of policies referred to collectively as "Americanization Programs." In short, these reform-minded citizens, many of them women, sought to Americanize the "giddy masses" of immigrants by imposing their own middle-class values on them. Indeed, both male and female progressives believed it their moral duty to address and enforce public and political morality, and these "progressives" succeeded in effecting real change in and wholly new policy regarding the state's response to immigration, social welfare, sexual behavior, and medical care.[2]

Progressive social reform grew out of the antebellum reform activities begun in the 1830s. It was not until after the Civil War, however, that political and social reform groups composed of and run by women made headway in crafting and forcing legislative change. The late nineteenth century witnessed marked growth in the number of women-headed social reform groups, with mission statements ranging from the prohibition of alcoholic beverages to woman suffrage. Between 1909 and 1918, California progressive reform boomed. In 1911, Hiram Johnson reigned victorious to become the one and only Progressive party governor; his victory fueled the Progressive party heyday. By 1930, the progressive influence in California politics had all but dried up, with a new administration less committed to social reform policy. But while the Progressive party's time in the sun may indeed have been short lived, its legacy lives on through legislative policy.[3]

Women helped build the legislative framework for reform, and it was women who led the call for and banded together to try to establish new laws to improve child welfare and public health, prohibit the consumption of alcohol, protect the chastity of young women and mandate a legal age of consent, and change the educational system. In particular, women's central role in the California Americanization Program—designed to facilitate the assimilation of new immigrants into the mainstream society and focused on the cultural "uplift" of immigrant women—demonstrates the level of women's influence. In addition, a consideration of the successes and failures of the California Americanization program shows how female reformers helped build and expand political and professional opportunities for women. Clearly, these reform-minded women gained new access as educators, social workers, and nurses. But while the gains made by the reformers behind the Americanization programs were concrete, only a small number of immigrants actually participated in their educational offerings. Historian Vicki Ruiz argues, for example, that Mexican immigrants adopted a system of "cultural coalescence," whereby they mixed the cultural traditions of their homeland with new experiences in the United States. Ultimately, navigation between cultures affected both immigrants and reformers in different ways, often with mixed results. In any case, a look at progressive reform provides a window into the cross-cultural interactions between women and illustrates the creation of a "female dominion" in California education and educational policy.[4]

CALIFORNIA PROGRESSIVE HEYDAY

From 1900 to 1920, California experienced unparalleled growth. No longer a pioneer outpost, California saw its population increase from 1.5 million persons in 1900 to 3.4 million in 1920. This explosive growth was in part fueled by the expansion of the Southern Pacific Railroad, which connected California to the Midwest. Families from across the United States steadily entered the Golden State, many of whom envisioned setting down agricultural roots. Immigrants from England, Germany, Ireland, and China arrived as well. By 1920, Mexicans composed the largest immigrant group, with 88,771 arriving that year, while the Italians trailed close behind with 88,504. Obviously farming would not sustain the hordes of newcomers entering the state, the majority of which now flocked to the big cities, from San Francisco to San Diego. Los Angeles, for example, became home to immigrants from around the globe, with most of them settling in the designated foreign sections of town, including the Mexican barrio, the second-largest community of Mexicans outside of Mexico City. The mass arrival of Mexican immigrants, coupled with the growth of the Eastern European and German population, provided local female reformers with vast new opportunities to apply their skills as civic housekeepers through new educational programs.[5]

THE EMERGENCE OF
A FEMALE DOMINION

The election of Hiram Johnson as California governor in 1910 marks the kickoff for education reform. A committed progressive, Johnson began his tenure as the state's chief executive by shaping policy changes around his Progressive ideologies. He succeeded in passing legislation designed to protect laborers, including a provision for workmen's compensation and new minimum-wage and maximum-hour laws. For women, his election brought the passage of the state's female suffrage bill, in 1911.

Attempts to secure female suffrage began in the early 1890s with the California Women's Congress, an organization that brought together women from different groups to build a statewide woman's movement. This coalition became the first women's civic organization to bring together women from across the state to fight for suffrage. Male progressives helped to secure the final passage of the constitutional amendment enfranchising women in 1911, yet many of these men supported female suffrage only halfheartedly. For his part, Governor Johnson believed that female suffrage would undermine the traditional role of men in politics and would debilitate the success of the Progressive party. Nevertheless, he understood the importance of retaining the female vote, and he was indebted to female fundraisers. His appointment of women to six different state commissions ensured women's continued support of the governor, and the moves opened new possibilities for women's political participation. The successful fight to achieve suffrage dovetailed nicely with the struggle of female educational reformers anxious to address the growing problem posed by increasing numbers of foreign immigrants.[6]

Female Progressives shared many of the same characteristics as their male counterparts. Most hailed from middle- to upper-middle-class families, and they were typically white, protestant, and directed by their religious ethos. But different women participated in the various reforms groups for different reasons. Many of them were motivated by their personal and religious convictions, some entered social reform for philanthropic reasons, while others sought to challenge the second-class status of women in society by fighting for suffrage and participation in politics. Once gained, the vote provided female reformers the opportunity to enlarge their political participation and to redefine the meaning of citizenship.

Unlike today, male and female roles were clearly defined by distinct spheres; women's domain was the home, wherein they exercised moral authority over husbands and children and helped to ensure the natural social order of society and government. The ideal woman was pious, nurturing, sentimental, and selfless, while the ideal man was competitive and materialistic. "Female moral authority" became the social and political gateway for women wanting to pursue social reform and eventually politics. Progressive women's success in state and national politics demonstrates the importance of female moral authority in promoting the Americanization program. These reformers believed that new immigrants could be assimilated through a comprehensive program designed to instill middle-class values through homemaking and educational programs, and immigrant women became the primary target group. Framing their political participation around the concept of female moral authority, they argued that no less than national security depended on the Americanization of new immigrants, particularly women. Instilling middle-class values through imparting lessons in patriotism and homemaking, the reformers posited, would ensure conformity and secure the nation. Their argument concluded that proper assimilation of foreign immigrants could only be accomplished through women's political activism and their professional management of educational programs.

California clubwomen provided the backbone for Americanization policy development.[7] Women's clubs provided a venue for both self-betterment and social reform. Women joined a variety of clubs and worked through a large network to remold society, but together these clubs represented "organized womanhood"; as municipal housekeepers, women transformed their role as moral guardians of the home to the civic environment. Historian Judith Raferty, writing on the role of clubwomen in Los Angeles, observed "California women began developing a reformist political culture through women's clubs. . . . And they worked through a series of complex networks to play a significant role in shaping statewide progressive programs." Influenced by the dramatic social and economic changes brought on by industrialization, clubwomen turned reformers transformed work experience in charitable organizations into political action and eventually political influence.[8]

THE IMMIGRANT "MENACE"

Tensions between native-born Americans and immigrants escalated with the dawning of World War I. In California, all newcomers faced some hostility: anti-German hostilities ran particularly high during the war years, but Mexicans experienced the brunt of whites' ire. The Mexican population boom between 1910 and 1920 focused the attention of white nativists in California on the "growing menace" of new immigrants. Then, as now, Mexicans came to the Untied States in search of jobs, but, at that time, most of them never intended to resettle permanently. Therefore, they were less likely to assimilate on the same level as other immigrant groups. According to historian George Sanchez, the Los Angeles barrio became the largest Mexican community in the world outside Mexico City. In L.A., the barrio provided most of its residents' needs; but life in an ethnic enclave tended to retard assimilation into mainstream American culture. Meanwhile, the anxiety and xenophobia triggered in the white manstream by World War I had helped to boost prewar programs designed to educate immigrants. Public education, it was proffered, might offer the solution by eliminating the "menace" of immigrants through programs designed to "Americanize" the newcomers.[9]

Yet the solution had costs. The Compulsory School Act of 1903 had escalated the need for Progressive educational reform, as increasing numbers of immigrants placed new demands on already pinched social services provided by the state. Reformers concerned over what appeared to be a rise in juvenile delinquency and school truancy sought to tighten their control on family behavior, and they proceeded to formulate and advocate the adoption of policies based on their own middle-class values.[10]

California's Americanization program developed out of the experience of settlement house work. The philosophy behind educational reform sprang from social gospel principles to help the poor, in this case by providing a full range of social services for poor and immigrant communities. The primary example of settlement house work was Jane Addams's Hull House in Chicago. California settlement-house workers adopted the methodologies of Addams by setting up neighborhood homes wherein they, too, could commingle with immigrants and thereby gain acceptance into their community to educate them. In short, they hoped to provide immigrants needed services while at the same time shepherding them in the assimilation process.[11]

Most progressive female reformers came from white upper- and middle-class families. And while the platform varied from group to group, most female reformers shared a common religious heritage as Protestants and were committed to women's political activism. Not all such volunteers, however, were white Protestants; California had a rich tradition of Catholic and Jewish organizations, which provided certain communities a wealth of social services, from orphan asylums to settlement housing.[12] In any case, the suffrage victory of 1911 brought together educators, settlement-house workers, and clubwomen to try to influence the meaning of citizenship through Americanization programs.

In Los Angeles, volunteers from across the social spectrum petitioned the Los Angeles School Board for new services, including native-language courses, kindergartens, free transportation to and from school for children, and school playgrounds and libraries. Because the school board lacked the funds to meet the pressing demands of the community, it relied heavily on benevolent societies to provide many of these amenities and services. In time the network of white female volunteers led to the formation of several programs including kindergartens, penny lunch programs, after-school playgrounds, and in-school health care. The successful institution of these programs had given middle-class women the opportunity to promulgate WASP values, set educational policy, and create new professional career opportunities for themselves and other women in teaching, nursing, public health, and social work.[13]

The professionalization of such volunteer organizations coincided with the expansion of local and state-sponsored services to the immigrant population; World War I–inspired xenophobia merely advanced educational programs already in place, while inducing a more "professional" approach to the assimilation of immigrants. The impact of overcrowded foreign quarters and the mix of languages heard in Los Angeles provoked new, more forceful programs. Albert Sheils, the newly appointed superintendent of schools, helped launch English-language programs for adults. These programs ostensibly were designed to teach newcomers how to speak and read English, yet they became forums in which to teach the tenets of American patriotism. As war fever, along with America's first "Red Scare" spread, compulsory registration of all aliens revealed a static immigrant population, but a dramatic increase in the number of foreign-born schoolchildren. In 1920, approximately 41 percent of the total Los Angeles student body was foreign born; this fact not only heightened the imperative to install new Americanization classes, but it provided the impetus to target immigrant mothers with new legislation entitled the Home Teachers Act.[14]

THE CALIFORNIA HOME TEACHERS ACT OF 1915

The Johnson administration turned from the protection of workers to the problems posed by foreign immigration. In 1913 Governor Johnson established the California Commission of Immigration and Housing (CCIH), which consisted of twelve different administrative sections, including a separate department for education and housing. According to the mission statement on education, the goal was to provide immigrants, children as well as adults, with educational and citizenship opportunities. In short, it sought to turn recent immigrants into good Americans. Johnson now appointed the first and only woman, Mary Simons Gibson, to serve on the new commission, which she did until 1921. Gibson believed that assimilation lay at the heart of the immigrant problem and that immigrant women held the key to the Americanization of their families.[15] She designed a program to bring education *to* immigrant women, with teachers entering private homes to teach women English, civics, and home economics. This became the basis for the Home Teachers Act of 1915.

Mary Gibson's entrance into politics was not happenstance but the outgrowth of her long involvement in civic reform. Prior to her marriage to George A. Gibson (Los Angeles School Board president) in 1881, Mary worked as a schoolteacher in Los Angeles. She committed most of her life to charity and reform work, and the goals of the associations she helped ranged from woman suffrage to the social purity of young women. Her support of Hiram Johnson for governor, her success in raising over $10,000 to support the woman suffrage bill, and her administrative role as the chair of the Women's Rally Committee Chorus and subsequent rallies all testified to her abilities—and earned her sufficient notice by Johnson. A lifetime spent in civic volunteerism, particularly her association with the California Federation of Women's Club and the Los Angeles Friday Morning Club, now proved important as Gibson set out to design an Americanization program revolving around home teaching and struggled to build a coalition to support passage of the California Home Teachers Act (CHTA) to legitimize and fund her programs.[16]

The goal of the Americanization program was to transform poor immigrants into productive and responsible American workers. This was especially true for rural Mexicans who had crossed the border with the goal of working in modern urban industries. Earlier programs had focused on Mexican males, who worked in a variety of migratory industries. But as such industries began to prefer to employ men with families, and as the program itself professionalized, the focus of the program moved from single men to women and children. Immigrant women became the primary target, since it was assumed that they, like women in general, held the moral authority in the family and were chiefly responsible for transmitting family values. Thus, reformers designed the curriculum around homemaking to teach Mexican women proper American housekeeping skills while simultaneously inculcating their civic responsibilities as loyal American citizens. Per this model, moral superiority and a happy home provided the foundation for a secure nation. Domestic education thus created domestic stability, ensured a happy and productive workforce, and taught immigrant women "American" homemaking skills for potential employment outside the home as maids, seamstresses, and laundresses.[17]

As Gibson launched the home teachers program, she identified the female immigrant as the top educational priority. Relying on the "cult of domesticity" as her model, Gibson formulated policy that emphasized the pivotal role of immigrant mothers in the Americanization process. She developed a three-tiered argument to gain support for her legislation. First, immigrant women fit prominently into the program design. She believed that assimilation of immigrant mothers was an urgent problem that needed resolution. The lack of female students attending the existing English-language nightclasses pointed to the isolation of immigrant women. It also indicated that they were not being inculcated in proper American values, or on their way to becoming responsible citizens. By extension, this isolation diminished the influence the mother had over her children and ultimately derailed all such efforts at assimilation. While the children and husbands of immigrant women might be exposed to the mainstream culture at school and work, learn English, and interact in the larger society, no such opportunities extisted for the women themselves. The rise in juvenile delinquency also supported the view of reformers that immigrant mothers had lost control of their children, and that the former's isolation from the workforce and American education diminished their role as the moral authority of their families. The home education of immigrant women, therefore, would close the gap, thereby restoring these women to their former place as the moral guardians, saving their families and ultimately the nation. Second, Gibson appealed to her fellow Americans' sense of patriotism and the premise that women's political imperative was to build a "home defense," one designed to strengthen family and social order. In short, she endorsed the idea of "Republican Motherhood" to instill civic responsibility, ambition, and intelligence. Finally, she appealed to the state educators by arguing that the proposed CHTA would promote the professionalization of the teaching profession, thereby removing the stigma of "girl teachers" and eliminating the reliance of the school system on untrained volunteers teaching English-language classes. Fundamentally, Gibson and other reformers approached immigrant education through rose-colored glasses. They never really understood the needs of the immigrant women they purported to help, and they never designed a program flexible enough to accommodate the cultural diversity of those they hoped to serve.[18]

Gibson's legislative campaign for passage of the CHTA proved more difficult than she had imagined. Many educators and church groups opposed the Americanization program because they feared it might interfere with family autonomy. Gibson went on the defensive and called on the support of the California Federation of Women's Clubs (CFWC) legislative council. With the assistance of the CFWC and other associations, Gibson took a softer approach focused on family stability in order to gain widespread support. Juxtaposing immigrant women's isolation with the broad-based experiences of their children and husbands, she succeeded in emphasizing the negative impact of native cultural traditions taught at home by nonassimilated mothers. Furthermore, Gibson and her supporters argued that the general loss of respect and prominence of mothers in the household, the rising rate of juvenile delinquency among immigrants, and the collapse of the family all could be rectified through the CHTA. In order to appeal to the educational community she argued that the act would enlarge the status of the teaching profession and supplant the current practice of using volunteers to teach English-language classes. By connecting citizenship and patriotism to the woman's sphere, and to the professionalization of education, Gibson appealed to a much larger constituency. Yet, the focus of the program on immigrant women remained a tough sell. State educators overwhelmingly believed that the role of public education was to benefit children, not adults. They followed the conventional wisdom of the day that if you "Americanize the children, the children will Americanize the home."[19]

Nevertheless, Gibson and her supporters succeeded in pressuring the state legislature to pass the California Home Teachers Act of 1915, without the support of most state educators. The statute permitted city school boards to employ "home teachers" whose responsibility it was to "work in the homes of pupils, instructing children and adults in school attendance and preparation . . . and to provide instruction in the English language, sanitation, household duties . . . and fundamentals of American citizenship and government."[20] The code clearly laid out the role of home teachers in educating immigrant families from providing lessons in basic civics to basic household duties. At its core, the act spoke to the concerns of progressive reformers regarding immigrant family life. Overcrowded cities, unsanitary living conditions, and the economic forces that drove women into factory work disturbed the maternal model of the female-centered home.[21]

The success of the CHTA depended on financial and educational support at the local level, due to the lack of funding by the legislature. State funding and administrative support was not benchmarked until the 1920 appointment of Ethel Richardson as the assistant state superintendent of public education for Americanization, and even then the apportioned funding was not enough to implement the program without community contributions. Therefore, Gibson had to garner firm public support, both in helping to subsidize teacher salaries and in the gathering of data to help convince other benefactors of the serious need to assist immigrant families. Therefore, the Los Angeles branch of the CFWC scoured the records of juvenile and divorce courts as well as those of the L.A.P.D. to document the necessity of public expenditures on immigrants. Gibson, a veteran fundraiser, played on the purse strings and fears of the middle class by emphasizing the rise in the rates of juvenile delinquency and crime among immigrants. She astutely argued that new tax expenditures in education would be better spent on helping to educate immigrants than on building bigger and better prisons.[22]

Gibson recognized that in order to increase funding for her program, she needed a successful test case. Los Angeles, her home base, became the obvious choice of places in which to conduct the experiment. Los Angeles presented all of the right conditions including a large immigrant population and established literacy, adult education, and citizenship programs already in place. The support of the Los Angeles school superintendent and Gibson's connection with the Friday Morning Club and the CFWC were equally important, in the selection of Los Angeles.[23]

The next step was to choose a sponsor and a teacher. In both cases, Gibson's connections paid good dividends. She garnered the support of the Daughters of the American Revolution (DAR) and convinced Amanda Matthews Chase to volunteer as the first teacher. Chase initially agreed to work without pay, but the DAR stepped in and agreed to furnish her salary. Chase's credentials were excellent: she had a long history of settlement work and teaching experience; she was university trained, she had spent several years teaching in Mexico; and she was fluent in Spanish. She exemplified the change from volunteer to professional educator. A member of the National Educator Association (NEA), Chase took the campaign to the next level in appealing to local teachers and administrators. She began her work as the first home teacher in 1915, and she reported back to the commission that she had made contact with 123 families and visited some 482 neighborhoods.

Chase gained entrance into the homes of immigrants by first making key contacts with female leaders in the immigrant community. Once in their homes, Chase conducted lessons in English and proper housekeeping. She attempted to balance education with socialization, while teaching basic principles of government and citizenship. Through her remarkable energy Chase succeeded in conducting a successful CHTA pilot program. At the year's end, the Los Angeles School District offered her a job. By 1918, the Los Angeles School District claimed to have employed forty-four home teachers, and in 1927 they had more than sixty-three. Other school districts throughout the state employed home teachers, but not at the same rate as Los Angeles, and even then the dropout rate among the other districts was a high 80 percent.[24]

EDUCATIONAL HOUSEKEEPERS

The opening of the Panama Canal in 1915 increased whites' fears that a new flood of immigrants would pour into California. The imagined deluge did not occur, but the demographic changes in the national origin of the immigrants to California changed significantly. Between 1900 and 1910, Northern Europeans composed the largest immigrant group, but, as mentioned, after 1910 Mexicans and Italians dominated.[25]

Now reformers perceived the rapidly growing Mexican community in California as their biggest problem, yet racial prejudice by reformers was particularly virulent against Mexicans. Indeed, reformers described Mexicans as "shiftless and thriftless," based on their observations of Mexican laborers. Mary Gibson and Amanda Chase shared the views that Mexicans lacked industry and ambition, and they believed that Mexican culture was innately flawed. Chase, despite having worked in Mexico, felt that there were major deficiencies in Mexican culture that limited Mexican immigrants' social mobility and ultimately their ability to assimilate. Ironically, however, she did not believe Mexicans a "hopeless proposition," but capable of transformation. What they needed, she argued, was a "peculiar sort—education that shall be a disciplinary tonic—that shall give them standards—that amounts to evolution." Mary Gibson expressed a similar view in the *California Outlook* in 1915: "These families are with us and make up a definite part of our civilization—whether that part shall be valuable or a menace to the body politic, rests on us." In short, progressive policy and educational programs were designed to remake Mexicans into 100 percent Americans, eliminating their native language and cultural traditions.[26]

The Mexican American family as a whole created a challenge for reformers, but the real "menace" was the immigrant mother, who lived in isolation and was unwilling to interact with mainstream culture and more importantly resisted "Americanizing" their homes. By focusing on immigrant women, reformers hoped to accelerate Americanization of Mexican families, while at the same time giving elite women (themselves) control over that process. Gibson tied female emancipation to municipal responsibilities in reshaping immigrant culture when she argued that suffrage brought the "responsibility of the education and protection of alien women; and to so establish and sustain the mother in her own domain, is to protect the state from delinquent children and an ignorant vote."[27]

By focusing on the immigrant home environment, and developing the curriculum around home economics, elite women justified their position as educators, as protectors of immigrant women, and ultimately as the setters of the standards of civic participation. Now, home-teacher curriculum centered on instructing immigrant women to keep clean, orderly homes. Chase and Gibson collaborated to design the new curriculum, and with the appointment of Ruby Baughman as supervisor of immigrant education in Los Angeles, all three women began to implement a professional program. In launching the program, Baughman insisted that the CHTA use professionally trained teachers with knowledge in basic childcare, home economics, government and civics, and a degree of familiarity with the native customs and language of those they served.[28]

Pearl Ellis, another Los Angeles reformer and author of *Americanization through Homemaking*, provided valuable instruction for home teachers, including how to conduct lessons on the importance of clean underwear, changing cooking techniques, and recommending the replacement of ethnic food such as beans and tortillas with American fare such as lettuce and white bread. Ellis further recommended "conservation cooking,"—choosing inexpensive ingredients and developing budgeting skills, which would preserve the family from hunger during lean times and eliminate "criminal tendencies" and "labor problems." Lessons described in the 1916 edition of *The Home Teacher* covered the basics from sewing, ironing, mopping, and laundering. Each lesson built on the prior one, and each concluded with home-decoration tips, such as setting a tea table complete with white linen and flowers. To this end, reformers hoped to address the whole gamut of assimilation issues from sanitation, public heath, cooking, and total emersion into American homemaking, which ultimately provided vocational training for low-level domestic services.[29]

Clearly, racial superiority and ethnocentrism dominated Progressive Era reforms. Yet, at the same time, reformers used a variety of techniques to attract immigrant interest to their programs, including bilingual instruction and cultural music, art, and folk festivals. Reformers tangentially promoted "cultural gift" programs that featured immigrant culture through dance, music, and art. In Los Angeles, Gibson organized the "Homeland Exhibit of Arts and Crafts," wherein immigrants celebrated their national culture through dress, dance, and music: the goal was to create a sense of national unity. In the end, the reformers determined which cultural gifts "to accept." And, as mentioned, the reformers placed very little value on Mexican culture. Vicki Ruiz, in her study of the Houchen Settlement House in El Paso, Texas, wrote: "Some immigrant traditions were valorized more than others. Celebrating Mexican heritage did not figure into the Euro-

American orientation." Los Angeles reformers, to be sure, valorized some cultures over others, and clearly they believed that Mexican culture needed reform, not validation.[30]

THE IMMIGRANT VIEW

Reformers committed to educating the masses of new immigrants naively assumed that their programs would succeed. The time and energy spent by Mary Gibson alone reveals a strong commitment to immigrant education. Yet, the Americanization program never really appealed to the larger immigrant population. Historian George Sanchez theorized that the program failed to do so because: "Mexicans . . . never fully committed themselves to integration into American life," and ". . . the various forces behind Americanization programs never assembled an optimistic ideological approach that might attract Mexican immigrant women. Instead, they presented a limited, inconsistent scheme which could not handle the demographic realities of the Mexican immigrant community." Other contributing factors include the rapid expansion of Los Angeles barrio, which sustained a self-sufficient community wherein interaction with white society was limited. The migratory existence of Mexican families further limited the ability of reformers to attract Mexican women to their programs. Surveys during the program reveal an 80 percent dropout rate among female night school attendees. Class attendance and dropout rates were high for all immigrants attending night classes—out of an immigrant population of 122,131, only 3,448 attended, and only 322 finished the program.[31]

Insensitivity to the immigrant culture further limited the success of the program, particularly in regard to Mexican women. The mission goals of the reformers failed to offer real solutions or opportunities to the immigrants themselves. Rather than studying immigrant culture and adapting their goals to meet the reality of life for these women, reformers focused on middle-class housekeeping. It is not too surprising given the poverty in which immigrant women lived that housekeeping instructions failed to entice new recruits in the assimilation process. Furthermore, the migratory experience of Mexican immigrants in particular reveals a separate reality from that of the idealized stay-at-home mother.

While the program simply failed to address the real needs of the immigrant population, reformers were genuine in the their efforts to educate immigrant women. Vicki Ruiz stated it well when she wrote: "As a Chicana historian, I am of two minds. I respect the settlement workers for their health and child-care services, but I cringe at their ethnocentrism and their romantic idealization of 'American' life." Home teachers and the administrators of the home-education program in California mirrored the ethnocentrism of the settlement-house workers in Texas, yet both groups provided education and needed social services to a segment of the population generally ignored by city, state, and federal government—immigrant women.[32]

EDUCATIONAL LEGACY

The Home Teachers Act and the Americanization program illustrate how Progressive women molded policy to create a unique female niche in California politics. Gibson and her followers created a new space for elite women to hold administrative positions within state government and most significantly in the Department of Education. Federal funding helped push state education into a highly bureaucratic structure, which led to the professionalization of the teaching profession. In 1921, California's State Board of Education and the office of the Superintendent of Public Schools merged into the Department of Education. Immigrant education moved from the CIHH to the Department of Education, headed by Ethel Richardson, a long-time associate of Gibson. Political and economic changes, however, turned the tide away from a focus on immigrant women.[33]

In 1923 California elected a conservative Republican governor, Friend Richardson, who proved to be less than a "friend" to public education and certainly was no supporter of immigrant education. The new governor proposed to cut the entire state education budget by 60 percent. He went so far as to fire Ethel Richardson, but political pressure forced him to re-hire her; now she no longer headed the division of immigration, but the newly formed Division of Adult Education. The move from "Immigrant" to "Adult" education reflected a new atmosphere of immigrant restriction and a significant reduction in the immigrant population. Thus, the imperative to educate immigrant women diminished, as the entire Americanization program lost its resiliency. Instead, adult education replaced courses previously defined as immigrant classes.[34]

The success of the Home Teachers Act is difficult to measure. The women who worked as home teachers believed they were very successful. Mary Gibson estimated that her teachers had reached some 50,000 families, adding that school districts across the state employed home teachers, suggesting public support of the act. The pilot project in Los Angeles served to illustrate the ability of women to organize and implement policy at the state and local level. That they also succeeded in gaining wide public financial support for the program, in light of their prime focus on immigrant women, is remarkable. Yet, their effectiveness in the immigrant community and the small number of successful graduates from their programs reveal the limit of the curriculum in fostering middle-class family ideals in poor communities. Furthermore, Mary Gibson and her associates, for all their good intentions, failed to understand the realities of life in the barrios, the little Italies, and the Chinatowns. The relatively small number of CHTA workers, the lack of state and local funding, and the ethnocentrism of the reformers limited their effectiveness. Meanwhile, ethnic communities offered similar courses in English—without devaluing cultural traditions and native languages. For example, the Catholic Church fostered religious loyalty through cultural diversity, and after World War I that institution launched a nationwide Americanization program. Thus, the conservative methodology combined with a strong Protestant ethos guaranteed limited success in reaching a large Catholic immigrant population.[35]

Nevertheless, Los Angeles provided a springboard from which state and national publicity brought accolades to Mary Gibson's work, so much so that Richard Campbell, U.S. commissioner of education, applauded the work of the CHTA and the efforts of Mary Gibson. Moreover, he intimated that California women were an example of the success of female suffrage and why female civic education was important.[36] However, the true success of the program is hard to assess because the state neither sufficiently funded nor required that school districts report on the activities of home teachers. As a result, the number of home teachers is difficult to quantify. Los Angeles claims to have had forty-four home teachers in 1918, and more than sixty-three in 1927. The program, though seemingly successful in L.A., never received the funding needed to carry out its goals. Funding of the program varied. In some cases, school districts allocated funds to cover the home teachers; in others, local benevolence was expected to cover salaries and supplies. The program lacked formal guidelines and reporting requirements, which ensured that its implementation would be decentralized by each individual school district.[37]

For all the ups and downs of the Home Teachers Act of 1915, as well as the Americanization programs during the heyday of the Progressive party, the idea of the home teacher is still with us. California, always a hotbed for education reform as well as a center for immigrant settlement, continues to deal with the resurgence in assimilation programs to educate its expanding immigrant communities. The same fears that provoked Progressive reform have resulted in a second look at the immigration "menace" today. The "home visitor" has received recent attention as a possible solution, reinforcing the legacy of female progressive education reform. To be sure, the original program was not perfect, but Mary Gibson's belief that the tax dollar would be better spent on education than on building prisons rings true today. The real testament to the success of the programs, then, was not the advancement of the immigrants they hoped to serve, or in the building of a democratic education system; rather it was the emergence of a female dominion in education and a reshaping of the meaning of citizenship.[38]

Notes

1   There are numerous articles documenting recent immigration issues. For the most recent article, see Eric Schmitt, "Americans (a) Love (b) Hate Immigrants, in *The New York Times*, Week In Review Section, Sunday, January 14, 2001 (Section 4). There are, of course, several text-

books on California as well as scholarly studies that describe different aspects of the immigrant conflicts and the laws they generated.

2 Richard Hofstadter, *The Age of Reform: From Bryan to F.D.R.* (New York, 1959); William Deverell, "The Varieties of Progressive Experience," in William Deverell and Tom Sitton, *California Progressivism Revisited* (University of California Press, 1994), 1–4; Judith Raferty, "Los Angeles Club Women and Progressive Reform," in *California Progressivism*, 146; Spence Olin argued that "moral absolutism" dictated the various platforms and served as the driving force behind much of the reform, including education, immigration, social welfare, sexual regulation, and medical-care reform. See Gerald Woods, "A Penchant for Probity: California Progressives and the Disreputable Pleasures," in *California Progressivism*, 99–100. Benjamin Parke De Witt, *The Progressive Movement: A Non-partisan, Comprehensive Discussion of Current Tendencies in American Politics* (University of Washington Press, 1915, 1968), 3–5, 17-25.

3 Paula Baker, "The Domestication of Politics: Women and American Political Society, 1780–1920," in *Unequal Sisters: A Multi -Cultural Reader in U.S. Women's History*, edited by Vicki L. Ruiz and Ellen DuBois (Routledge, 1994), 88–96; Diane Claire Wood, "Immigrant Mothers, Female Reformers, and Women Teachers: The California Home Teacher Act of 1915" (Ph.D. diss., Stanford University, 1996), 14–16; Gerald Woods, "A Penchant for Probity: California Progressives and the Disreputable Pleasures," in William Deverell and Tom Sitton, *California Progressivism Revisited* (University of California Press, 1994), 99–101.

4 The early history of the progressive movement as recreated by Mowry and De Witt is instructive in outlining the basic male political activities. These histories nevertheless fail to reveal the diversity of progressivism, and they completely ignore the centrality of gender, class, and race. New scholars looking to address some of the old questions such as who the progressives were, have made significant contributions in uncovering those traditionally ignored. *California Progressivism Revisited* serves as the springboard for this essay. See William Deverell's introduction for a brief historiography, 1–11; Vicky Ruiz, "Dead Ends or Gold Mines? Using Missionary Records in Mexican American Women's History," edited by Vicki L. Ruiz and Ellen DuBois, *Unequal Sisters: A Multicultural Reader in U.S. History* (Routledge, 1994), 311–312; Robyn Muncy, *Creating a Female Dominion in American Reform, 1890–1935* (New York, 1991), xii.

5 Wood, "Women Teachers," 13–16; According to the work of Vicki Ruiz and George Sanchez, Mexican migration to the United States between 1910–1930 reached 1 million. See Vicki L. Ruiz, *From Out of the Shadows: Mexican Women in Twentieth Century America* (Oxford University Press, 1998), 6; George J. Sanchez, *Becoming Mexican American: Ethnicity, Culture, and Identity in Chicano Los Angeles, 1900–1945* (Oxford University Press, 1993), 17–20, 94–107.

6 Wood, "Women Teachers," 19–20; Gayle Gullett, "Women Progressives and the Politics of Americanization in California, 1915–1920," *Pacific Historical Review* (February 1995), 80–81; Raferty, "Los Angeles Club Women," 153–154; Gayle Gullett, *Becoming Citizens: The Emergence and Development of the California Women's Movement, 1880–1911* (University of Illinois Press, 2000), 74–75.

7 Linda Kerber, *Women of the Republic: Intellect & Ideology in Revolutionary America* (W. W. Norton & Company, 1980); Baker, "Domestication of Politics," 86–91.

8 John Higham, *Strangers in the Land: Patterns of American Nativism, 1860–1925* (Rutgers University Press, 1955), 235–239; Gullett, "Women Progressives," 72–76; Raferty, "Los Angeles Club Women," 144–145; Gullett, "Women Progressives," 80-86. There are several good studies documenting the role of women in settlement and missionary reform. See Sarah Deutsch, *No Separate Refuge: Culture, Class, and Gender on an Anglo-Hispanic Frontier, 1880–1940* (Oxford University Press, 1987); Peggy Pascoe, *Relations of Rescue: The Search for Female Moral Authority in the American West, 1874–1939* (Oxford University Press, 1990).

9 Sanchez, "Go After the Women," 285–286; Raferty, *Land of Fair Promise,* 63-68.

10 Wood, 15–30; Judith Rosenberg Raferty, *Land of Fair Promise: Politics and Reform in Los Angeles Schools, 1885–1941* (Stanford University Press, 1992), 14–18; George Sanchez, "Go After the Women": Americanization and the Mexican Immigrant Woman, 1915–1929," *Unequal Sisters: A Multicultural Reader in U.S. History* (Routledge, 1994), edited by Vicki L. Ruiz and Ellen DuBois, 284–285.

11 Raferty, *Land of Promise,* 14–15, 27–32. Collaboration took place on many fronts, including the fight for sexual purity. The Women's Christian Temperance Union for example collabo-

rated with many other women's organization to combat immoral behavior, and specifically the quest to save young girls from sexual ruin. See Mary E. Odem, *Delinquent Daughters: Protecting and Policing Adolescent Female Sexual Purity in the United States, 1885–1920* (North Carolina University Press, 1995), 8–12; Elizabeth Ewen, *Immigrant Women in the Land of Dollars: Life and Culture in the Lower East Side, 1890–1925* (New York, 1985), 77–84; Muncy, *Female Dominion*, 9–13.

12 Raferty, *Land of Fair Promise*, 18–21; Gullett, "Women Progressives," 71–72; William H. Slingerland, *Child Welfare Work in California: A Study of Agencies and Institutions* (Russell Sage Foundation, 1916), 25–30.

13 Raferty, *Land of Fair Promise*, 21–44.

14 Raferty, *Land of Fair Promise*, 62–68.

15 Ibid.

16 Raferty, "Los Angeles Club Women," 153–155; Mary Gibson, *A Record of Twenty-Five Years of The California Federation of Women's Clubs, 1900–1925* (The California Federation of Women's Club, 1927), 204–209.

17 Sanchez, *Mexican American*, 98–101; Gullett, "Women Progressives," 74–75.

18 Raferty, *Land of Fair Promise*, 72–75; Wood, 28–32; Sanchez, "Go After the Women," 288; Maxine Seller, "The Education of the Immigrant Woman, 1900–1935," *The Journal of Urban History* (Volume 4, 1978), 317; Wood, 28–29. There are several studies that point to the importance of "Republican Motherhood," and ways in which women used this ideology to gain entrance into the public sphere. See Linda Kerber, *Women of the Republic: Intellect & Ideology in Revolutionary America* (W.W. Norton & Company, 1980); Baker, "Domestication of Politics," 86–91.

19 Wood, "Women Teachers," 28–32; Patriotism and elevation of the teaching profession were other components of her argument. Raferty, *Land of Fair Promise*, 72–75.

20 Wood, "Women Teachers," 28–32, 50. The California Home Teachers Act is quoted in verbatim in Wood from the code: *California Legislature, Final Calendar or Legislative Business, History of Bills, etc., Introduced and Index of the Senate and Assembly, Officers and Standing Committees,* compiled by Edwin F. Smith and L. B. Mallory, 41st Session, (California State Printing Office, 1915), 167.

21 Wood, "Women Teachers," 31–33.

22 Wood, "Women Teachers,"50–55; Raferty, "Los Angeles Club Women, "156.

23 Wood, "Women Teachers, " 51–59.

24 Wood, "Women Teachers,"55–61.; Raferty, *Land of Fair Promise*, 74–76; Ewen, *Land of Dollars,* 83–84; Muncy, *Female Dominion*, 11–15; Raferty, "Club Women," 156–157; Sellers, "Immigrant Women."

25 Gullett, "Women Progressives," 82; Raferty, "Club Women," 156; Sanchez, "Go After the Women," 285–286.

26 Gullett, "Women Progressives," 82–83; Mrs. Frank A. Gibson, "Educating Parents—A California Problem," *California Outlook,* XVIII (1915): 9–10; Sanchez, *Becoming Mexican American,* 92–101; Ruiz, "Dead Ends and Gold Mines," 290–305.

27 Gullett, "Progressive Women," 86–87.

28 Raferty, *Land of Fair Promise*, 73–80.

29 Sanchez, "Go After the Women," 288–293; Seller, 311–312; Ruiz, "Dead Ends and Gold Mines," 302–305; Gullett, "Progressive Women," 87–88; Raferty, *Land of Fair Promise*, 79.

30 Ruiz, "Dead Ends," 302–304; Gullett, 91; Sanchez, "Go After the Women," 288; Raferty, *Land of Fair Promise*, 91–92.

31 Sanchez, "Go After the Women," 293–294; Seller, "Education of the Immigrant Woman," 311; Gullett, "Progressive Women," 90.

32 Sanchez, "Go After the Women," 294–296; Seller, "Education of the Immigrant Woman," 318; Ruiz, "Dead Ends and Gold Mines," 305.

33 Wood, "Women Teachers," 120–123, 134–151.

34 Ibid.

35 Wood, "Women Teachers," 154–157; Seller, "Education of the Immigrant Woman," 320–322.

36 Wood, "Women Teachers," 62–63.

37 Wood, "Women Teachers," 64–69.

38 Wood, "Women Teachers," 154–157; Raferty, *Land of Fair Promise*, 198–200; Gullett, "Progressive Women," 71–72, 93–94.

CHAPTER SEVEN

Black Faces for Black Audiences: The Lincoln Motion Picture Company of Los Angeles

John Anderson

No discussion of California history would be complete without mention of the development of the motion picture industry, the roots of which reach back to the early twentieth century, the era of silent films. Early movie producers sought refuge from Thomas Edison's East Coast "trust," his attempt to control the production of motion pictures in the United States by licensing out his patent on film-making equipment. Those "renegade" producers who landed in the Golden State discovered that southern California was a nearly ideal place to make films. Low corporate taxes, cheap land, year-round sunshine, and a strong anti-labor union sentiment soon enabled the owners of California's nascent film studios to expand dramatically their operations. Indeed, as early as 1915 the informal process of shooting films in the field with small crews gave way to a studio system with a specialized division of labor and strict production standards. This increased productivity allowed the industry to integrate the crucial elements of the business: production, distribution, and exhibition. By the 1920s, renegades such as Adolph Zukor and the Schenk brothers had become monopolists themselves. The enlarge-

Publicity still from *The Realization of a Negro's Ambition*, the first film produced by the Lincoln Motion Picture Company. *From the Robert S. Birchard Collection.*

125

ment of production capacity enabled the "major" studios to make longer and more lavish films that appealed to a growing and movie-hungry middle-class audience.[1]

The "movie" business quickly reciprocated the favors bestowed upon it by the City of Angels. The studios enhanced L.A.'s "booster" image created by the area's major financial interests. Local parks, streets, and other physical landmarks served as backdrops to glamorous silent narratives stressing the theme of personal reinvention in a land of infinite possibility. Soon, tourists from all over the country began to arrive in Los Angeles to gawk at the mansions of movie "stars." Real estate magnate Charles Toberman remodeled the business district along Hollywood Boulevard, and civic leaders encouraged impresario Sid Grauman to build exotic, "orientalist" movie palaces such as the Egyptian and Chinese Theaters along the main drag. By 1920, films had replaced orange-crate labels and picture postcards as the primary promoter of L.A.'s legendary arcadian splendor.[2]

During this period, Los Angeles's black community also underwent a process of reinvention, albeit one not played out before the city's motion-picture cameras. These changes had more to do with the evolution of black America as a whole rather than with the uniqueness of Los Angeles. The 1910s and 1920s saw an intense African American migration from the rural South to modern cities, where jobs and a vibrant urban culture awaited new arrivals. In Chicago, the black population soared from 9,000 in 1910 to more than 320,000 in 1930. During the same span, New York City saw its number of African American residents rocket to more than a quarter of a million persons—the vibrant art, music, and poetry of Harlem promising a cultural renewal inspired by the metropolis. While not of the same magnitude, Los Angeles saw a similar jump in the growth of its black neighborhoods. Initiated by the expansion of the railroads, but later fueled by the lure of successful black-owned businesses such as the Golden West Insurance Company, the African American population of the city grew from 2,000 to more than 16,000 between 1900 and 1920. Numerous civic and political clubs flourished in the black community during the period, and Los Angeles seemed poised to create a new motion-picture industry catering expressly to the nation's black audiences.[3]

There was a strong demand for a "black Hollywood" during the period. For if the movies were teaching whites what to think of southern California or, for that matter, the United States, they also were teaching blacks what southern Californians, indeed most Americans, thought of them. The normative movie protagonist during the period was white, with blacks relegated to roles of menial servitude (maids, porters, field hands) and other demeaning stereotypes. Early feature-length films ("features") such as David Wark Griffith's wildly successful *Birth of a Nation* (1915), portrayed black aspirations toward economic, social, and political equality as dangerous threats to the natural social order. While the release of this film led to national protests by prominent African American civil rights groups, several black leaders countered Hollywood racism cinematically, making films that refuted *Birth of a Nation*'s negative portrayals of African Americans. Backed by Booker T. Washington's assistant, Emmett J. Scott, *The Birth of a Race* (1918) celebrated African contributions to Western Civilization, particularly in combating German militarism during World War I. The Frederick Douglass Film Company in New York likewise expressed a commitment towards civil rights with its 1915 release of *A Colored American Winning His Suit*. Despite their desire to produce films depicting blacks in central and positive roles—vehicles dubbed as "race" films by the contemporary media—these filmmakers faced serious distribution problems. At the time, black audiences constituted a small percentage of the total film audience, and exhibitors generally assumed that "race pride" would not appeal to white audiences. Discrimination in Hollywood at the production end meant that the prospects for developing talent for race films was limited as well.[4]

In this racially charged climate, and seemingly in defiance of the odds, a handful of associates founded the Lincoln Motion Picture Company in Los Angeles. Originally described as "a Negro company organized to make, buy, and distribute motion picture films, principally high class productions and special features featuring the Race in a dignified manner in which we desire to see ourselves portrayed," Lincoln became the first studio to portray dramatically the aspirations of certain segments of the African American community.[5] Knowing that they, unlike the owners of the major studios, lacked the resources to establish a vertically integrated mode of production and distribution, Lincoln's founders sought investors and promoters from within the nation's black urban cores. And they hoped to play a significant role in the rise of a new black urban culture by producing works that championed the values of an older, bourgeois black community and condemned the cosmopolitanism embodied by "easy" money and spendthrift consumerism. By portraying protagonists with strong moral character, individual initiative, self-reliance, and personal honor, Lincoln's early contributions to the race film movement expressed the view that the values of the emerging mass culture hindered the advance of the African race in the United States. In addition to rejecting Hollywood's celebration of self-expression through consumerism, Lincoln's products also reflected Booker T. Washington's vision of race advancement through entrepreneurial initiative. The prolific neo-Washingtonian black film auteur Oscar Micheaux owed his filmmaking career to Lincoln, which optioned his novel *The Homesteader* for an aborted adaptation.

Noble Johnson, the principal founder of the Lincoln Motion Picture Company (LMPC), was born in Marshall, Missouri, in 1877. When Noble was six years old, his father moved his family to Colorado Springs, Colorado, where he had gained employment as a resident horse trainer for mining magnate Richard DeVignerie. Upon entering his teen years, Noble, following in his father's footsteps, took to the road, toiling at a number of odd jobs and eventually ending up working as a cow puncher back home in Colorado. Seeing that one of Noble's schoolmates was none other than the famous actor Lon Chaney, it was not entirely far fetched to assume that motion pictures might play a significant role in the life of Noble Johnson as well. In 1914, Johnson was hired as a wrangler for Philadelphia-based Lubin Pictures. Impressed by the horseman's skill and photogenic face, director Reginald Fielding signed Johnson to an acting contract. Shortly thereafter, Johnson garnered noticeable supporting roles in two Lubin serials, *The Red Ace* and *The Eagle's Nest*. The following year, he signed with Hollywood-based Universal Pictures, where he worked throughout the early 1920s.[6]

It was the nature of Johnson's assigned roles that undoubtedly inspired him to start his own film studio. A publicity booklet printed by Universal for their 1918 serial *The Bull's Eye* described Johnson as, "one of the busiest heavies in the whole Universal camp." The booklet lists more than thirty film credits for Johnson, lauding the actor's versatility in playing a variety of "types." Tellingly, the characters Johnson portrayed were not delineated by proper names or professions, but by their racial characteristics. In *The Red Ace*, for example, the booklet notes that he played an American Indian, a "role" that he reprised in at least five other Universal Westerns before 1918. In *Across the Rio Grande, A Western Governor's Humanity*, and *Species of a Mexican Man*, he portrayed a person of Mexican origin. In *The Bull's Eye*, his character, a rogue cowboy called Sweeney Bodin, is described as, "a dark, foreign type giant." The list acknowledges Johnson's portrayal of a person of African descent in only two films: the first one *The Lion's Ward*, a "Southern" drama in which he played an "old Negro servant," and the second an unnamed biblical epic.[7]

The brochure provides a revealing look at racial typecasting during the period. While Johnson's race is not explicitly mentioned, the literature nevertheless infers that his versatility as an actor derived from the pigmentation of his skin, which allowed him to "pass" as other racial or ethnic types (including, from time to time, whites). Johnson's success was not so much defined by his acting abilities, but by his appearance. Johnson realized that if he ever hoped to be recognized as a skilled actor, he needed to land serious roles in which he could portray real African Americans, not thoughtless stereotypes thereof. Afraid to stray from the stereotypes and risk offending white exhibitors in the South, neither Lubin nor Universal offered Johnson the opportunity to make movies about black life in authentic situations and surroundings.

In 1916, Noble Johnson and a cadre of black Los Angeles businessmen founded the Lincoln Motion Picture Company, its production offices located on the 2400 block of Central Avenue, in the heart of L.A.'s black business district. Lincoln's first president was J. Thomas Smith, a druggist who moonlighted as a casting agent for black talent in the Hollywood movie industry. Clarence Brooks, Dudley Brooks, and A. L. Shumway, a trio of local actors, were among the studio's other chief investors. Signed on to direct Lincoln's fledgling efforts was white cinematographer Harry Gant, a friend of Noble Johnson from Universal. George P. Johnson, Nobles's younger brother, booked Lincoln's films from an office in Omaha, Nebraska.

The younger Johnson established crucial links between his own connections and the company's operations. Upon reaching his teens, George was enrolled (likely by the DeVignerie family, his father's employers) at Hampton Institute, a black trade college in Virginia where Booker T. Washington received his education. As a Westerner, however, George felt culturally isolated from his fellow scholars, whose educational levels and world views were shaped by segregation and Southern culture. In his eighties, George P. Johnson looked back upon his Hampton days, regaling interviewers with his hearty disdain for the molasses-drenched cuisine dished out at the school commissary. Like his brother, George took outside jobs during the summer, earning money as a Pullman porter while experiencing the pleasures (and travails) of the open road.

The rails eventually led George Johnson to Muskogee, Oklahoma, where in 1909 he founded the town's first black newspaper, the weekly *Muskogee Phoenix*. In the *Phoenix*, Johnson reprinted articles and stories from the city's main daily that he felt were of interest to the local African American community. Although it was far from the pinnacle of the black press, the paper nevertheless gave Johnson the opportunity to travel among other journalists promoting African American interests. When Missouri began to tilt towards Jim Crow, Johnson closed shop and moved to the somewhat more tolerant clime of Omaha, Nebraska, in 1913. There, he became an assistant postmaster and a member of the town's more prestigious black social organizations. He also began booking films for the Lincoln Theater, where local blacks went to see movies. Johnson's personal experiences and theatrical contacts were invaluable to his brother's new enterprise.[8]

Several reasons underlay why those who invested in the Lincoln Motion Picture Company believed that a serious black cinema would reap profits and prestige. Considering the overt racism of much Hollywood fare, it seemed sensible to assume that black audiences might pay to see black persons realistically and sympathetically portrayed. Furthermore, their personal research led them to conclude that there was a large and lucrative market of "250 Negro Theaters, 500 mixed, 500 Negro colleges and normal schools, 42,000 Negro churches, 161 Negro high schools, lodges, Y.M.C.A.'s Army posts, lodges, fairs, parks, and exports," to which they might provide films.[9] They also were convinced that the cinema—like the press and the pulpit—was a good medium for delivering the message of race progress to large audiences. While newspapers and journals might appeal to an educated and professional elite, fascination with the cinema crossed boundaries of taste and class. In short, Lincoln's founders believed that the movies had the potential to expand the popularity of black uplift discourse beyond the ranks of the previously converted.

The Lincoln Motion Picture Company was chartered with $30,000 worth of assets and was bonded to sell up to $75,000 worth of stock: $50,000 of common stock, and $25,000 of preferred stock paying an 8 percent dividend. Ninety percent of this stock was distributed equally among the cofounders, who also split 600 shares of capital stock.[10] By the end of its first year of production, LMPC issued a report (prepared by one of the principals, presumably George Johnson) boasting gross returns of $2,863.83, an increase in rentals by more than 100 percent over the first three months of 1917, and net assets totaling nearly $75,000. The cofounders considered this a remarkable achievement, "taking into consideration the fight we had to make in overcoming the almost insurmountable obstacles of prejudice, doubt, suspicion, and lack of proper releasing agencies."[11]

Despite this early success, the LMPC faced tall hurdles placed in its way by the large motion-picture distributors. By the mid-1910s, theaters were becoming integrated into production and distribution alliances. Because of the financial rewards reaped through this vertical consolidation, Hollywood studio monopolies controlled the most famous stars, bankrolled the highest film budgets, and developed a regimented but highly efficient system of production in order to feed the almost weekly demand for new programs.

In the face of this lopsided competition, black movie producers struggled mightily. The 1910s and 1920s, the heyday of the silent film, witnessed the formation of more than 200 black-owned filmmaking ventures, of which approximately 40 actually succeeded in making a film. Even those companies with a product to sell faced a serious challenge in getting their movies booked into theaters—this in a dwindling market for low-budget, message-driven pictures. Investment in race film companies naturally held little attraction to major lenders.

Lincoln's executives understood that their working capital had to come from the black business elite and civic leaders. In order to appeal to the class interests of their potential investors (and to stay within a stringent budget of $2,500 per reel of film released) the film scripts Lincoln touted stressed socially conservative themes of self-empowerment and proper moral conduct. Apparently, these themes struck a chord, for Lincoln's principals found enthusiastic backers who helped them produce and distribute their pictures across the nation.

The building of a black motion-picture studio was portrayed in the Lincoln advertisements as morally elevating. By offering only a limited number of shares in the company to the public, Noble Johnson and his colleagues stressed that they could break the skepticism of the black middle class regarding investments. In a brochure entitled *Why the Public is Allowed to Invest,* Lincoln's board of directors stipulated,

> The reasons few are wealthy and the masses poor is because of the superior foresight of the former, and not their better education and environment. The few followed their judgement; the masses try to get the combined judgement of all their friends and acquaintances, many of whom through jealousy, envy, spite, or personal interest, discourage them. Investment opportunity, such as the stock of the Lincoln Motion Picture Corporation offers is usually financed by a few capitalists, as surprise is expressed as to the company's plan of disposing its stock among the small investors. As the success of the Lincoln Motion Picture Inc. depends entirely upon the public, they feel confident that the interests of this company and its stockholders will be best served by having the stock in the hands of the small investor in the different localities where their advertising, cooperation and advice will be of great value. In other words the Lincoln Corporation is a Mutual Company, owned by the masses who attend the theaters and make the corporation a possibility.[12]

The principals maintained that investing in the company was vital to improving the black community and that the gesture might uplift the investors themselves from the evils of, "jealousy, envy, spite, or personal interest." While several prominent African American capitalists assisted the company throughout its life (most notably Ms. C. J. Walker, the cosmetics queen who bought 100 shares), 90 percent of Lincoln's shares remained the property of its board of directors. This strategy not only kept potential profits in the hands of the founders, but it also ensured that the financial and creative control of the pictures remained the domain of the corporate inner circle. By limiting the likelihood of a buyout, Noble Johnson and his partners hoped to guarantee the existence of an independent African American cinema, one not only free from the pressure to advance certain stereotypes, but freely sympathetic to the aspirations of certain members of the black community.

While Lincoln managed to raise enough money to produce a number of films, getting those booked into theaters remained highly problematic. Integrating with the mainstream motion-picture industry was not an option, since the major studios were not interested in releasing all-black pictures. Even had such a desire existed, it would have robbed Lincoln's directors of control over the content of their films. In short, they had no choice but to circumvent the industry's system of vertical consolidation. Professional alliances with African American business and community leaders assisted Lincoln in this goal.

In this endeavor, the black press became one of Lincoln's best allies. Journalists and film critics such as Tony Langston of the *Chicago Defender* and D. Ireland Thomas from Kansas City served as investors and agents for the company. Both men used their personal contacts with theater owners to generate positive word of mouth about Lincoln pictures. They also kept an eye out for the competition and secured advertising for other venues in nearby territories.

Langston was one of the first newspapermen to establish a relationship with the LMPC. Recognizing that the company's success would enhance his own prestige, as well as that of his newspaper, he joined on early in 1917. Langston encouraged the recruitment of journalists such as himself as booking agents for Lincoln. Employees who were ignorant of the ins and outs of the film business, he argued, would undoubtedly cost the company income, as exhibitors would naturally take advantage of a novice's naivete. Throughout his tenure with Lincoln, Langston insisted that hiring journalists would enhance public confidence in the studio's product:

> We will get the names of the class of fellows that I mentioned (the newspaper gang) together, and I will write them each a personal letter making them any proposition that you and I decide to be a good one; I can offer them a record of my own transactions as an incentive, and am sure that I can convince them that it will mean easy money for them. We will take the man on the New York Age, or the Amsterdam News in New York; the man on the Tribune in Phil.; the man on the Bee for Maryland and Washington; the Man on the Guardian in Boston, etc., and in this way consummate exactly the plan that I mentioned before. This plan can be worked in every section where there is a newspaper that has any following at all and even though the booking is slow there will surely be some out of the lot who will make it go and go good. It is a cinch that if you or I were on the spot agencies would spring up like mushrooms. Personal touch counts so much in a game that has so many angles as this one, and the experienced man can do so much more than the other kind that it seems too bad indeed that it will be necessary to break a crew of men in through the mail.[13]

In short, those possessing ties to community organizations and some knowledge of show business would better promote the interests of the company to theater owners than those merely blessed with good intentions.

Langston graphically detailed his service for Lincoln in the Midwest. He reported the size of particular theaters he contacted and the managers' level of interest in running race films. He also used his expertise to determine whether to settle for a straight fee, a daily rate, or a percentage of the house when dealing with theater managers in placing Lincoln films. He also served as an able collector. When an exhibitor who rented on a per-day rate "doubled" the film in another house, Langston fought to get the money properly owed the studio. He also extorted an exhibitor who threatened to cancel a Lincoln booking because of a dispute concerning conditions in the company's rental agreement. On more than one occasion, Langston implied that his reputation gave Lincoln preferable bookings over the offerings of inept black studios. In reference to a certain competitor Langston said,

> Your reply to that ham Cameron was a coocoo. He nor the Unique either one amounts to a damn. The Unique made one release, Shadowed by the Devil, and it was a joke. It had four days here in all and with the entire cast and settings right here in Chicago. Can you beat it? If Cameron has 160 theaters he doesn't look it. Ten cats could catch one rat in the seat of his pants he's so raggedy. When you hear from that class you will do me a favor by referring them to me. Oh my. 90% of that bunch are so crooked that they couldn't hide behind a cork screw.[14]

Despite newspapermen's ability to promote the fledgling studio in unfamiliar territory, Lincoln's directors had reasons to be wary of them. Journalists were also businesspersons, and they often demanded exorbitant advertising fees (for guaranteed space ads in their respective papers) on top of the percentage of the house they received for their bookings. Replies to the early solicitations for stock sales made by Lincoln to African American journalists always included information regarding advertising rates. Romeo Dougherty of the *New Amsterdam News,* for one, was, "not at all pleased at the idea of seeing your "ad" appearing in the other New York papers when the truth of the matter is that I took a personal interest and from what I saw of "The Trooper of Troop K" [I convinced] Mrs. Downs to play "The Law of Nature." Due to the LMPC's tight financial circumstances, the owners could not always reciprocate their agents' favors. While the black business community was cooperative, it was hardly a co-op, and market factors complicated Lincoln's attempts to create a viable distribution network.

Lincoln also looked outside the press to promote its pictures. The principals recruited representatives by telephone or correspondence, making a good assessment of an applicant's level of competence difficult. Langston was quick to remind the studio that hiring well-meaning but inexperienced agents could damage the corporation's professional image. In a letter to George P. Johnson, Langston noted:

> Then again the wildcatting of films is a thing of the past, no matter what the subject is, and the minute you start anything that kind of hustling, away goes your prestige. In my own personal experience as booker and manager I have always been leery of the man with the thing under his arm; I learned this along with the Jews, and you know that they are the last thing in smartness when this game is concerned.[15]

Other journalists shared Langston's opinions. When William Bayless, manager of the *Pittsburgh Courier,* was asked to give an assessment of the performance of representative Emery Crane, he candidly responded that while the subject, "—is a young man filled with honesty of purpose, but not over endowed with enthusiasm, and has not a striking personality. I would rate him as an insistent plodder, a little above the mediocre."[16]

Another wrinkle in Lincoln's system of distribution was that it better accommodated relatively prosperous urban locales, as opposed to rural territories where potential audiences were large but business networks were weak. It became increasingly difficult for Lincoln to penetrate the Deep South, where black economic engines and civic support languished. In these areas, films were distributed through professional exchanges often referred to in the industry as "states righters" because they handled film bookings in regionally defined territories, usually within the borders of a particular state. These firms rented prints of films directly from the producers and then booked the films with exhibitors. Such middlemen would then share a percentage of the profits with the producers. According to the only record in the Lincoln archive pertaining to such bookings, its films were shown mostly in schools, churches, and lodges, instead of in the preferred venues of theaters or vaudeville houses. Although Lincoln's films may have made money in the South due to their novelty, the informal, even makeshift, nature of their showings emphasized the economic gap between the producers, their middle-class sponsors, and residents of the "black belt" living under the indignities of Jim Crow.[17]

Positive reception of LMPC films depended on their ability to tell stories of interest to investors and clients alike—a consideration not lost on the Lincoln production staff. The protagonists in these pictures shared the ideals of the black business community. In each outing, the hero achieved success in one of the various enterprises available in black urban America. These conventions reinforced a Booker T. Washington-like belief that economic inequality between the races might be realized through individual resolve rather than through social activism.

Lincoln's first film, a two-reeler called *The Realization of a Negro's Ambition* (1916), chronicled the rise of a young engineer in California's growing oil industry. After obtaining a degree in geology at the prestigious Tuskegee Institute, the hero is denied work at a prominent refinery due to racial prejudice. Then, after saving the life of a white oil magnate's daughter, he is rewarded with a job searching for oil in the Los Angeles foothills. Because of his training, the protagonist discovers high-grade crude on land that his boss thinks is worthless. The hero ultimately buys the land, drills for oil, and strikes a gusher. In the end, he buys a home, marries his employer's secretary, and lives off the wealth generated by his discovery. The hero's dual achievement of economic self-reliance and domestic tranquility coincides perfectly with the ideology of the film's distributors and financiers—if not the realizable hopes of its entire audience.[18]

Later in 1917, Lincoln released a picture that celebrated the contribution of the United States Army to black uplift. *A Trooper of Troop K* tells the story of "Shiftless" Joe, an unmotivated soul whose inability to hold a job undermines his attempts to catch the eye of a responsible, morally upright young woman with whom he is enamored. As the woman's attentions drift instead toward a well-heeled suitor, she suggests to Joe that he join the army, which might teach him the self-discipline he needs to become a productive citizen. Thus inspired, Joe ships off to Fort Huachuca, Arizona, home of the Tenth Cavalry, where he makes a poor initial impression upon the troops and his white commanding officer. Nevertheless, Joe soon excels at grooming horses, doing such a good job of it that he eventually becomes the troop's mascot. While on patrol in Mexico, Joe and his comrades suffer an ambush by guerrillas. At the height of the danger, the once-shiftless Joe valiantly carries his wounded commander from the combat zone to safety. The hero's exploits are duly reported back home, where, upon his return, he wins the leading lady's hand in marriage. Like *Realization, Trooper* shows how rehabilitation through work and loyalty brings about upward social mobility.[19]

The story of *Trooper* was based upon a true incident that received a considerable amount of attention in the black press at the time. In 1916, a band of Mexican revolutionaries led by Francisco "Pancho" Villa raided the town of Columbus, New Mexico, killing more than seventy U.S. citizens. In response, President Woodrow Wilson sent a large number of troops (most of whom were black) into Mexico in what proved to be a futile two-year attempt to bring Villa to justice. During the deployment, Troop K of the U.S. Tenth Cavalry was ambushed by a party of Villaistas at Carrizal. The factual basis of the film enhanced its themes: it showed black soldiers making considerable sacrifices for the defense of the United States, and it presented the case that African Americans deserved a greater reward than what society generally dealt them.

In Lincoln's next film, *The Law of Nature* (1918), the theme of race progress was filtered through a decidedly more feminine sensibility. Here, the protagonist is a young woman traveling from Chicago to the plains in order to vacation with family. She meets up with Johnson's character, a wealthy, industrious, upstanding, although socially awkward, rancher. The two fall in love and eventually marry, but the rancher's rustic mannerisms cause significant embarrassment for the couple when they go back to the city and move among black society's "smart" set. In time, the heroine becomes attracted to a professional gambler and betrays her upstanding husband. Dejected, the hero returns to the ranch with the child of his ill-fated union. Meanwhile, the heroine takes up with the ne'er do well, who quickly squanders her fortune. Her financial decline is soon coupled with a fatal dose of consumption. Realizing all too late the error of her ways, the ailing heroine musters enough strength to take the train back West, where she reunites with her loving husband before expiring in his arms.[20]

By eliminating stereotypes and slapstick situations, the Lincoln Motion Picture Company presented feasible, if idealized, depictions of African American professionals. They represented Western locales such as California as places offering unique opportunities for personal advancement. *Realization* emphasized how an educated tradesman could make a modest fortune in California's booming oil fields. In *Trooper*, the protagonist's redemption occurs within a Southwestern military institution, as he and his comrades defend American soil. In *Nature*, Lincoln exploits tensions between rural and urban societies in order to dramatize the conflict between self-reliance and social conformity. As in mainstream "Westerns," in Lincoln films the frontier settings contrast the rugged masculinity of the physical world against the effeminate material world of affluence and inherited social class.

Lincoln's principals were well aware of how Hollywood marketed its wares, and in this respect, they mimicked the studio system in several profound ways. Lincoln's advertising emphasized adventure and romance, only subtly inferring to the messages behind the romance. Their movie posters were printed in vivid reds and blues and depicted characters performing feats of courage (such as Shiftless Joe saving his wounded commander's life) or frozen in melodramatic poses (such as the rancher in *Law of Nature* stoically resisting his wife's plea that he "go east"). Noble Johnson's name and association with mainstream Westerns tied his presence to an image of heroism that Pathé (a French firm) and Universal Studios had already developed. Stars from African American theater troupes, such as the Lafayette Players, also appeared in Lincoln films. Featuring the talents of acclaimed thespians lent the films an aura of professionalism.

Based on surviving correspondence from Lincoln's records, the formula partially succeeded in pleasing its intended audience. Numerous exhibitors testified in the company's promotional literature that Lincoln made the best race films that they had yet seen, and that they were well received by black audiences. The Dunbar Theater in Columbus, Ohio, reported having, "—enormous attendance in a blizzard."[21] Likewise, G. J. Smith of the Dunbar Theater in Lincoln, Nebraska, reported that Lincoln's pictures, "—fill up my house in the worst possible weather."[22] Managers also testified that the race angle gave smaller, less-established houses a competitive edge in the African American community. In New Orleans, for example, the Creole managers of the Star Theater mentioned,

> We showed their picture on the same day that our opposition opened up their new $100,000 colored theater, seating 1400 opposite to ours and we played to a big matinee and S.R.O. and both night performances, while the big house

opposite looked like a joke. Our second day was if anything better than the first as this is a picture that the Negroes will rave about and I can strongly recommend that you play it, as you can clean up with it.[23]

Joining the exhibitors' praise were other spokesmen for the urban African American elite. Professors, teachers, and ministers also praised the films' socially uplifting content. One J. A. Hodge, who attended a screening of a Lincoln film at a black college in Missouri, expressed the feelings of many other community leaders when he proclaimed:

I wish to say that I have never seen a cleaner play anywhere and in fact I think that there are few plays on the various circuits that can boast of the wholesomeness which characterizes your play. No one could object to their children seeing such as play, and I really think many of the white corporations would do well to purify many of their productions of the drinking and gambling features. Your company has shown that these bad features can be eliminated and still have a play that will interest and please all classes. As a Negro, I feel proud of the height that you have suddenly reached in this new line of endeavor, and I predict a great future financially for the Lincoln Film Co. You have my best wishes as pioneers in a new field.[24]

As the letter indicates, many viewers felt that films should not just entertain, but that they should also instill proper values—without resorting to gratuitous sensationalism.

In order to demonstrate further the sincerity of their intentions, Lincoln bypassed preferred theatrical venues and set up special screenings at institutions renowned for promoting black social uplift. At the famous Tuskegee Institute, for example, a screening of *Realization* and *Trooper* attracted 1,800 people from the school and surrounding community. Smaller schools and colleges also provided dignified settings for Lincoln presentations. The President of Wiley College, for example, boasted that, "Could Mr. Noble Johnson have heard the applause and the singing of "My Country "Tis of Thee" during the battle scene he would have felt rewarded for his clever acting."[25] Lincoln's product therefore provided a public forum wherein African Americans could mix race pride with patriotism. Lincoln's endeavors also made print in national magazines such as *The Crisis*, the newsletter of the NAACP.[26]

As one might expect, all-black units of the U.S. Armed Forces enthusiastically received Lincoln films. C. J. Ballinger, a Captain in the Twenty-fifth Infantry, rented three Lincoln films for eight days in 1918, showing them to 3,000 black and white soldiers, officers, and civilians. By his own estimation, "For the past week there have been an average of six or seven letters a day coming in from them, expressing their appreciation for the

Lincoln photo-plays."[27] H. P. Strichland, an officer of the Tenth Calvary, witnessed the enthusiasm with which African American soldiers responded to serious black films:

> At first we had a Mutual Weekly, then a Wm. Fox production, and all the time the crowd was getting impatient. At last it was all over. The house suddenly got dark as they were getting reels in. The silence was almost painful as they waited for what was to most of them an introduction to a new adventure, a novelty, a movie with an all Negro cast. Then they sat and watched a story that might happen to any of them any day, so ably acted and unravelled by a Negro company. I don't know what they really wanted to do, you could feel their pride and pleasure popping out all over them; it was grand from start to finish. I was really surprised, it was beyond my expectations. You can't hear anything today but, "The Law of Nature". I am more than glad that I had the opportunity to see your pictures.[28]

This testimony is surprising considering that Lincoln was initially rebuffed by the military when *Trooper of Troop K.* was released. In 1917, the army cancelled a screening of *Trooper* either out of sympathy for those lost at the battle, or fear that the film's depiction of combat might disturb the unit. Nevertheless, Lincoln obtained greater support from the army than the mere collection of rental fees. Lincoln continued recruiting military officers and chaplains as agents for the company; they booked Lincoln films into nearby civilian theatrical venues while the prints were still on base.[29]

Lincoln's films appealed largely to those who believed that advancing the cause of race progress inherently raised the quality of the cinema. Compared to the slapdash, mostly comic, one-reel shorts produced by other filmmakers such as William Foster of Chicago, Lincoln's professionalism and seriousness of purpose made the idea of viewing a race film more respectable. In a testimonial to Lincoln, exhibitor Chester Paul wrote:

> There is no use talking. They will all have to take their hats off to the Lincoln Company. Their features are so far superior to the other all colored productions that there is absolutely no comparison. I consider The Law of Nature as fine as story and as well an acted one as I have shown on the screen here in a long time, and that is saying a lot when you consider our programs are always very carefully selected. The Realization and the Trooper features showed progress, but a story of the description of this last release would even be attempted is an indication of the great possibilities of the future, as this last effort certainly is an artistic and well portrayed success. I will always be glad to use the Lincoln company's productions, as they are uniformly excellent and I consider them good, box-office attractions.[30]

Praise for the artistic quality of Lincoln's film was significant, for in the mind of the audience the entertainment value of the works probably was qualified. Budgetary constraints posed hardships for the company, problems revealed by the production values of the films. While the major Hollywood studios spent more than $1 million on some features during the period, Lincoln remained restricted to a budget of $2,500 a reel. Its first two efforts each ran for two reels, *Nature* to three. In short, Lincoln's production values certainly fell below that to which most moviegoers were accustomed. Even the company's stock literature acknowledged certain aesthetic shortcomings of the products, arguing all the while that idealized portrayals of black aspirations compensated for any such flaws.

While many individuals who shared Lincoln's drive for economic success praised the company's work, the general black audience was probably more varied in its opinion. As the Great Migration grew, working class tastes predominated. Despite the prevalent racism in most films, both black and white spectators were enchanted by Hollywood's ability to spectacularize action and romance. This set certain production and story standards that Lincoln simply could not match. Producers who ignored the changing tastes of the audience did so at their risk once the novelty of race films wore off.

Performance spaces and venues were changing as well. In Chicago, exhibitors held lotteries, booked live entertainment, and paid orchestras to underscore the silent melodramatics playing on the screen with comedic music. All this created a sideshow atmosphere in the black cinema district. Across the nation, "the movies" were becoming a place where the class fissures of the urban black community were on display, a sensibility that challenged Lincoln's high moral purpose.

And Lincoln's message-driven cinema was probably less appealing to those not part of the race movement. Despite the rising optimism of the 1910s, most African Americans were members of the growing black working class or lived in parts of the country where the inspiring words of Booker T. Washington held little influence. Where segregation and job discrimination limited economic advancement, Lincoln's messages of self-improvement found limited support. As exhibitor A. P. McCaffee told actor and Lincoln cofounder Clarence Brooks in August 1918, ". . . Louisville (KY) is about the "haryest" [sic] place this side of Germany. Negroes here do not ordinarily support race movements of any kind. That's characteristic of this berg." Even black troops temporarily stationed in the vicinity seldom viewed Lincoln's offerings. This was due to the false impression that the Palace Theater (which Mcafee managed) was off-limits to black servicemen, that soldier's pay was too small, and that, "80% do not care for pictures or if they do there are OTHER DIVERSIONS they have access to which is more preferable, seldom available but always desirable. Get me?"[31] Simply put, Lincoln's pictures were probably not universally embraced outside large cities.

Nevertheless, by integrating some of the more sensationalistic elements of the Western genre into stories of race improvement, Lincoln possibly expanded the appeal of its films to a broader audience. The action-packed format of *Trooper* tried to catch the emotions of audiences, often at the consternation of censors and other monitors of public decency. One of the more graphically violent (and emotionally troubling) moments of *Trooper* involved the shooting of a buffalo soldier's corpse by a Mexican bushwhacker; the scene was censored in several states. On the other hand, the violent retaliation for the attack was, not surprisingly, one of the most popular scenes in the film. At one screening, Tony Langston noted that, "When Joe shot 'the greaser' off the horse at the 8:00 show there was a yell let out that almost raised the roof."[32] Dramatizing the conquest of the West through violent spectacle helped Lincoln conceal their didacticism and bridge class divides.

Even the vast popularity of the Western genre, however, was not enough to keep the company afloat. Despite its relatively low production costs and overhead, Lincoln was not hugely successful. By the end of its first year, it had broken even, but by 1919 it was $1,000 in the red. Low costs of admission and the necessity to take a percentage of the house, as opposed to a flat rental fee, forced the filmmakers to reduce their financial expectations. With most of the stock still resting in the hands of the board of directors, and with box-office revenue marginal at best, Lincoln only produced and distributed films as profits allowed, not on a regular schedule. In an era when major studios were churning out features on a weekly basis (as well as short-subject films and animated featurettes) theater owners could not rely on the steady arrival of new Lincoln product. Because of the major studios' efficient mode of production, major distributors pressured theater owners to book their films exclusively or else lose the opportunity to get films with major stars and production values. This practice of "block booking" made increasingly fewer commercial venues available for "independent" film companies such as Lincoln.

Things became particularly difficult once the United States entered World War I. Shortages in household income imposed by mobilization limited the discretionary income of would-be moviegoers. Since theaters usually had to screen Lincoln films at the relatively high admission price of 10 cents (to cover the high rental costs) some theaters, such as the Bison in Lincoln, Nebraska, declined showing Lincoln films: people simply could not afford to see them.[33]

The war posed problems for all filmmakers, and the number of films produced in the United States fell considerably during the conflict. Products vital to motion-picture production were in short supply and subject to rationing by the National War Board. The principals of Lincoln tried to get J. Emmett Scott (then an undersecretary in the War Department) to authorize army funds for the production of documentaries showing black soldiers' contribution to the war effort. George Johnson proposed that black entertainment impresarios Robert Levy (of the Quality Amusement

Company and owner of the Lafayette Players), Grant Williams (owner of Dunbar Amusement), Noble Johnson, and other Lincoln agents form a group to be "supported and operated by colored people under Government supervision during the period of the War." To do this, the company's supporters had to buck current spending priorities in Washington. In 1918, the War Department granted the Motion Picture Directors Association, a white industry trade group, with $7 million in subsidies—this under the supposition that Hollywood pictures satisfied the tastes of all Americans. In pointing out that this program inadequately reached black audiences, George P. Johnson argued,

> Owing to obvious reasons the colored people are not represented by the Motion Picture Directors Association; hence the suppositions are that the plan to take care of the colored citizens will be merely to stage some humiliating farce in the way of a burlesque comedy staged by white directors and actors or inexperienced colored actors. . . ."[34]

Such accusations were met cavalierly in Washington. In response to Johnson's concerns about the demeaning portrayal of blacks in government funded films, Frank Wilson replied,

> That various publicity departments of federal organization invariably treat colored American citizens in a humiliating way is correct. It may be that some of the motion pictures portray the colored Americans in a humorous way just as they do the Southern Colonel, the Irish, the stupid Englishman with his monocle and cane, the dude, the Western cowboy, the New England prude and the bloated bond holder.[35]

In other words, the government took the rather peculiar position that stereotyping was a respectable artistic devise for unifying the nation in wartime. Such a position stood in sharp contrast to the government line during World War II, when pictures such as *The Negro Soldier* and *Daybreak* highlighted African American participation in the war and promised their fuller integration into white, mainstream society once victory had been achieved.

In any event, as to whether Lincoln would have been able to pull off George Johnson's grand plan is doubtful. Strapped for cash, Lincoln executives found it difficult to make contacts outside of their primary offices in Los Angeles or Omaha. When Robert Vann, owner of *The Pittsburgh Courier*, expressed interest in a Lincoln proposal to join forces, George Johnson found it impossible to travel east in order to discuss the deal. Whether the cause for the breakdown was financial or wariness on Johnson's part is not known, but the ability of Lincoln executives to expand their networking was definitely compromised during the war.

Lincoln faced an even more severe problem than rationing, cash short-ages, or the risk of alienating constituencies of the black film audience by their highbrow attitudes. At the end of 1917, the studio lost one of its co-founders and its biggest star. The official minutes of the meeting of LMPC executives note that Noble Johnson had decided to leave the company be-cause it was technically inoperable, and therefore unable to give him sub-stantial work.[36] George P. Johnson claimed, however, that his brother's extracurricular activities (i.e, involvement with the LMPC) violated the terms of his contract with Universal Studios, which might have given Uni-versal grounds to fire him. Since Lincoln's films outgrossed Universal's in or near black residential areas, the latter may have instigated a showdown in order to protect its interests. While audiences enjoyed seeing Johnson play African American leads, the actor ultimately protected his career by severing his ties to Lincoln. Johnson continued as a prominent character actor for more that thirty years, appearing in such films as *The Ten Com-mandments* (1924), *Uncle Tom's Cabin* (1927), *The Four Horsemen of the Apocalypse* (1928), and *She Wore a Yellow Ribbon* (1948).

Despite these serious setbacks, Lincoln resumed operations once the war ended. Although the hazards of networking were well known to the company's board of directors, their blueprint for a revived system of dis-tribution was incredibly ambitious. They planned weekly releases of news-reels, shorts, and features, doubling the budgets on features to $5,000 per reel. In order to accomplish these feats, they intended to double their in-vestment pool, as well as maximize returns through releasing a larger vol-ume of output. In reality, however, few things changed. The majority of the company's stock stayed in the hands of the board of directors (with George P. Johnson now holding a slightly larger share than his associates). Financ-ing was limited to one source, P. H. Updike, a wealthy white borax manu-facturer who put up all of the investment capital for Lincoln's last three pictures.[37]

Although social change rocked the black community in the aftermath of World War I (most notably, the "bloody summer" riots of 1919) Lincoln's films still emphasized the moral conservatism of the black entre-preneurial class. In *A Man's Duty* (1921), the hero (now played by Clarence Brooks) is tricked into thinking that he impregnated a prostitute. Being a man of honor, he leaves his fiancé in order to marry the disgraced woman and take care of their expected child. But before taking his vows, he learns that his less-than-honorable friend is the actual father, thereby releasing the protagonist of his obligations to the woman and freeing him to follow his own ambitions. In *By Right of Birth* (1922), the heroine is a young orphan found wandering the Great Plains after the massacre of the rest of her pio-neering family by Indians. Rescued by a white family, the girl, who is of fair complexion, is raised in a Caucasian household without any knowl-edge of the nature of her adoption. When it is discovered that her departed parents' claim rests on a pool of crude oil, her stepmother conspires with a lawyer to take title to the property. In the end, it is up to the hero, an African American USC track star, to rescue the young woman from the extortionists, restore her rightful fortune, and create her true sense of racial identity. While films such as *By Right of Birth* featured fully fleshed out melodrama (more so than Lincoln's earlier two- or three-reel efforts) the basic values of education, character development, and economic advancement still underlay the narratives.[38]

The principals of the LMPC still maintained their belief that the U.S. military provided a path for race advancement. In 1921, Lincoln released a one-reel documentary called *A Day with the 10th Cavalry*, which showed regimental drills and daily life at Fort Huachuca, Arizona. Even as *By Right of Birth* was being released, the company was developing a screenplay about a decorated but now aimless veteran who reclaims his masculine birthright by fighting drug traffickers on the Mexican border alongside the Tenth Cavalry. In this film, the military still seems to provide a standard by which the contributions of blacks were measured as equal to that of whites.[39]

And Lincoln still used the same techniques for distributing films that it had used before the war. Generally, community networks and "states righters" made sure that Lincoln pictures received attention from the targeted African American audience. In Southern California, Lincoln experimented with a more ambitious exhibition scheme. For the premiere of *By Right of Birth*, the company staged a big premiere at Trinity Hall in Downtown Los Angeles. Hiring an orchestra and printing huge ads in the local papers, they easily filled the auditorium's 1,500 seats. They repeated this feat the following night in Riverside, this in front of a white crowd, which, according to Clarence Brooks, received the film quite well. Nevertheless, distribution problems still plagued the LMPC. Then, when their financial angel backed out, the company immediately folded.[40]

The failure of the Lincoln Motion Picture Company sadly exemplifies the transformation of American film culture from one that reflected the interest of ethnic communities to one that subordinated diversity for the sake of creating a mass audience. In order to maximize the efficiency of its distribution networks, corporate Hollywood homogenized the various ethnicities of U.S. cities into a mass "white culture." Subsequently, in the motion pictures of the 1930s and 1940s, images of ethnic and racial difference were cleansed of controversy, made "quaint" by comic relief or simply deleted by corporate or state censorship. With the exception of Oscar Micheaux, the cause of "race uplift" was almost entirely eliminated from the big screen. As a result, the strivings of black America would remain silenced in American movies for another thirty years.

Notes

1 For a particularly detailed discussion on the vertical consolidation of the studio system, see, David Bordwell, Kirstin Thompson, and Janet Staiger. *The Classical Hollywood Cinema: Film*

Style and Mode of Production to 1960 (New York: Columbia University Press, 1985), pp. 85–154.

2 For a discussion of the impact of the movies on the culture of Los Angeles, see Neil Gabler, *An Empire of their Own: How the Jews Invented Hollywood* (New York: Doubleday, 1988), pp. 187–265, and Lary May, *Screening Out the Past: The Birth of Mass Culture and the Motion Picture Industry* (Chicago: University of Chicago Press, 1980), pp. 167–199.

3 Alan Spear, *Black Chicago: The Making of a Negro Ghetto 1890–1920* (Chicago: University of Chicago Press, 1967, p. 12); Quintard Taylor, *In Search of the Racial Frontier: African Americans in the American West, 1528–1990* (New York: Norton, 1998), pp. 222–27.

4 Thomas Cripps, *Slow Fade to Black: The Negro in American Film, 1900–1942* (New York: Oxford University Press, 1993), pp. 41–69. See also Cripps, "The Making of The Birth of a Race: The Emerging Politics of Identity in Silent Movies," in *The Birth of Whiteness: Race and the Emergence of U.S. Cinema* (New Brunswick, NJ: Rutgers University Press, 1998), pp. 38–55.

5 *Why the Public is Allowed to Invest,* The George P. Johnson Collection, University of California, Los Angeles.

6 George P. Johnson, *George P. Johnson: Collector of African American Film,* Regents of the University of California, 1969, pp. 39–42.

7 This is based on a partial list of credits from 1915 to 1918 on a publicity packet on Noble Johnson supplied by Universal Pictures in the George P. Johnson Collection, University of California, Los Angeles.

8 Johnson, op. cit., pp.1–16, 165–191.

9 From an undated report on the finances of the Lincoln Motion Picture Company, George P. Johnson Collection, University of California, Los Angeles.

10 Lincoln Motion Picture Company Stockholders contract, George P. Johnson Collection, University of California, Los Angeles.

11 Undated report of the Lincoln Motion Picture Company, George P. Johnson Collection, University of California, Los Angeles.

12 *Why the Public is Allowed to Invest,* The George P. Johnson Collection, University of California, Los Angeles.

13 Correspondence from Tony Langston to George P. Johnson dated November 24, 1916, George P. Johnson Collection, University of California, Los Angeles.

14 Correspondence from Tony Langston to George P. Johnson dated October 23rd, 1916, George P. Johnson Collection, University of California, Los Angeles.

15 Ibid.

16 Correspondence from William P. Bayless to George P. Johnson, dated 10/13/17, George P. Johnson Collection, University of California, Los Angeles.

17 Lincoln Motion Picture Company minutes dated 9/2/17 and 12/3/17, Financial statements from Brady and Mowery, undated, George P. Johnson Collection, University of California, Los Angeles.

18 Synopsis of *Realization of a Negro's Ambition* in the George P. Johnson Collection, University of California, Los Angeles.

19 Synopsis of *Trooper of Troop K,* George P. Johnson Collection, University of California, Los Angeles.

20 Synopsis from draft of advertising copy for *The Law of Nature,* George P. Johnson Collection, University of California, Los Angeles.

21 Advertisement for Lincoln Motion Picture Company Stock. George P. Johnson Collection, University of California, Los Angeles.

22 Letter from C. J. Smith to the Lincoln Motion Picture Company dated 6/28/17, George P. Johnson Collection, University of California, Los Angeles.

23 Letter of introduction for D. Ireland Thomas by Mess. Bennett and Bendreaux dated 7/16/20, George P. Johnson Collection, University of California, Los Angeles.

24 Correspondence from J. A. Hodge to the Lincoln Motion Picture Company dated 6/28/17, George P. Johnson Collection, University of California, Los Angeles.

25 Correspondence from M. W. Dugan to D. Ireland Thomas, undated, George P. Johnson Collection, University of California, Los Angeles.

26 Testimony from Charles Bailey, others in publicity materials for the Lincoln Motion Picture Company, George P. Johnson Collection, University of California, Los Angeles.

27 Letter from Colonel C. J. Ballinger to the Lincoln Motion Picture Company dated 3/6/18, George P. Johnson Collection, University of California, Los Angeles.

28 Correspondence from H. P. Strichland to the Lincoln Motion Picture Company, dated 8/29/17, George P. Johnson Collection, University of California, Los Angeles.

29 Letter from Battise to the Lincoln Motion Picture Company dated 4/27/17, George P. Johnson Collection, University of California, Los Angeles.

30 Draft of advertising material for Lincoln Motion Picture Company dated 7/22/18, George P. Johnson Collection, University of California, Los Angeles.

31 Correspondence from A.P. McCaffee to Noble Johnson, George P. Johnson Collection, University of California, Los Angeles.

32 Correspondence from Tony Langston to George P. Johnson dated 10/30/16, George P. Johnson Collection, University of California, Los Angeles.

33 Correspondence from R. A. Perkins to the Lincoln Motion Picture Company dated 6/26/18, George P. Johnson Collection, University of California, Los Angeles.

34 Correspondence from George P. Johnson to S. Hart, dated 8/12/18, George P. Johnson Collection, University of California, Los Angeles.

35 Correspondence from Frank Wilson to the Lincoln Motion Picture Company dated 10/18/18, George P. Johnson Collection, University of California, Los Angeles.

36 Minutes from the Lincoln Motion Picture company dated 9/3/18, George P. Johnson Collection, University of California, Los Angeles; Johnson, op. cit., pp. 152–53.

37 Financial report drafted in 1920 by the Lincoln Motion Picture Company, George P. Johnson Collection, University of California, Los Angeles.

38 Synopsis for *A Man's Duty* and *By Right of Birth*, George P. Johnson Collection, University of California, Los Angeles.

39 Synopsis for *A Day With the 10th Cavalry* and *The Forgotten American,* George P. Johnson Collection, University of California, Los Angeles.

40 Thomas Cripps, *Slow Fade to Black: The Negro in American Film, 1900–1942,* (New York: Oxford, 1993), pp. 86–89.

CHAPTER EIGHT

Stigmatizing Okies

Nancy J. Taniguchi

"We weren't Okies."—Woody Guthrie

OKIES IMAGINED

Today, *Okie* is not a dirty word, or so says $37,500 of California tax-payers' money. In 1991, Mary Lynn Rasmussen won a lawsuit to continue to advertise her "Okie Girl Restaurant" with a billboard alongside Inter-state Highway 5 where it becomes "the Grapevine," the nickname for the snaking section of blacktop that crosses the Tehachapi Mountains, the natural upthrust that separates California's lush, agricultural Central Valley from the city sprawl and orange groves of the southland. CalTrans of-ficials, employees of California's Department of Transportation, had filed suit over her sign, claiming it was "in poor taste and offensive to some trav-elers," thereby prohibited by law on an interstate highway. Rasmussen countered that the name was no longer a slur and, in winning, brought a legal, if not a visceral, conclusion to the stigmatization of the Okies.[1]

No one would deny, however, that Californians used *Okie* as an insult for most of the twentieth century. In America at large, this subculture is known largely through a series of artistic works dating from the Great Depression: the images of photographer Dorothea Lange (the best-known of which is "Migrant Mother," shot in 1936); the scholarly studies of economist Paul Schuster Taylor and lawyer/historian/activist Carey McWilliams; folksinger Woody Guthrie's *Dust Bowl Ballads* (1940), and John Steinbeck's 1939 novel, *The Grapes of Wrath*, converted in 1940 into a feature-length film. These works portrayed Okies as poor, unlettered, earnest, and frequently hopeless, using a single negative stereotype to rep-resent a much more complex group.[2] Despite intervening decades, Ameri-cans continue to picture Okies based on *The Grapes of Wrath*. Its protagonists, the Joads, driven off their dried-up Oklahoma farm, pile their

Publicity still from *The Grapes of Wrath* showing the Joad family at a migrant worker camp. *Courtesy of the Museum of Modern Art, Film Stills Archive.*

tired belongings onto a jalopy and head west on Route 66, bound for a new start in California. A wiser migrant warns them of what to expect there: "Well, Okie use' ta mean you was from Oklahoma. Now it means you're a dirty son-of-a-bitch. Okie means you're scum."[3] By the end of the novel, the Joads have arrived in California's Central Valley and found nothing as they expected. There is no work. No one wants them. Rain pours down, drowning the ramshackle migrant camps, and the flooded-out Joads take dispirited refuge in a stranger's barn. There, another migrant boy and his starving father shiver from the storm. The Joad's eldest daughter, Rose of Sharon, who has just delivered a still-born baby, offers her milk-full breast to the starving stranger out of pure necessity.[4] While one part of the reader gasps at her selflessness, another cries out, "How raw! How shocking! How disgusting! How could anyone ever be *that* poor?!"

HISTORICAL OKIES

They weren't that poor, or, at least, all of them weren't. This point was partly behind Woody Guthrie's proclamation, "We weren't Okies." Fundamentally, Okies came from Oklahoma, but there the stereotype stopped for Guthrie. Although he was a native of Okemah, Oklahoma (and Guthrie used the Okie association to claim his audience), he remembered wealth no Okie would have. His family, he said, had owned a two-story, brick home in town (stereotypical Okies were all from the farm). His folks were middle-class (Okies were all at the bottom of the social ladder).[5] As late as 1989 he was proudly remembered by a fellow Okemah native as being named "after President Woodrow Wilson. His father was a businessman, politician, a respected member of the community. His mother gave her all to [her] family."[6] Nonetheless, Californians made no such fine class distinctions.

Census data, as analyzed by contemporary historian James Noble Gregory, bears out the variety of this migrant subculture. Gregory noted that, immediately prior to their forced migration from the Midwest, only 43 percent of the people Californians called *Okies* had been engaged in agricultural pursuits.[7] Furthermore, not all *Okies* hailed from Oklahoma; they came also from Arkansas (sometimes also known as *Arkies*), Texas, and Missouri, predominately. The infamous 1936–37 "Dust Bowl"—allegedly the impetus for mass migration westward—technically affected only the areas of eastern Colorado and contiguous western Kansas, the Oklahoma panhandle, and North Texas.[8] This environmental disaster came well after other forces that drove people west: the long agricultural depression of the 1920s, leading into the Great Depression of the 1930s; the introduction of machinery to do the work of many men, resulting in so-called technological unemployment; and, for some, poverty born of decades of share-cropping.[9] Hundreds of thousands of migrants drifted to California, looking for work, looking to settle down and make a new home in a more hospitable climate. But in following this long-cherished American dream of moving westward to seek greater opportunity, these white, Protestant, family-oriented people ran head first into the hard realities of California history. They drove a wedge into previously settled notions of race, occupation, and land tenure. Their behavior—and their desperation—shocked and scared the already settled white landowner.

From today's standpoint, it is easy to confuse art with history, and to confuse cause with effect. Californians' prejudice against Okies came first—the hopeless, ignorant, fictional Joads came later. As Charles Shindo noted in his 1997 book, the creation of the Okie stereotype—in photographs, words, and images—says more about its creators than any historical reality.[10] Nonetheless, the anti-Okie prejudice was searingly real. But what caused the prejudice against Okies? Why were they stigmatized?

No one was an Okie before they landed in California, because California created the Okie. Transients were commonplace nationwide in the 1930s as drifters crisscrossed America, but in the Golden State vagrants were met with particular dislike.[11] Three principal reasons underlay this. The first was shared by the entire nation.

The Great Depression was America's greatest stagecoach ride, a metaphor created by Utopian socialist Edward Bellamy in 1887, following the eastern industrial depression of 1881 that culminated in 1886 in the bloody clash between organized labor and police in Haymarket Square in Chicago. Bellamy envisioned American society as a huge stagecoach, with the rich riding comfortably atop, out of the dust and the mud, hunger holding the reins and lashing at the poor, who pulled the coach "along a very hilly and sandy road." As Bellamy wrote:

> These seats on the top [of the coach] were very comfortable [but] . . . the seats were very insecure, and at every sudden jolt of the coach persons were slipping out of them and falling to the ground, where they were instantly compelled to take hold of the rope and help to drag the coach on which they had before ridden so pleasantly. . . . [Sometimes] the vehicle came to a bad place in the road, . . . or to a particularly steep hill. At such times, the desperate straining of the team, their agonized leaping and plunging under the pitiless lashing of hunger, the many who fainted at the rope and were trampled in the mire, made a very distressing spectacle. . . . [T]here was always some danger at these bad places of a general overturn in which all would lose their seats.[12]

In the 1930s, the very real threat of "general overturn" made everybody fearful.

A second reason for the rise of Okie-hating stemmed from California's own unique history. Since the heady years of the Gold Rush, questions of race, class, and land ownership had been settled in favor of white emigrants from the eastern United States, especially from the Northeast. American Indians were largely eliminated, the survivors of the once numerous groups socially marginalized.[13] California, although a "Free" state in the great pre–Civil War controversy, maintained a stringent fugitive slave law and, in fact, permitted slavery within its borders.[14] With such palpable discrimination, the black population of California remained relatively small.

Xenophobia also abounded. Foreigners, such as Peruvians, Chileans, Mexicans, and Chinese were forced out of the state by the Foreign Miners Tax of 1850 (and its revised form, in 1855) and accompanying vigilante action.[15] Even native-born persons of Hispanic descent were largely dispossessed. The Land Act of 1851 resulted in the ownership of huge landed estates shifting from the *Californios* to white speculators.[16] In short, a racial hierarchy with whites at the top and all other peoples beneath them had been established in early California and maintained ever since. To return to the stagecoach analogy, the possibility that the traditional coach riders—the white landowners—could now slip to the level of their traditional workers—people of color—was never raised, that is until the sudden appearance of the *white*, Okie fieldworkers. To those on top, it was a horrifying thought.

Finally, the Okies were southerners, a fact made obvious as soon as they opened their mouths. In Steinbeck's approximation, the Joad family, upon reaching the east bank of the Colorado River, rested a while before making the crossing. One of the boys grew apprehensive, remarking about California, "Get to thinkin' they ain't no such country. I seen pitchers like that."[17] His drawl branded him as forever an outsider. Furthermore, there was no place like the California of his imagination, as the Joads would soon find out.

Being southerners carried heavy implications in California in the 1930s. Like most attitudes, this one was rooted in history. While the Gold Rush of 1849 had lured northerners and southerners alike (although the former predominated), by the Civil War, California was leaning politically toward the North. Leland Stanford got himself elected governor of the state on the Republican (pro-northern) ticket in 1861. Power became wedded to wealth when, by 1869, he and three colleagues had become the "Big Four," the richest men in the state. They made most of their money as the builders of the western segment of the transcontinental railroad.[18] Together with their company lawyer they dominated all aspects of California government until 1910. They maintained their connections to northern politicians and federal officials as, by the turn of the century, sectional differences were replaced by political splits between wealthy industrialists and poor laborers. Southerners remained the "out-group" in California.

However, the Old South, by the twentieth century, had developed a new mystique. With sectionalism safely in its grave, a new look at the South's "quaint" history emerged in early silent films which established a slick, one-dimensional image of gracious southern landed gentry and their happily singing slaves.[19] This California-made cinematic view was widely accepted—even embraced—nationwide. The mainstay of this portrayal was the maintenance of the racial divide: white masters, black underlings. Yet now, in the height of the depression, here came the Okies to California, taking jobs that no white man, woman, or child would do. When these white people crossed that barrier, they lost the privilege Californians granted to their state's dominant race. In the eyes of settled white Californians, the Okies became a breed apart: inferior, despised, and stigmatized.

BROWNS AT THE BOTTOM

Until the 1930s, the underclass in California had been brown; the elite, white. This pattern developed out of dispossession of the *Californios*, begun by law and completed with the drought and flood cycles of 1862–64.[20] American migrants to the Golden State first replicated the *Californios'* ranching economy but soon thereafter turned to growing wheat. In the 1870s and 1880s the Central Valley was known as "the breadbasket of Europe," a feat spurred by a series of technological inventions led by the combine popularized by Benjamin Holt of Stockton.[21] California produced more wheat than any other state in 1874 and 1875, with yields soaring to an all-time high in 1884.[22] Hoboes who drifted into California on its spreading railroads in response to the economic panics of the late nineteenth century harvested the wheat and moved on, following the call of their transient lifestyle.[23] By the turn of the century, California landowners increasingly turned to planting orchards and row crops (tomatoes, strawberries, and beets, for example), all of which required great numbers of pickers during the few critical weeks of the harvest.

By the time row crops predominated, however, the Chinese, who had succeeded the hoboes as the main fieldworkers, were dwindling in number. The national Panic of 1873, which reached California two years later, brought widespread layoffs, resulting in Chinese scapegoating by angry whites. Chief among these was Irish immigrant and anti-Chinese agitator Denis Kearney. In his sandlot oratory aimed at organizing the Workingman's Party of California, he regularly included the refrain, "The Chinese must go!"[24] With stalwart backing from a variety of other sources, this sentiment emerged in Congress as the Chinese Exclusion Act of 1882, placing a ten-year restriction on Chinese immigration.[25] In 1902, Congress extended Chinese exclusion indefinitely.

Only one year after the act's original passage, California growers began to worry about a farm labor shortage. In September 1883, an editorial in the *Pacific Rural Press* asked where replacement labor would be found. The older states of the Union were not the answer, since their laborers were "paid as well or better . . . than similar laborers are paid here."[26] That same month, members of the State Horticultural Society suggested recruiting city schoolboys for the crucial harvest weeks, with the approval of school authorities. Of course, the boys would have to be given comfortable quarters and treated "as fellow creatures who are capable of being our own equals—capable of some day filling the positions we now occupy—not as slaves but as freemen."[27] Such an arrangement was out of the question for Chinese fieldworkers; indeed, as of 1870, the law denied the extension of U.S. citizenship to Chinese on racial grounds. By the late 1880s, some Californians went so far as to theorize that the departure of the Chinese farm workers might prove beneficial in forcing open an occupational niche for the married white farmer, "who [naturally] must have his cottage and garden, and a reasonable employment within a few miles [of his home]. . . . This is the normal condition of American life. The Chinaman had denied it to California." While this line of thought is a perverse example of blaming the victim, it does expose a double standard that, for their own selfish reasons, the owners of large farms espoused. Typically, Chinese laborers had been single men with a propensity to move on once a particular job was finished, but such would hardly have been the case with married white laborers, who might well demand that the landowners subdivide part of their vast agricultural tracts in order to clear space for the construction of nearby homes and communities.[28] This process would obviously have cut into the wealth of the elite; it was unacceptable. Instead, big growers started seeking more tractable, mobile laborers.

The economic downturns of the late nineteenth century provided a sufficient workforce of transient poor—but that situation disappeared by 1902, when the Chinese Exclusion Act became permanent. By then, Japanese immigrants had entered the fields, and even they exceeded the number of Chinese in the beet harvest. As the resident Chinese farm workers grew increasingly elderly, growers tended to hire young, vigorous Japanese to replace them. So in the fields as well as in the state's imagination, the Japanese replaced the Chinese as the "yellow peril." However, the Japanese workers differed from their Chinese counterparts in significant ways: the newcomers were members of a more powerful Asian nation, and many of them decided to stay in California and raise families. The first overt sentiment expressed by the white majority toward the Japanese surfaced in San Francisco in 1906, and it resulted in the federal "Gentleman's Agreement" of 1907, in which Japan agreed to refuse exit visas for the laborers bound for the United States. That same year, one of the papers read at the annual Fruit-Growers Convention stressed California's dependence upon Asian workers to perform tasks that white laborers refused to do. The organization unsuccessfully petitioned Congress to admit Japanese laborers (contrary to the "Gentleman's Agreement") and readmit Chinese laborers (contrary to the Exclusion Act). A growers committee even generated a pro-Japanese report for the state legislature in 1910, which met with highly unusual disapproval from the state senate, which usually followed growers' recommendations.[29]

This disapproval was a bellwether of changing attitudes, for Japanese success, especially in agriculture, was making this new group of Asian immigrants increasingly unpopular among jealous whites in California. Increasing discrimination against Japanese in the cities had driven many Japanese families out to the rural areas. They brought with them means enough to buy land and set up their own farms in competition (however minor) with white growers.[30] Now a growing fear of a rural-based takeover by the new "yellow peril" merged with preexisting urban prejudices. One result, the Alien Land Act of 1913, forbade any future land purchases by aliens ineligible for citizenship (meaning the Chinese and Japanese, although the former had already been excluded from buying property for over thirty years). In 1920, a ballot initiative that plugged loopholes in this law passed by a 3-to-1 vote. In 1923, California passed a third alien land act, this one forbidding the leasing of land to Asian immigrants as well. The federal Immigration Act of 1924 finally, and effectively, ended Japanese immigration.[31]

In the early twentieth century, other nonwhite immigrant groups also entered California agriculture, though in lesser numbers. While the Japanese were gaining a foothold in this occupation, workers from the Indian subcontinent were imported for the 1907 to 1910 harvests—perhaps a fearful reaction to the potential effects of the Gentleman's Agreement. This new group was evaluated by the California writer Carey McWilliams, who coined the phrase "factories in the field" to describe California's agricultural system:

> From the [white] growers' point of view, the Hindus fitted nicely into the pattern of farm labor in California. Not only were they good workers, but they could be used as one additional [non-white] racial group in competition with other [non-white] racial groups, and thereby wages could be lowered. A notable fact about farm labor in California is the practice of employers to pay wage scales on the base of race, i.e. to establish different wage rates for each racial group, thus fostering racial antagonism and, incidentally, keeping wages at the lowest possible point.[32]

The obvious but unspoken assumption here was that brown people got paid less than whites, and new immigrants got paid less than older ones. With this race-based wage scale in place, Indian fieldworkers initially served to keep wages depressed. However, like the Japanese, they eventually became landowners, some of them operating rice farms and others moving to the cities. The Immigration Act of 1917, which excluded people from certain "barred zones," effectively ended Indian immigration, once again necessitating new searches for workers to fill the agricultural labor pool.[33]

Between 1923 and 1929, one final wave of Asians came to harvest California's crops. During this time, roughly 30,000 Filipinos arrived in California straight from America's Pacific colony. These immigrants were mostly young males without families, English-speaking, educated in American schools, yet willing to accept the accommodations previously accorded the Chinese and Japanese farm workers. Nonetheless, growers generally did not want to hire Filipinos, except for the asparagus farmers of the San Joaquin Delta.[34] The Filipinos' very level of acculturation prompted the hatred whites expressed for them: here were Asians who could easily form social and sexual liaisons with white Californians. V. S. McClatchy of the *Sacramento Bee* conjured images of a "Third Wave" of yellow peril washing over America's shores. Anti-Filipino vigilante actions broke out in the San Joaquin Valley and in Watsonville in 1929 and early 1930, respectively.[35] Clearly, the Filipinos were not the solution to California's agricultural labor problems, although they nevertheless added to the racial mix of the workforce.

Finally, overlapping the Filipino immigration, Mexicans came to the fields in increasing numbers in the 1920s. Although they worked in the citrus orchards in the first decade of the twentieth century, the "conception of [a] dependence on Mexican labor first began to become generalized among farm employers during the spring of 1926."[36] The Mexican fieldworkers came with the spreading cotton culture, bringing with them skills learned in the Mexican regions of Durango and Baja California. Following higher wages into the San Joaquin Valley, by 1926 Mexicans made up 80 percent of the cotton pickers, often 95 percent on ranches of 300 acres or more.[37] California growers vigorously resisted any suggestions that Mexicans be added to the immigration quota system established by federal law in 1924. To combat any such quota, employers made specious and racist arguments in favor of Mexican labor including: 1) without Mexican labor, less desirable Filipinos, southern blacks, or Puerto Ricans would have to be recruited to work the fields; 2) white workers would not perform "stoop labor," but Mexicans were not only suited for it but were content with it; 3) without Mexican labor, the state's agriculture would stagnate and/or consumer prices would rise; and 4) Mexicans would willingly return to Mexico when the harvest was over, thereby avoiding the perceived racial or social problems associated with other migrant fieldworkers in California.[38] While these arguments were patently false and self-serving, they did help form public policy.

In 1926, newpaper editor Chester Rowell succinctly summarized his view of the current development of the "racial problem," with emphasis on the Japanese.

> In California the Chinese largely did the work which there were no white workers to do, and the Japanese have improved land which we left waste, and developed products which we overlooked. There is no economic conflict here, but there is still hostility. Into the places vacated by departing Orientals now flow, not Americans, but Mexicans. Nobody objects, because nobody else wants those jobs. . . . [but] When Japanese move into a city neighborhood, Americans move out . . . because they will not live where persons of a different physical race live. . . . It is sheer racial caste. But it makes the American farmer move out [too], even at an economic loss.[39]

Racial tensions heightened as the thirties began. As the Great Depression deepened, those at the bottom became targets of increased animosity. For example, when many Mexicans did not willingly return to their homeland after the harvest, American officials forcibly "repatriated" them. The idea of "returning" Mexicans to their homeland—the meaning of *repatriation*—effectively disguised the fact that many of those sent to Mexico had never actually been there. Instead, thousands were United States citizens, born of Mexican immigrant parents, for whom Mexico was a foreign country. However, in the collusion between the governments of the United States and Mexico, the Constitutional rights of these American citizens hardly mattered. Repatriation reached its height in 1931 and 1932, when over 65,000 (American statistics) or over 200,000 (Mexican statistics) individuals were sent [back] to Mexico.[40] Some Mexicans stayed in

California, however, and others quietly returned, so by the time the Okies arrived the lowest labor rung in agriculture, especially in the cotton culture, was Mexican-occupied.

Other nonwhites faced other forms of prejudice as the depression began. By 1929, the second-generation Japanese had become a "problem" worthy of study by Stanford University psychology professor Edward K. Strong. Armed with a $40,000 grant from the Carnegie Corporation, he analyzed the vocational aptitudes, public reception, and public school education of Japanese-Americans. His results, published in 1934, summarized Californians' continuing prejudice, which he lumped into three categories: racial grounds (intermarriage was dismissed as "unthinkable"), political grounds (an alleged continuing allegiance to "the Mikado," or Japanese emperor), and issues of personal character. He found all these negative views exacerbated by "the comparatively large number of Japanese in the state, emphasized particularly by their concentration in certain localities," foremost among them the agricultural areas where the Okies would soon congregate.[41] Strong concluded this section of his hopeful study with the belief that, since Japanese immigration had stopped, these prejudices "are no longer bitterly urged. In all probability, however, they have had their effect in an unconscious bias of the whites against the Japanese."[42]

That bias, coupled with Japan's military advances in China and Korea and its growing competitiveness in world markets, soon threatened California's status quo, according to editor and pundit Carey McWilliams. "In 1935, 1937 and 1939," he wrote a few years later, "various anti-Japanese measures were introduced in the California legislature . . . and in the spring of 1935 the [California-based] Hearst press began to inveigh against the 'inequitable Oriental competition sapping the economic life of America and retarding recovery.'" McWilliams noted the appearance of a mysterious "Committee of One Thousand" in Southern California in the thirties, which began spreading anti-Japanese rumors: "Japanese truck gardeners [in California] were spraying their vegetables with arsenic; using human excrement as fertilizer, thereby creating epidemics of 'bacillary dysentery'. . . and so forth."[43] When the Okies arrived, some would work for Japanese growers, undercutting the wages paid Mexican fieldworkers. It was unthinkable.

THE OLD SOUTH IN CALIFORNIA

Southern thought regarding race had a steady influence in California disproportionate to the number of southerners living there. While the Gold Rush attracted people from all over the nation, northerners predominated among the new immigrants. Regular delegates to the state constitutional convention reflected the local mix and sectional roots. Of the forty-eight members listed by historian H. H. Bancroft, twenty-three had arrived from the North (including the Ohio Valley), fourteen hailed from the South (including the border states of Maryland, Kentucky, Tennessee, and Missouri), five were foreign immigrants, and six were *Californios*.[44]

Although the newcomers may have regarded California as the land of new opportunities, these argonauts never abandoned most of their old assumptions. Although California entered the Union as a free state in 1850, it had a stringent Fugitive Slave Law that did not give a black person "any more peace of mind than a Free Negro would have enjoyed in the heart of the Southland."[45] Any owner who claimed runaway slaves had only to procure a warrant for their arrest. Blacks could not testify against whites in court, and unless they could produce evidence of freedom (such as cherished "freedom papers") they could be enslaved by court order. This system remained in effect until 1858, the same year that the state legislature passed a bill that prevented the immigration of "Free Negroes and Mulattos." That law was repealed in 1859, but that move hardly augured any real change in ideas about white supremacy in the Golden State.[46]

Sectional differences also animated early California politics, as the state Democratic party (the state's only organized political party) split between the "Chiv" (southern) and "Regular" wings. Fiery orators clashed on views of slavery or freedom in public and in politics, focusing particularly on Kansas, which engaged in civil warfare over this question from 1854 to 1856. Harsh words spawned by this political partisanship led in 1859 to California's most famous duel. Judge David S. Terry, of the "Chiv" Democrats, killed David Broderick, originally of New York, discrediting the southern wing.[47] Thereafter and throughout the American Civil War, California elections remained under the sole control of pro-Union politicians. In the words of California native John Hays Hammond, born in San Francisco in 1855 of southern parents:

> California was a Union state, and the Southerners there were viewed with suspicion during the Civil War, yet we were so far removed from the scene of actual conflict that the bitterness of personal animus was greatly lessened. Some Southerners . . . were paroled, after giving their word to the northern officers that they would not join in the southern cause." He continued, "My father found his business enterprises made difficult by the war; his political activities ceased." But "friendly relations [with northern officers] were maintained throughout the struggle.[48]

The evaporation of political opposition meant that northern sympathizers needed no cause to trumpet in order to maintain the upper hand. Now, they could control state politics unchallenged, without having to abandon the ideas of racial superiority that had characterized all the sections of the antebellum United States.

In the late nineteenth century, California stayed with the national mainstream on racial ideas. As shown by historian C. Vann Woodward in *The*

Strange Career of Jim Crow, all America opted for increasing racial segregation in the years after the Union troops were withdrawn from the South in 1877.[49] The prevalent national pattern of a "separate but equal," two-tiered, black-white society was institutionalized by the Supreme Court in *Plessey* v. *Ferguson* (1896). California also practiced a more subtle segregation of the white and brown races, as already noted in the example of race-based wage differentials in agriculture. As psychologist Strong pointed out in his 1934 study, "It is interesting to speculate upon the possibility that if California had not had Chinese and Japanese for common laborers she might have had a great influx of Negroes in the early days."[50] Had this scenario developed, life might have been much simpler for the Okies. At least they would have known where they stood.

This nationally popular system of white supremacy over blacks became a touchstone of the fledgling film industry. Just seven years after the *Plessey* decision, a silent-film version of *Uncle Tom's Cabin* debuted, marking the beginning of the Southern genre in film. Its director, Edwin S. Porter, has been acknowledged as "the father of the story film," using a sharp eye for realistic content and pioneering the use of editing to achieve dual, simultaneous narrative lines.[51] Because of the lack of dialog to achieve character development, scenes had to be devised clearly to indicate who was the villain and who the hero. Consequently, in this and other early adaptations of Harriet Beecher Stowe's famous novel, "the typical Southerner is invariably well clothed and well mannered and is kind to his slaves." In return, the slave owners "receive commendable service from their charges." The villain, by contrast, is unkempt, ill-mannered, and brutal.[52] The Porter rendition of the story ended with two men shaking hands, personifying the reunion of the nation after the Civil War. In the words of a modern cultural historian, "in view of how bluntly stereotyped the grinning, singing blacks were and how satisfied they seemed under Caucasian guidance, it was hard for an audience not to be charmed by the genteel atmosphere which so strongly implied that the South knew best how to care for the Negro."[53]

This cinematic orientation flowered in California under the directorship of David Wark Griffith. In 1914, he sought suitable stories for film and was offered *The Clansman*, written in 1905 by a southern clergyman. Griffith then raised "an astonishing $110,000, rehearsed for six weeks and filmed in nine, edited in three months, and presented an epic of twelve reels and three hours running time . . . [that] altered the methodology of American filmmaking: *Birth of a Nation*."[54] This movie also made film a medium for the enjoyment of the elite, as tickets sold for a munificent $2.00 and forty- to one hundred-piece orchestras accompanied the action. Most important, "the stereotyped South finally became eminently respectable to many who had before shunned film."[55] *Birth of a Nation* was shown in the White House for President Woodrow Wilson and, over the protests of African Americans, became wildly popular all over the nation. In California, Governor Hiram Johnson supported its views. This single film set a pattern that would be followed for seven decades. The popularity of the Old South stereotypes "pointed not to the industry's concept alone, but to what the audience had come to expect and believe was accurate."[56] The genre reached an apex in 1939 with *Gone with the Wind*, released even as the Okies were struggling into California.

In short, the southern epic film was one with the cotton culture. Blacks were routinely portrayed as happy workers of the cotton fields, and movie posters sometimes were bordered with cotton bolls. Furthermore, the Old South film portrayed only two classes—rich whites and poor blacks. The whites sat about drinking mint juleps while the blacks uncomplainingly worked. "Characterizations of the Southern herdsmen, mountain people, farmers, town dwellers, and merchants, or the average planter with his few slaves and modest home were entirely absent."[57] By the late 1930s, with this conceptualization of southern culture well-entrenched in the American psyche, the horde of impoverished Okies seeking work in the cotton fields came as a very nasty shock to California landowners and townspeople alike.

LIFE BACK HOME

The Okies arrived without any knowledge of California's racial stratification. Oklahoma, like California, had a tradition of commercial farming, but one that relied on tenants rather than migrant labor. Between 1909 and 1919, cotton production in Oklahoma doubled, making the state the fourth-largest producer in the country. Men filled in the time between growing seasons with work in the oil fields or coal mines, but many fieldworking families stayed put.[58]

Racism certainly existed in Oklahoma, as in other states from which the Okies had arrived, but it was aimed at the few resident nonwhite groups. Missouri, Arkansas, and Texas all had been slave states, and their residents retained strong ideas about white supremacy and black inferiority. Oklahoma had been Indian Territory until 1907. At statehood, Oklahoma legislated a white-black society with "colored" (people of African descent) at the bottom and "whites," which included Indians, above them.[59] Ten years later, in August 1917, the multiracial Green Corn Rebellion wreaked widespread destruction in the southeastern counties of the state, as poverty-stricken blacks, Indians, and whites rose up against the white-dominated power structure. The uprising was rapidly squelched and caused a severe backlash. In the Green Corn Rebellion's wake, the Ku Klux Klan prospered, physical repression silenced any "deviant" group, and propaganda, including D. W. Griffith's *Birth of a Nation*, helped solidify white supremacy. In Oklahoma as in other states of the region, a sense of being better than all the non-whites became the last bastion of hope for otherwise dispossessed, white, landless farmers.[60] The presence of "colored" people on the bottom, including and identified with blacks, trumped any notions of a middling status for browns and reinforced the national black-white dichotomy.

Instead of examining brown/black/white racial subtleties, white Oklahomans celebrated their superiority. Self-acknowledged Okie Roxanne Dunbar-Ortiz wrote of the glue that bound Okies together: a shared enthusiasm for "country music, evangelism, romanticism, patriotism and white supremacy." Growing up in Oklahoma, she never heard the term "white trash" until she saw *Gone with the Wind*. The film portrayed low-class whites as "some pretty creepy people, dirt poor, sneaking, conniving, violent tenant farmers, or perhaps migrant cotton pickers. At the time I saw the movie my father was alternately a tenant farmer, migrant cotton picker and ranch hand, but I did not for one minute identify with those whom the planters and the enslaved Africans called 'white trash.' I identified with Scarlett."[61]

THE WORLD THE OKIES ENTERED

California once had been a desirable destination for people from all walks of life. Well before the Great Depression, southern Midwesterners were no strangers to California. "By 1910, 103,241 Southwesterners, two-thirds of them Missourians, were already living in California. More than 300,000 others joined them during the big surge of the 1910s and 1920s."[62] These emigrants wrote home about their prosperity; sometimes other family members joined them. Likewise, the cotton culture, with which many of the Okies were intimately familiar, also entered California at this time, dominated by large-scale agriculturists, most originally from the American South. By 1920, five nationally based firms controlled the California cotton industry; by 1925, four home-grown cotton magnates were challenging the control of the majors.[63] However, the more sobering fact hidden in this story of competitive success was that only nine companies controlled virtually all of California cotton.

The same pattern prevailed in the cultivation of all other crops, and by the 1930s California had a solidified agricultural system based on large landholdings, migrant labor, and a repeated failure to subdivide huge estates to provide land for the landless poor. In the 1930s, economist Paul Schuster Taylor of the University of California at Berkeley noted that almost four-fifths of California's crops grown in 1929 were the result of intensive agriculture, not family farms. He added that "More than one-third of all large scale farms in the entire country are located in California in 1930."[64]

This system had developed despite arguments, begun by economist Henry George in the 1870s, that this pattern of landholding encouraged a reprehensible social imbalance. To rectify this problem, state attempts at creating rural communities rather than agribusiness began shortly before World War I. A Commission on Land Colonization and Rural Credits, created in 1915, issued a critical report a year later. It claimed that the holding of 4 million acres of land by just 310 proprietors had led to arrested rural development. In order to achieve political stability and satisfactory social conditions, two demonstration agricultural colonies were attempted at Durham and Delhi (the latter in direct competition with the nearby Japanese colony at Livingston). Neither was a conspicuous success.[65] The State Commission on Immigration and Housing in 1919 even recommended that a graduated tax on unimproved land value would encourage subdivision, but in the economic roller coaster of the 1920s, this suggestion died.[66]

The state simultaneously tried to deal with the transient poor, many of whom were the result of reliance on migrant labor by California agribusiness. In 1901, the California State Legislature passed its first Indigent Persons Act, prompted by a request from the San Joaquin County sheriff and his deputies to "solve the tramp question."[67] A 1913 survey of cheap San Francisco boardinghouses found nearly 40,000 single men and boys holed up for the winter, after the harvest had ended. A concurrent survey in other cities located almost 25,000 more in Los Angeles, and lesser numbers in Stockton, Fresno, and Bakersfield.[68] A year later, the State Commission on Immigration and Housing convened by Governor Hiram Johnson again found severe unemployment, especially in the winter months. When the Commission interviewed 222 laid-off migratory workers, almost one-fourth of them admitted having lost their last regular job somewhere outside the state, but had come here believing: "You cannot freeze to death in California; you cannot starve to death in California."[69] A resultant governor's directive to begin a relief program for the unemployed was accompanied by a vigorous press campaign that stressed that "California offered no special inducements, either of relief or of employment."[70]

Sixteen years later, the Great Depression undercut all such governmental attempts at amelioration. The goal became survival, pitting the physical survival of the Okies against the survival of California's baronial landholding system. Each contradictory impulse got some support. Never immune to human misery, the state took the lead in unemployment relief. It created the State Emergency Relief Administration in 1931, establishing approximately 250 migratory labor camps, of which two were outstanding demonstration projects. But Mexicans were not welcome at these state-sponsored facilities, and an estimated 160,000 Mexicans were repatriated (or, in the case of American-born children of Mexicans, exiled).[71] The Federal Emergency Relief Act passed in 1933, with a subsidiary Federal Transient Service.[72] Already pressed to provide relief, Californians hoped this federal legislation would help migrants in their state.

At the same time, conditions in the fields grew more desperate. Cotton, a crop familiar to the Okies, serves as one example of falling wages and increasing labor dislocation. In 1928, cotton pickers earned $1 per hundred pounds, which dropped to 40 cents per hundred pounds in 1932. Prices mirrored this drop: in 1927 cotton was worth 20 cents a pound; by 1932, only 6 cents. As a result, many small growers lost their farms and joined the migrant labor force, spreading the grip of poverty. The federal National Recovery Act of 1933 explicitly excluded agricultural workers; from the fieldworkers' perspective, there was nothing left to do but strike.[73] A previously quiescent labor force stood at the edge of desperation in 1933. Not only had jobs evaporated, wages, if available, had bottomed out, and workers had to maintain residency in order to obtain any measure of relief. So, hundreds of them struck for better wages in the cotton fields in 1933 and 1934 under the leadership of the Cannery and Agricultural Workers Industrial Union (CAWIU).[74] Between April and December 1933, thirty-seven such strikes, involving roughly 50,000 Mexicans and whites, shook California agriculture. In Pixley, growers killed three men and wounded eight others. In Arvin, one striker was shot to death. Photographs depicting the ugly incidents appeared in newspapers throughout the country, bringing pressure on the growers for the first time to consider the welfare of their workers.[75] Federal mediation led to a pay raise and the end of the strike, but the union was not recognized.[76] In 1934, 3,600 Mexican vegetable pickers struck in the Imperial Valley.[77] Then, on August 27, 1934, a strike by lettuce pickers began in Salinas as Mexican, white, and Filipino laborers walked out of the fields.[78] As in the 1933 strikes, vigilante violence targeted the strikers. A binding agreement was finally forged covering the period from October 1934 to September 1935. Nonetheless, prejudice remained high against ethnic workers, as reflected by a Salinas sign, "This is a White Man's County. Get Out of Here if You Don't Like What We Pay."[79]

While 1935 was relatively quiet in the fields, the federal think tanks kept churning out ideas to combat the depression. In April 1935, the federal government instituted the Resettlement Administration to implement "the resettlement of destitute or low income families, in both rural and urban areas, . . . land conservation projects, . . . [and help] farm families on relief become independent by extending to them both financial and technical assistance."[80] The Resettlement Administration then took over California's two demonstration camps and added thirteen more permanent settlements and five "Mobile Camps," which could be moved to the area of greatest need.[81] The hope existed that, combined with the Transient Service, drifters could be aided and resettled. Then, on on September 30, 1935, the Federal Transient Service was disbanded when appropriations dried up.[82]

The California legislature, while providing its own "carrot" of aid to workers, also legislated a "shield" to keep others out. In June 1933, it had passed a revised version of the 1901 Indigent Act, which made it a misde-

meanor to bring a known indigent into California. Increasingly, this statute was vigorously enforced, not against big growers but against individuals
who brought family members to California.[83] Since the preferred destination for most of these migrants remained southern California, Los Angeles police chief James E. Davis came up with his own response. He reasoned
that if California could not take care of the Okies, the only solution was
physically to keep them out. He sent more than one hundred of his own
men to staff border crossings, instituting what became widely known as
the "bum patrol." Under intense pressure from a variety of sources, including the American Association of Social Workers, the American Civil Lib-
erties Union, the governor of Nevada, the attorneys general of Arizona and
Oregon, and the chief of the California Highway Patrol, the Los Angeles
police were withdrawn in April 1936.[84]

Meanwhile, hundreds of thousands of willing workers continued to
pour into California, most of them now "Okies." Those coming by mo-
tor vehicle could be counted; one study found that 259,654 migrants in
need of employment entered the state from June 16, 1935 to December 31,
1937.[85] Additional thousands rode the rails, walked, and otherwise slipped
across the border uncounted. In the winter of 1935–36, according to a state
survey, "69,731 transients and homeless asked for aid from 124 public and
private agencies in 19 cities in California."[86] This survey covered only half
the state and made an incomplete count of those turned away. In short, the
human deluge was reaching crisis proportions. Most who landed in California could not afford the trip back home and were willing to take any
job offered. Initially, Californians were ambivalent about the presence of
the Okies. One train of thought claimed that they would claim the "white
man's right," long articulated, to a permanent home and a piece of land,
that they would demand higher wages [from the large growers] than foreigners, and would not submit to being "tractable labor." On the other
hand, reasoned others, the sheer number of Okies might be the answer to
the growers' problems with increasingly demanding Mexican and Filipino
laborers. Acting on the latter assumption, Joseph DiGiorgio, one of the
state's largest growers, openly hired Okie labor in 1936.[87] Other growers
followed suit, and the Okies, hungry, tired, but stubbornly willing to work,
suddenly became the mainstay of California agricultural labor.

S TIGMATIZING   O KIES

By the summer of 1939, a sign appeared in a San Joaquin Valley theater foyer: "Negroes and Okies upstairs."[88] What, Okies asked, had happened? How could poor southern whites who maintained their social
standing largely by seeing themselves as better than blacks arrive at this
level in California?

The answer lies in racial perceptions of the period. Despite common illusions of white supremacy in the 1930s, the southern Midwest and California had very different concepts of a racial hierarchy. In reality as well as on film, only two races, whites and blacks, generally inhabited the South. When the other races were present, such as in Texas and Oklahoma, they endured the same sort of legal discrimination and segregation approved nationwide by the *Plessey* decision. In the country as a whole, whites, including Okies, felt superior.

Multicultural California had a whole different perspective on race. The racial hierarchy in the fields has already been described: white growers at the top, a variety of brown people at the bottom. African Americans lived largely in urban areas; they did not figure in the racial equation. But even California cities were different from those Okies knew "back home." Los Angeles, the home of Hollywood and the cradle of the bum patrol, was, in many ways, the greatest crucible for change.

Different views there were fostered, in part, by sudden, unprecedented growth. More than 2.5 million people poured into California between 1920 and 1930, most to Los Angeles, which grew in population from roughly 100,000 at the turn of the century to 1.2 million by 1930.[89] Most of these new residents came from largely white states like Illinois and Iowa, bringing with them less-pronounced racial prejudices than their southern counterparts.[90] In California, they saw few African Americans.

The number of blacks in California had remained relatively low. After their inhospitable reception in the 1850s, African American migration to California had slowed to a trickle. When they began to arrive, starting in the 1880s, they, too, predominately chose Los Angeles, creating what was known as a Pullman Car colony of middle-class, railroad-employed individuals. But even in L.A., their numbers remained small: only 188 in 1880, 7,599 in 1910, 30,893 in 1930—this in a city of 1.2 million persons. They unobtrusively mixed with the newly arrived whites, building a different type of urban society. According to Carey McWilliams, "Los Angeles by 1900 had outgrown most of its early hostility toward Negroes. A tradition survives that Los Angeles was one of the first, if not the first, city in America to employ Negro firemen and policemen."[91] Given this atmosphere, California blacks remained a largely urban population. They avoided the racist jungle of fieldwork, where, allegedly, "'the Japanese and Mexicans drew off much of the racial hostility which otherwise might have been concentrated on the Negroes.'"[92]

In other words, Japanese and Mexicans, as already shown, were at the bottom of society in the fields. When the Okies entered California, they entered a world that shocked them. They were appalled by what they saw as "race mixing"; they shuddered at working side by side with Mexicans.[93] Yet they fought for any work they could get. Some of them went to work for Japanese landowners.[94] They often refused to join unions for racist reasons; as one woman put it, "you can't equalize me with no nigger."[95] Okies considered blacks as the lowest social class and were unaware of the California hierarchy. In fact, some Okies insisted they would not take a job that "niggers would do." Secure in their racial status above African Americans, they instead took jobs even less prestigious than the work blacks were doing in California. Okies went to the fields to do work they knew well, undercutting Mexican and Filipinos, unknowingly assuming the very lowest rung of the social ladder.

Now, the rest of white California, appalled by Okie fieldworkers' deprivation, had to make a decision. Either they paid the Okies a "white man's wage" to provide them the "American lifestyle" of a cottage and garden, or they had to justify their refusal to do so. In 1933, it took nothing short of a strike involving 18,000 pickers, lasting 27 days, spreading over 100 miles and four counties, and forcing federal arbitration to effect higher wages in California cotton fields.[96] No voluntary wage increase, no matter the race of the employee, was going to be forthcoming. Furthermore, unlike previous migrant groups, the Okies did not withdraw to the cities once the seasonal fieldwork was done. Instead, they stayed near the farms, even though the residents of nearby towns were inhospitable to them.[97] Their poverty became increasingly visible. One letter received by the Rural Resettlement Administration described "inadequate . . . care for the influx of pickers" and whole families "squatted out . . . without any sanitary conditions what-so-ever." It added, "Some of these people are living in tents, some in improvised shelters made up of cardboard packing cased [sic] and burlap and anything that can be picked up in the junk pile, and in such places as these women and children are sleeping on the ground."[98] These living conditions were nothing new for those who toiled in California's factories in the fields, but they had been unremarkable to the majority until white people lived that way.

In the desperate days of the Great Depression, the growers came to an uncomfortable realization: no longer would white skin keep anyone from sliding to the bottom of society. For the white elite, the repeated excuse for providing pickers poor wages and working conditions—that the brown races were getting all they deserved—had just evaporated. In the face of the growers' unwillingness or inability to provide better wages and working conditions, the only other alternative was to stigmatize Okies.

California opinion makers rose to the challenge. For example, Madera's health director warned against providing Okies with houses of more than one room, because they would tear down the partitions. He added, "One has to deal with a people whose cultural and environmental background is so bad that for a period of more than three hundred years no advances have been made in living conditions among them . . . [in spite of living] in close proximity to an advancing civilization and culture."[99] In short order, the ignorant, bigoted, bumpkin became the stereotype representing *all* Okies, and the image entered art, literature, movies, and the public consciousness. This image has taken three generations to mellow.

Neither Dorothea Lange, John Steinbeck, Paul Schuster Taylor, nor Carey McWilliams was seeking to stigmatize Okies by their portrayals. In fact, the film version of *The Grapes of Wrath,* at the hands of director John Ford and screenwriter Nunnally Johnson, conveyed quite a different message than the novel that inspired it. "By having the Joads arrive at the peach ranch before the government camp (reversing the order of events in Steinbeck's narrative), Johnson traces a progression from the squalor of the Hooverville to the oppression of the peach ranch to the benevolence of a government camp."[100] The end of the film is far more optimistic than that of the novel. In the former, the Joads become part of a great movement of people. The final image is that of a parade of cars and trucks moving out, with the still-pregnant Rose of Sharon presumably "making it" along with the rest of the family. The final soliloquy belongs to Tom Joad, the main protagonist: "Wherever there's a fight so hungry people can eat, I'll be there. . . . I'll be in the way kids laugh when they're hungry an' they know supper's ready. An' when our people eat the stuff they raise, an' live in the houses they build, why I'll be there too."[101] Here, again, is the good old "American dream" of "a cottage and a garden," as expressed as far back as the 1888 study of the desires of a white agricultural workforce. In the thirties, for the Okies, it was only a dream.

In his factual study written at the same time as Steinbeck's novel, Carey McWilliams acknowledged the unpleasant reality facing California's migrant farm workers. As McWilliams wrote in his *Factories in the Fields,* he hoped for "The End of A Cycle," in which the white race of the Okies would trump a long history of discrimination in agricultural work. He concluded:

> There is no longer any equivocation in California: The problem of migratory labor, dramatized and intensified by the influx of dust-bowl refugees, has forced public recognition of an acute social problem. . . . The race problem has, in effect, been largely eliminated. . . . The anachronistic system of ownership by which they [the workers] are at present controlled must be changed.

Even McWilliams acknowledged, however, "That day, as it now seems, is far distant."[102] He was correct. Race did not triumph over economic interest. In 1970, Walter Packard, the former national director of the Rural Resettlement Administration, was asked to reflect back on the success of his agency. He said that in California it was "not very successful," since few farms had been established due to lack of available land. The pattern of large landholdings and poorly paid workers had not altered since the 1930s. He added that labor organization and collective bargaining was the only route to better conditions. When the interviewer suggested, "The Delano strikers are doing something about that," Packard replied, "They sure are, and they deserve public backing."[103] This brief reference to "the Delano strikers" encompassed the new agricultural labor movement of the sixties, in which Filipinos, Mexicans, and others made common cause as fieldworkers in opposition to the big growers. Their inception at Delano, between Fresno and Bakersfield, marked their strongly felt presence in California's Central Valley. By 1967 their union, the United Farm Workers of America, through a national boycott of table grapes, had successfully negotiated field labor contracts for the very first time. Yet those strikers, led by Larry Itliong, Cesar Chavez, and Dolores Huerta, were Filipinos and Mexicans.[104] Where were the Okies?

THE OKIE LEGACY

Due to their own strong efforts, white skin, and the passage of time, the Okies became assimilated in California, and California became molded to the Okies. This dual transformation took place concurrently. First of all, California prospered as the nation boomed economically in World War II. The American West—the nation's "underdeveloped region"—attracted ample federal defense dollars and, within this region, California benefited most of all. Consider, the national government spent $60 billion in the West between 1940 and 1945, with almost half of this amount enriching California to develop an aircraft industry, maintain military installations, and support a wide range of war-related work.[105] In this economic upsurge, everybody got jobs, including Okies. Therefore, the poverty that had originally marked them as California's "white underclass" gradually disappeared. At the same time, earlier Okie segregation had created strong cultural bonds that carried through subsequent generations. In hard times, Okie strength could be found in their religion, their music, their southern origins marked by their speech patterns and cadences.[106] These distinctive qualities became a source of pride, lifted to national prominence by musician Merle Haggard. Born in Bakersfield, California in 1937 of parents who had left Oklahoma in 1934, Haggard spent a checkered boyhood in and out of jail, turning twenty-one in San Quentin Prison.[107] When he got out, he threw his energy into his music, topping national charts in 1969 with "Okie from Muskogee." According to historian James Noble Gregory, "Conservatives loved it. Hailing its flag-waving slams at hippies, draft-dodgers, and campus radicals, President Nixon [another California native] sent him a letter of congratulations."[108] Writer Gerald Haslam summed up his career to date: "By 1995 Haggard had written forty-two number-one songs, the second-largest total in the history of this [country] music and produced perhaps the finest repertoire written by anyone in the country."[109] Through his achievements and those of many others, including Gene Autry,

Bob Wills, Buck Owens, and, recently, Dwight Yoakam, among others, California has become known as "Nashville West," the home of a special, California brand of music.[110] Californians' attitudes and Okie predilections melded in other ways, too. The huge war industries boom of World War II brought unprecedented numbers of African Americans to California, particularly to the Los Angeles region. Partly to control this influx, the Los Angeles police force hired Okies or their children, some of whom retained strong views of white supremacy over blacks. These racial attitudes emerged in a confrontation recounted by self-described Okie, Roxanne Dunbar-Ortiz, during the height of the anti-Vietnam War protests and hippie counterculture. She and a [non-white, male] foreign student friend were stopped by Los Angeles police suspecting a curfew violation:

> My friend had the good sense to raise his arms, palms open, way above his head, and I followed suit. However, the cops remained in firing position. . . . But they gave themselves away: I recognized the way they moved, the way they talked, not just their Okie accents but as if they moved and talked in slow motion, compared with most Californians I knew. . . . I was no longer scared, I said, "Where y'll from? I'm from near El Reno." The effect was immediate. Suddenly the two cops . . . became friendly Okies. We chatted. . . . their parents had been Dust Bowl Okies from Choctaw and from Prague in southeastern Oklahoma . . . and then they drove away. They never even checked our identification.[111]

Dunbar-Ortiz herself embodies another side of the Okie character—the racial solidarity traced back to Oklahoma's Green Corn Rebellion. Thus, the two sides of the coin found each other in Los Angeles. The Okies had become Californians.

Many Okies, like Dunbar-Ortiz (a professor at Cal State Hayward) combined a sense of compassion with a love of education. David Smith, founder of the Haight-Ashbury Free Clinic, was born in Bakersfield in 1939. As he described his background: "My grandparents lost their farm in Oklahoma and came out to California, where they were farmworkers. So I had that strict, "Grapes of Wrath" Okie background. . . . In the Central Valley of Bakersfield, there was a lot of discrimination against Okies." He added:

> This had a far greater impact than I realized because it had such an enormous impact on my parents, especially my mother. . . . She described humiliating experiences during the Depression when she and her sisters went out with my grandmother to the fields to try to get a job. The boss asked, "What can you do?" and my grandmother, who I love dearly said, "We'll do anything." The most consistent message I heard from my mother when I was growing up was, "never say you will do 'anything.' Say you are something, like a doctor or a dentist."[112]

Smith fulfilled his mother's dreams, getting his medical degree at the University of San Francisco and simultaneously earning a master's degree in pharmacology. On the way to these achievements, he had moved from a binge-drinking alcoholic to taking hallucinogens. He was working at San Francisco General Hospital during the 1967 "summer of love" and remembers walking home at night, after doing research on LSD, past "these thousands of kids" high on the same drug. This made him realize that "love needs care." Consequently, on May 13, 1967, he incorporated the Haight-Ashbury Free Clinic. It opened its doors on June 7 with fifty people already waiting in line. The medical clinic is still open; it is still free, and there are 300 more like it.[113] In a 1996 interview, the internationally recognized Smith articulated what it felt like to be an Okie descendent in California. He said "I am beginning to realize that I started the clinic to heal myself; that I identified with these outsiders. No matter how much I accomplished externally, I had this void, feeling different; feeling 'not as good as.' . . . The clinic . . . became the centerpoint of my life and helped heal the void, although I didn't understand that at the time."[114]

For a long time, like Woody Guthrie and Dave Smith, no one felt good about being an Okie. Since the original Okie stereotype was partly the product of creative sources, it is fitting that much of Okie rehabilitation has been literary. The prose giant of Okie portrayal is Gerald Haslam; in poetry, Wilma Elizabeth McDaniel. In describing his hometown of Oildale, Haslam, a retired Sonoma State University professor, writes:

> Oildale has been to Bakersfield as Bakersfield has been to California, a scapegoat; "You're from *Oildale*?" I've heard at genteel parties, tone saying it all. . . . In Oildale you cannot be unaware of this nation's class system because this is a cusp where hopelessness and hope, or at least the *hope* of hope, abut . . . [But] most of Oildale is populated by folks who have established themselves in the middle class by dint of hard work. . . . Oildale's citizens pay their taxes, frequently resent welfare and shake their heads at punk rock, at "Fit 'n' Forty" medallions, at sprout sandwiches, but accept the churning present anyway.[115]

In Oildale, Bakersfield, Modesto of the Central Valley; over in Salinas, and wherever Okies worked and settled, their voices and dreams remain. Roxanne Dunbar-Ortiz, who wrote *Red Dirt: Growing Up Okie*, admits, "[I]t wasn't often that I revealed my roots. . . . Even when I began working on this book I still had no desire for any relationship or interchange with those people like me out there. . . . I identified myself as working class, part poor white, part Indian, anything but 'Okie.' Then I met Wilma Elizabeth McDaniel,"[116] who wrote from life:

Picking Grapes 1937

Magic seventeen
and new in California

working in bursting
sweet vineyards

hot sand on soul
one strap held by a
safety pin

a girl could be whatever
she desired

the first breath of
Eve in Paradise

the last gasp of Jean Harlow
in Hollywood.[117]

Hollywood—the maker of dreams, the purveyor of stereotypes, the creator of a fantastical South from which the Okies never came. Myth and reality each have their own, strong grasp on the American mind. For the Okies, it is time to sort out the difference.

Notes

1   "Owner Gets $37,500 from state after legal battle with CalTrans," *Merced Sun-Star,* Oct. 31, 1991.
2   Charles J. Shindo, *Dust Bowl Migrants in the American Imagination* (Lawrence: University Press of Kansas, 1997), 2–3.
3   John Steinbeck, *The Grapes of Wrath* (New York: Viking Press, 1939), 213.
4   Steinbeck, 472–73.
5   Shindo, 132–141, 167–188; Alan Lomax, *Woody Guthrie: The Library of Congress Recordings* (Washington, D.C.: Department of the Interior, 1940).
6   Clayton Troy Wyse, letter to the editor, *Okemah News Leader,* April 30, 1989.
7   James Noble Gregory, *American Exodus* (New York: Oxford University Press, 1989), 15.
8   Gregory, 5–12.
9   Ibid.
10 Shindo, 5–10.
11 Migratory agricultural workers in Arizona, New Mexico, and Texas also experienced prejudice, but such hatred never reached public consciousness or lingered as long in those places as it did in California. See Works Progress Administration, *Migratory Workers of the Southwest* (Westport, Conn.: Greenwood Press, 1978).
12 Edward Bellamy, *Looking Backward, 2000–1887.* Edited and with an Introduction by Daniel H. Borus (New York: Bedford Books of St. Martin's Press, 1995), 34–35.

13 See James Rawls, *The Indians of California: The Changing Image* (Norman: University of Oklahoma Press, 1984), especially 171–201; Albert L. Hurtado, *Indian Survival on the California Frontier* (New Haven: Yale University Press, 1988), especially 211–18.

14 The best example of this is the Archy Lee case. See George H. Tinkham, *California Men and Events* (Stockton: Record Publishing Company, 1915), 134–37; Hubert Howe Bancroft, *History of California,* Vol. VI (San Francisco: The History Company, 1888), 715, n.52.

15 Leonard Pitt, *The Decline of the Californios* (Berkeley: University of California Press, 1970), 60–82; Tinkham, 127–34.

16 Pitt, 83–119.

17 Steinbeck, 211.

18 David Lavender, *The Great Persuader* (Garden City, N.Y.: Doubleday & Company, 1970), 74–76, 100–243; Oscar Lewis, *The Big Four* (New York: Alfred A. Knopf, 1938, reprint, 1959).

19 Edward D. C. Campbell, Jr., *The Celluloid South* (Knoxville: University of Tennessee Press, 1981), 3–72.

20 Pitt, 244–48.

21 Wallace Smith, *The Garden of the Sun* (Fresno: Max Hardison—A–1 Printers, 1939), 217–258.

22 Smith, 251.

23 Edward F. Treadwell, *The Cattle King* (Fresno: Valley Publishers, 1931), 319–329.

24 Alexander Saxton, *The Indispensable Enemy* (Berkeley: University of California Press, 1971), 117–18.

25 Saxton, 174–78.

26 From an editorial in the *Pacific Rural Press*, XXVI (September 8, 1883), 29, quoted in Varden Fuller, *Hired Hands in California's Farm Fields* (Berkeley: Giannini Foundation, 1991), 12.

27 Quoted in Fuller, 12.

28 From an editorial in the *Pacific Rural Press* (February 11, 1888), quoted in Fuller, 16.

29 Ibid., 21–30.

30 Kesa Noda, *Yamato Colony: 1906–1960* (Merced: Livingston-Merced JACL Chapter, 1981), 1–15; Valerie J. Matsumoto, *Farming the Home Place* (Ithaca: Cornell University Press, 1993), 29–31.

31 Edward K. Strong, Jr., *The Second-Generation Japanese Problem* (Stanford: Stanford University Press, 1934; reprint, New York: Arno Press, 1970), 42–45.

32 Carey McWilliams, *Factories in the Fields* (1939; reprint, Santa Barbara: Peregrine Smith, Inc., 1971), 17–18. Although McWilliams used the commonly accepted term of his day, *Hindu,* most of these immigrants were of the Sikh religion. See Karen Leonard, "California's Punjabi-Mexican Americans, 1910s–1970s," in Sucheng Chan et al., eds. *Peoples of Color in the American West* (Lexington, Mass.: D.C. Heath and Company, 1994), 308–320.

33 Ibid., 119.

34 Fuller, 52–53.

35 Howard De Witt, *Violence in the Fields* (Saratoga, Calif.: Century Twenty One Publishing, 1980), 32–37.

36 Fuller, 50.

37 Devra Weber, *Dark Sweat, White Gold* (Berkeley: University of California Press, 1994), 35.

38 Fuller, 50–51.

39 Chester Rowell, "Western Windows to the East," *Survey* LVI (1926): 174.

40 Paul Schuster Taylor, "Mexican Labor in the United States: Migration Statistics, IV," *University of California, Publications in Economics,* Vol. 12, No. 3 (Berkeley 1934): 24–25. The most recent study is Francisco E. Balderrama and Raymond Rodriguez, *Decade of Betrayal* (Albuquerque: University of New Mexico Press, 1995).

41 Strong, 133, 135–150.

42 Strong, 151.

43 Carey McWilliams, *Prejudice* (Boston: Little, Brown and Company, 1945), 70.

44 Bancroft, 288.

45 Delilah L. Beasley, *The Negro Trail Blazers of California* (Los Angeles: n.p., 1919), 82. See also Eugene H. Berwanger, *The Frontier Against Slavery* (Urbana: University of Illinois Press, 1967), especially Chapter 3, "El Dorado."

46 Tinkham, 134–37; Beasley, 78.

47 Bancroft, 718–739.

48 John Hays Hammond, *The Autobiography of John Hays Hammond* (New York: Farrar & Rinehart, 1935), 18.

49 C. Vann Woodward, *The Strange Career of Jim Crow*, 2nd. rev. ed. (London: Oxford University Press, 1966).

50 Strong, 46.

51 Lewis Jacobs, *The Rise of the American Film* (New York: Columbia Teachers College Press, 1968), 35.

52 *Ibid*, 38–39.

53 Ibid., 39.

54 Ibid., 46.

55 *Ibid*, 58.

56 *Ibid*, 60, 19.

57 *Ibid*, 90, 15.

58 Roxanne Dunbar-Ortiz, *Red Dirt: Growing Up Okie* (London: Verso, 1997), 15–18.

59 Donald A. Grinde and Quintard Taylor, "Slaves, Freedmen, and Native Americans in Indian Territory (Oklahoma), 1865–1907," in Chan et al., eds., 299.

60 Dunbar-Ortiz, 15–17, 46–48.

61 Ibid., 47.

62 Gregory, 8.

63 Weber, 22–23.

64 Quoted in Walter E. Packard, "Land and Power Development in California, Greece, and Latin America," interviewed by Willa Klug Baum, Berkeley, California, 1970, Regional Oral History Office, Bancroft Library, University of California, Berkeley, 309 [hereafter Packard interview].

65 Fuller, 40–41; James R. Kluger, *Turning on Water with a Shovel* (Albuquerque: University of New Mexico Press, 1992), 85–101.

66 Fuller, 41.

67 *California Statutes*, 1901, ch. 210, 636–38; "Some Legislation Sheriffs Want," *Stockton Daily Indpendent*, December 20, 1900.

68 *Interstate Migration Hearings . . . Pursuant to H. Res. 63 and H. Res. 491*, Pt. 6, San Francisco Hearings, September 24 and 25, 1940 (Washington, D. C.: Government Printing Office, 1941), 2234.

69 Quoted in Fuller, 39.

70 Fuller, 39.

71 McWilliams, *Factories*, 285, 296–97.

72 California State Relief Administration, *Transients in California* (San Francisco, 1936), 3. [Hereafter cited as SRA Report].

73 Weber, 80.

74 Paul Schuster Taylor, *On the Ground in the Thirties* (Salt Lake City: Peregrine Smith Books, 1983), 17–168; McWilliams, *Factories*, 285.

75 Cletus E. Daniel, *Bitter Harvest* (Ithaca: Cornell University Press, 1981), 141–166; Weber, 80, 100–101.

76 Weber, 104–11.

77 Stein, 224.

78 De Witt, 85.

79 Ibid., 99.

80 Quoted in Packard interview, 303.

81 Packard interview, 311a.

82 SRA Report, 24–25.

83 Nancy J. Taniguchi, "California's Anti-Okie Law: An Interpretive Biography, *Western Legal History* Vol. 8, No. 2 (Summer/Fall 1995): 278.

84 Ibid., 278–281.

85 Taylor, 225.

86 SRA Report, 285.

87 Stein, 226–28.

88 Ibid., 63.

89 Gregory, 7–8.

90 Carey McWilliams, *Southern California: An Island on the Land* (Salt Lake City: Peregrine Smith, 1973), 165–175. [Hereafter cited as *So Cal.*].

91 McWiliams, *So Cal*, 324.

92 Ibid., 325.

93 Weber, 149.

94 Interview with Izumi Taniguchi, September 13, 1998, Merced, California.

95 Quoted in Weber, 149. Some Okies were involved in the two main strikes in 1936 and 1937, in the Salinas lettuce packing sheds and Stockton's canneries, respectively. But most of the strikers were Mexicans and Filipinos. See Stein, 229–38.

96 Weber, 79.

97 Dan Morgan, *Rising in the West* (New York: Alfred A. Knopf, 1992), 72.

98 John Thompson to Jonothan [sic] Garst, 7 December 1937, Record Group 96 Farm Security Administration–San Francisco, General Correspondence 1940–1942, Box 2, Folder "General Suggestions, Cal., Kern County," National Archives Pacific Sierra Branch, San Bruno, CA.

99 Quoted in Stein, 60–61.

100 Shindo, 164.

101 Quoted in Shindo, 162.

102 McWilliams, *Factories*, 319–25.

103 Packard interview, 318–320.

104 Melvyn Dubofsky and Foster Rhea Dulles, *Labor in America*, 6th ed. (Wheeling, Ill.: Harlan Davidson, Inc., 1999), 374; see also Richard Griswold del Castillo and Richard A. Garcia, *Cesar Chavez: A Triumph of the Spirit* (Norman: University of Oklahoma Press, 1995).

105 Gerald D. Nash, *The Federal Landscape* (Tucson: University of Arizona Press, 1999), 42.

106 Gregory, 172–248.

107 Gerald W. Haslam, *Workin' Man's Blues* (Berkeley: University of California Press, 1999), 247–52.

108 Gregory, 239.

109 Haslam, *Blues*, 253.

110 Haslam, *Blues*, especially 13–24, 309–314; Gregory 241.

111 Dunbar-Ortiz, 221–22.

112 Richard Fields, "David E. Smith: The Quiet Revolution," *Professional Counselor*, April 1996, 8, enclosed in David E. Smith to Nancy Taniguchi, 13 May 1996.

113 Clark S. Sturges, *Dr. Dave* (Walnut Creek, Calif.: Devil Mountain Books, 1993), 2–5, 30–32, 40–41, 55–58; "Health Care Still Considered a Right at Free Clinic," *San Francisco Chronicle*, June 6, 1999; "The Haight's Community Clinic," *San Francisco Chronicle*, September 1, 1997.

114 Fields, 9.

115 Gerald Haslam, "Oildale," in Stan Yogi, ed., *Highway 99* (Berkeley: Heyday Books, 1996), 288, 290, 291.

116 Dunbar-Ortiz, 221.

117 Wilma Elizabeth McDaniel, "Picking Grapes 1937," in Yogi, ed., 64.

CHAPTER NINE

The Los Angeles Zoot-Suit Riots: Latin America Responds *

Ricardo Griswold del Castillo

In June of 1943, hundreds of United States servicemen went on a two-week rampage in Los Angeles, California, attacking scores of Mexican American youths clothed in the "Zoot-Suit" style. These civil disturbances were significant in a number of ways: the incidents constituted one of the largest riots involving Mexican Americans up to that time; the violent acts made Latin Americans aware, many for the first time, of the plight of Mexicans in the United States; and they proved a dramatic watershed in the cultural history of Chicanos, marking the political emergence of a large United States–born population of Mexican descent—one no longer willing to tolerate stereotyping and violence by their fellow Americans. In California history, this episode has been interpreted by Chicano historians as one in a long series of anti-Mexican reactions motivated by wartime frustrations and racism. In this case, however, the local news media and police, as well as city, state, and federal government officials, were responsible for fostering an anti-Mexican atmosphere and fueling the violence.[1]

But while there have been numerous studies of the implications of the Zoot-Suit riots in California and United States history, few scholars have considered the international significance of this event.[2] Nevertheless, there is a considerable body of information bearing on this topic, one that until recently has been fully exploited by historians. Thanks to files in the archives of the *Secretaria de Relaciones Exteriores* in Mexico City, it is possible to examine in detail the Mexican government's response to this affair. Also available are voluminous files from the U.S. Federal Bureau of Investigation (FBI) and the Department of State dealing with the suspected involvement of foreign agents in the riots, and providing an in-depth analysis of the social and political situation surrounding the Mexican colony in Los Angeles. Finally, there are the little-known or analyzed responses of the Latin American press—during and after the riots—as well as the commen-

*Parts of this essay originally appeared in *Mexican Studies/Estudios Mexicanos*, Vol. 16, No. 2. © 2000 by The Regents of the University of California. Reprinted by permission of the University of California Press.

Looking to pull off people dressed in zoot suits, a crowd of servicemen surrounds a trolley on Main Street, Los Angeles, during the Zoot-Suit Riots of June 1943. *Los Angeles Times Photo.*

tary and reporting about the disturbances in U.S. based Spanish-language newspapers.

These sources reveal and confirm that the whole episode was a deep embarrassment for both the Mexican and U.S. governments. For its part, the Mexican government could not adopt a strong position protesting the disturbances because of their wartime alliance with the United States. Indeed, the Mexican government's initial statements of concern were not followed by formal proceedings to produce a diplomatic protest, a public apology from U.S. officials, or compensation for damages. On the other side of the border, the riots sparked an intense effort on the part of the U.S. government to find foreign agents who might have been responsible for provoking them, as well as an official denial that racism underlay the violence.

Throughout Latin America, reaction to the riots ranged from anti-government protests to anti–Zoot-Suit diatribes. Many Latin American students seemingly identified with the Mexican youths victimized during the riots. And despite the best efforts of both the Mexican and U.S. government, the Latin American press often portrayed the whole affair as proof of the racial prejudice of white Americans toward Indian-stock mestizos. Indeed, some Latin American classifications of Mexican Americans reveal a degree of class prejudice against the so-called *Pachucos*. In any case, the riots alerted the general public in Mexico and other Latin American nations to the serious discrimination suffered by Mexican Americans.

During the late 1930s and World War II, the press in California usually referred to young Mexican Americans either as *Mexicans* or *Pachucos*, depending on the circumstances. The term *Chicano* was almost exclusively used by barrio residents to refer to recently arrived Mexican immigrants. Within the Mexican neighborhoods of large California cities such as Los Angeles, young people were in the process of rebelling against their parent's conventional values. In so doing, the young Mexican Americans created their own subculture, adopting their own music, language, and style of dress. The men favored an outfit known as a zoot suit, featuring a flamboyant longcoat, baggy tapered pants, a pork pie hat, a long key chain worn outside the pocket, and big, thick-soled shoes. They called themselves *Paychecks*, a term of unknown origin but generally referring to United States–born Mexican youths who dressed in the trendy style and spoke *Calo*, a highly inventive slang composed of English and Spanish.[3] Undoubtedly Pachuquismo had its origins in poverty and racism and the Pachuco gangs were bound to defined territories, as much by discrimination as by love of the barrio.

In the early 1940s, especially in Southern California, fears over Pachuco gangs had been mounting in white communities, as manifested by periodic mass arrests of Mexican Americans followed by sensational publicity in the *Los Angeles Times*. The summer of 1942 witnessed the so-called Sleepy Lagoon case, in which nine teenage members of the 38th Street gang stood trial for the murder of José Díaz in an abandoned quarry pit. The sensational case generated an outburst of anti-Mexican sentiment, and the press and the police began to characterize all Mexican American youths as "baby gangsters" and Pachucho hoodlums. Ultimately, the nine young men were convicted and sentenced to long prison terms at San Quentin.

Soon after Sleepy Lagoon, incidents of violence involving U.S. service personnel and Zoot-Suit–wearing Mexicans and other minorities took place in Los Angeles, San Jose, Oakland, Delano, San Diego, and elsewhere. The most serious outbreak of violence took place in Los Angeles.

Most observers believe that the infamous anti-Mexican riot in Los Angeles began on June 3, 1943, when, ironically, a group of Mexican American youths, members of the Alpine Club, were meeting at a local police substation to discuss how to reduce the rate of teenage delinquency. Either during or after the meeting—the observers' accounts are varied—words were exchanged between some of the young Mexican Americans and a small group of sailors.[4] According to Carey McWilliams, eleven sailors reported to the police later that night that they had been attacked by a gang of Mexican youths while walking along the street. Beatrice Griffith, a social worker, reported that a sailor yelled to a group of the boys who were sitting in a window in the police station that "You guys better beat it. There's about a hundred sailors hunting for you up at Alpine (Avenue)."[5] In any case, as a result of a complaint by the sailors, a group of off-duty policemen who happened to be at the station that night decided to form a

"Vengeance Squad" and go out to "clean up" the gang responsible for the attack. They were unable to find any Mexicans to arrest. Nevertheless, the publicity generated over the attack and the police sweep seems to have sparked the formation of a series of larger Vengeance Squads in subsequent days. These quickly evolved into patrols of servicemen roaming the city in taxis followed by the police in pursuit in their squad cars. The soldiers and sailors referred to their impromptu squads as "task forces," adopting military terminology. Upon sighting a Zoot Suiter the servicemen piled out of their cabs and attacked him, stripping him of his distinctive clothing. The police followed up by promptly arresting the hapless Zoot Suiter for disturbing the peace.

Every night for almost a week the Taxi Cab Brigades, as they were dubbed by the press, wended their way through the Mexican neighborhoods looking for Mexican American youths they supposed were gang members: anyone wearing a Zoot Suit not only fit that description but was deemed a probable draft dodger as well. Sadly, all this was fueled by the newspapers, which reported the military's war against the Zoot Suiters in lurid tones. Headlines such as "Sailor Task Force Hits L.A. Zooters," and "Wild Night in L.A.—Sailor Zooter Clash" only increased the number of servicemen taking part in the riots. Now civilians began to join the patrols, and some of the Mexican and African American persons they attacked were not even wearing a Zoot Suit at the time. At the height of the riot, June 7, 1943, a crowd of about 5,000 people milled through the streets of downtown Los Angeles searching out Mexican Zoot Suiters. Carey McWilliams, a lawyer and eye witness, described the scene in his book, *North From Mexico:*

> Marching through the streets of downtown Los Angeles, a mob of several thousand soldiers, sailors, and civilians, proceeded to beat up every zoot-suiter they could find. Pushing its way into the important motion picture theaters, the mob ordered the management to turn on the house lights and then ranged up and down the aisles dragging Mexicans out of their seats. Street cars were halted while Mexicans, and some Filipinos and Negroes, were jerked out of their seats, pushed into the streets and beaten with a sadistic frenzy.[6]

The riots lasted more than ten days and resulted in the beating and arrest of hundreds of Mexican youths. As Mauricio Mazon points out in his study of the psychological implications of the riot, the public had been preconditioned by the Sleepy Lagoon case and its surrounding publicity to think of young Mexican Americans as gang members deserving of punishment.[7] Just prior to the riot, Al Capp, the artist who drew the daily "Li'l Abner" cartoon for the newspapers, had portrayed Li'l Abner as a pawn in a conspiracy by clothing manufacturers to sell more Zoot Suits. The particular strip ended with a frame showing riots against the stores selling the Zoot Suits. In Mazon's view, this cartoon episode was "a gripping precursor of the symbolic developments that typified the riots."[8]

Another aspect of this episode was its misnomer, for the Zoot Suiters were not the ones doing the rioting. Clearly, it was a "riot" by U.S. military personnel. Indeed, the local military commanders recognized this and were immediately concerned over their inability to control their own recruits as well as the need to restore military order. Their communiques use such terms as *disorder* and *riot* to characterize the servicemen's behavior. General Maxwell Murray stated in a memorandum that "Military personnel of all ranks must understand that no form of mob violence or rioting will be tolerated . . . ."[9] News of the rioting spread to other military bases in Southern California, and soon servicemen were coming into Los Angeles by the truckloads, some from as far away as Las Vegas, Nevada. Many believed that the young Mexcians were convenient scapegoats, on which the U.S. servicemen cruelly released wartime frustrations, not only for the failure of the U.S. armed services to defeat the enemy but for other pent-up anxieties.

MEXICAN GOVERNMENT'S RESPONSE

On June 10, 1943, the Mexican ambassador in Washington, D.C., Dr. Francisco Castillo Najera, and the minister of foreign relations in Mexico City, Lic. Ezequiel Padilla Pefialosa, received copies of a coded telegram sent by the Mexican consul in Los Angeles. In the cable, the counsul, Lic. Alfredo Elias Calles, reported that in the previous week, riots against Mexicans had taken place in the city of the Angels. Specifically, he related how U.S. soldiers and sailors were attacking Mexican nationals within the "*barriados mexicanos*" or the Mexican section of the city. Padilla stated that, thus far, the police had not been able to control the violence and that it had spread from attacks against supposed delinquents to Mexicans in general, including women and children. The consul related that he had protested energetically to the mayor, sheriff, chief of police, and naval authorities, all of whom had promised to quell the disturbances but, as of the date of the telegram, had failed to act. The consul also took note of how the California press was sensationalizing the riots instead of criticizing the illegal activities of the servicemen.[10] This one-page telegram was the first official Mexican government notice of the infamous Zoot-Suit Riots of 1943, the first urban riot in Los Angeles's history directed specifically against Mexicans.* For the next month, these disturbances would pose a

*There were several vigilante mobs that threatened riot against Mexicans in the 1850s. A *riot*, however, is usually defined as a violent public disorder caused by a large crowd of persons. Under that definition, Los Angeles has arguably seen five large riots in its modern history. The first was a public rampage against the Chinese in 1870, when 500 citizens burned the local Chinatown and killed 19 Chinese. The second large-scale violent riot was the Zoot-Suit Riot in 1943. No one was killed in that riot, but many suffered injuries. Subsequent large-scale public disturbances include the Watts Riot in 1965, the Moratorium Riots in 1970, and the Los Angeles Riot of the summer of 1992, spawned by the acquittal of LAPD officers on trial for the beating of African American motorist Rodney King. Notably, all of the major riots in Los Angeles's past occurred in nonwhite areas of the city, largely involved interracial tension, and saw violence mainly directed against nonwhite citizens.

potential problem for U.S.-Mexican relations, as the whole matter had the potential to damage the important U.S. alliance with Mexico and other Latin American countries.

The delay in the formal response of the Mexican government to that of the United States after the former received news of the Los Angeles riots in June 1943 may have resulted from its uncertainty over the nationality of the victims. When the riots began, Adolfo de la Huerta, the inspector general of the consulates, sent his own report to the Mexican government. In it, he related that after five nights of continuous violence, hundreds of old and young people "of Mexican extraction" had been wounded. He said that the U.S. military police had intervened and promised to stop the disturbances. Additionally, de la Huerta reported that California Governor Earl Warren had asked the state attorney general to investigate the matter. De la Huerta also blamed the American press for having whipped up anti-Mexican sentiment.[11] The exact phrase used by de la Huerta to describe the victims was "of Mexican extraction," whereas the Mexican consul in Los Angeles, a day after the outbreak of hostilities, had clearly stated that the series of attacks had been made on Mexican nationals. This point was to prove important in the subsequent weeks and months as it slowly became clear that most of the casualties were not Mexican nationals but American citizens and hence, it was argued, were not the concern of the Mexican government.[12]

The first formal response of the *Secretaria de Relaciones Exteriores* (the Secretary of Foreign Relations) was to cable the Mexican ambassador in Washington D.C., Dr. Castillo Najera, to instruct him to meet with U.S. Secretary of State Cordell Hull as soon as possible. At that meeting, Castillo Najera was to inform Hull that the Mexican government was refraining from making any formal protest over the incidents until it had all the pertinent information in hand. Until then, the Mexican government would trust in the ultimate justice of its United States counterpart. Castillo Najera also was to ask Hull to make a public statement condemning the riots. Finally, the Mexican ambassador was to warn Hull that news of the riots would spread throughout Latin America, thereby handing Axis agents throughout the region an easy propaganda victory.[13] Even before these instructions had been sent to Castillo Najera, the Secretaria de Relaciones Exteriores had established a clipping file in which he began to collect all the stories on the riots appearing in the newspapers of various Latin American countries.

Prior to his meeting with Castillo Najera, Hull had been receiving reports about the riots from the military as well as the civilian authorities in Los Angeles, all of which deemphasized the racial nature of the violence. As early as June 6, Los Angeles mayor Fletcher Bowron had sought to assure Secretary of State Hull that the disturbances could be handled locally and that the riots ". . . were in no way directed against persons of Mexican descent."[14] This denial emerged as Los Angeles's civic leaders, as well as the local press, began to realize that the riots (and the news thereof) were creating an international incident that might well hurt the important United States-Latin American alliance. Therefore, after the first few days of the rioting, both the *Los Angeles Times* and the *Daily News* began to deny any racial motivations behind the riots and downplay the significance of the whole affair. Interestingly, these had been the principal newspapers that had encouraged the riots through their lurid headlines and sensational reporting on the Zoot Suiters.[15] Churchill Murray, the Los Angeles representative of the Office of the Coordinator of Inter-American Affairs, an agency dedicated to improving United States-Latin American relations, also denied the racial factor when he wrote, "The riots at Los Angeles formed a purely local and non-racial situation. The frequency of Mexican names among the 'zoot-suit' element was without acutal significance to relations between Mexico and the United States because most of the civilian figures in the clashes with men of the armed service are American citizens."[16] To Alfredo Calles, the Mexican consul in Los Angeles, however, it was clear that the Mexican population of the city was being threatened. His office printed and distributed a large number of circulars in Spanish warning all Mexican nationals to remain at home after dark "to avoid unpleasant happenings." The circular stated that "We are confident that the civil and military authorities will soon remedy this unpleasant situation."[17]

Needless to say, the State Department was not anxious to upset relations between the United States and Mexico in the midst of a World War. Prior to the formal meeting on the matter, Ambassador Castillo Najera sought to reassure the U.S. government that Mexico did not intend to present a formal protest over the attacks. In his June 15 meeting with Hull, he stated that he thought that the situation had improved and that the crisis was past and that, in any case, more than "90 percent of the 'so called' pachucos were United States citizens" and only a few Mexican nationals had been involved.[18] After Najera had finished expressing his concern about the riots, Secretary Hull assured him that a full investigation would be made into the affair and "expressed deep regret about any injuries that might have been sustained." Hull blamed the riots on both the "zoot suit" element, which he maintained were of "questionable character and possess a spirit of lawlessness," and a small number of American servicemen out of more than 8 million in arms, "who gets out of hand occasionally and commits some lawless act." At the end of the meeting, he urged the Mexican ambassador to try to influence the Mexican press "to take this view and make it clear along with other facts."[19] Two days after the meeting, the State Department issued a press release that read, in part: "If as a result of those investigations it is found that there are cases involving Mexican citizens (and none have yet been found) the resulting claims will be expeditiously handled by this government in accordance with principles of international law and the principles of justice and equity which the two governments jointly uphold."[20] Within a few days of this statement, the much-promised inquiry was completed and the secretary of state reported that "investigations revealed no cases where Mexican citizens were involved in recent fights in Los Angeles."[21] This conclusion was sustained by the Los Angeles County Grand Jury's investigations, which began about a week after the onset of the disturbances. In addition to interviewing many of the civilian and military officials who had been in charge during the riots, the Grand Jury also interviewed several Mexican officials including President Avila Camacho's chief aid, Zuno Femenedez.[22]

One day after the meeting between Castillo Najera and Hull, the Mexican Foreign Office issued a formal statement of its position on the affair. The public press release, reprinted in Mexico City newspapers and in the Spanish-language newspapers in the United States, stated that the Mexican government was gathering information about the "regrettable events taking place in Los Angeles between the Zoot-Suiters and groups of North American sailors." The Mexican government asserted that they had received "reports of damages suffered by some of our nationals" and that, accordingly, they had informed the U.S. State Department that after an official investigation into the riots they would demand punishment for those responsible and indemnification of the victims.[23] This statement was then dispatched to the various consulate offices throughout the United States and Latin America. The Mexican Foreign Office also asked its consular officials throughout Latin America to report on any articles regarding the Zoot-Suit riots appearing in the local press. The officials were further instructed not to discuss the Los Angeles disturbances. They were to remain observers, not instigators, of local reaction.[24]

Other than this statement of concern, and faith in the ultimate indemnification of the victims, the Mexican government made no further official protest or demand for a more thorough investigation into the riot. The strongest position it took was in a statement issued on June 16, in which it announced that it trusted the U.S. government to investigate the affair and punish those found guilty. Evidently, the Mexican government did not gather independent sources of information in Los Angeles. At least there were no instructions to do so coming from Mexico City, and, as of yet, no file has been found showing any effort to find and document the mistreatment of Mexican nationals.

The inaction of the Mexican government to protest the Zoot-Suit riots provoked criticism from Mexican nationalists. On June 13, *El Excelsior*, a pro-government newspaper in Mexico City, severely criticized the government's handling of the whole affair. Editorially, Diego Tinoco Ariza rebuked Ambassador Castillo Najera and the Office of Foreign Relations for a lack of action prior to the riots, since there clearly had been so much anti-Mexican sentiment in the California press. "The Ambassador had exactly ten months to do something to diminish the sad fermentation of hate of which our compatriots were the victims," Tinoco Ariza wrote.[25] The riots, he argued, were yet another example of American racism at work, similar to the activities of the Ku Klux Klan in the Deep South. The riots provided an occasion to contrast Mexican culture with that of the *norteamericanos*. The writer concluded that *mestizaje*, or the mixture of races that had been going on for 400 years, ensured that Mexico would remain free of the "racial obsessions" of its northern neighbor.

Now the Zoot-Suit riots in Los Angeles became front-page news in Mexico City, leading to public demonstrations against the Mexican and U.S. governments' actions. Some newspapers cited the Mexican government's response to the incident to criticize Minister of Foreign Relations Eziquiel Padilla, charging that he "did not complain early enough or firmly enough after the fighting broke out in Los Angeles between the United States sailors and young civilians, many of them of Mexican descent."[26] *Novedades*, another Mexico City daily, ran a front-page banner on June 20: "Foreign Minister Ezequiel Padilla Is To Blame for the Scandalous Acts Against the Mexican Race." The story went on to charge Padilla of being responsible for perpetuating anti-Mexican acts in the United States by his failure to take a harder line towards the government of that country.[27] Criticism of the government's handling of the riots eventually resulted in a street protest by students from the National Autonomous University on June 24, 1943. The demonstration was announced by a flyer that proclaimed that the Los Angeles riots had been caused by "Hearst interests, the Ku-Klux-Klan, United States imperialists, Fifth Columnists of all kinds, and those interested in bringing about a victory for Hitler, who therefore have provoked these street riots in which our compatriots have suffered great injuries.[28]

Two days before the demonstration, two Mexican youths dressed in the zoot-suit mode were beaten and stripped of their clothes as they passed by the Faculty of Medicine in downtown Mexico City.[29] Although no one was identified with this incident, it revealed that some Mexicanos harbored anti-Pachuco sentiments. Five hundred students assembled in the Faculty of Law on June 24. After marching downtown chanting "Down with Roosevelt and Padilla," the students assembled in front of the Ministry of Foreign Relations. There they were met by the rector of the university, Rodolfo "Brito" Foucher, who spoke in defense of Roosevelt but against North American racism. He said that Mexicans could not be military allies of a nation that encouraged racism: ". . . the North American public [must] realize that the people of Mexico, mostly of mixed Indian and Spanish blood, cannot fight in this war with enthusiasm side by side with a country that harbors racial prejudice." He continued, "As for the people (Anglo Americans in the United States), and above the people of the southwest of the United States, it is indubitable that they are possessed by a deep prejudice against the Mixed Mexican population . . . ."[30] After his speech, the students marched towards the American Embassy, where they were blocked by the police. They then turned the march to go downtown towards the Zocalo. According to one observer, "the students marched through the downtown area booing, jeering, and hissing every store that displayed American signs. Sanborn, (sic.) an American-owned restaurant, was the target for a particularly violent demonstration, as some of the students entered and mauled an American who was having luncheon."[31] The students ended the demonstration by establishing a Committee for the Defense of Mexicanos Abroad (*Comite de Defensa de los Mexicanos de Afuera*) the goal of which was to protest the treatment of Pachucos as well as the race riot against African Americans in Detroit, Michigan, and the actions of the Mexican government that exhibited "a lack of patriotism."[32]

Meanwhile, some conciliatory articles had begun to appear in the Spanish-language press in Los Angeles. For example, on June 19, *La Opinion,* the leading Spanish-language newspaper in Southern California, reprinted an article that had first appeared in *El Nacional,* in Mexico City. The article reported that, "there is no doubt that the investigators [of the U.S.] will arrive at a just decision . . . . The provocateurs of hate cannot destroy the Good Neighbor Policy, nor can they distract either of the countries from their war against the Axis."[33] A few days later, Padilla, the Mexican secretary of *relaciones exteriories,* sought to justify the attitude of the Mexican government toward the recent Pachucho Riots. In answer to critics publishing in the local Mexico City newspapers, he said that he had sent instructions to the consul in L.A. "authorizing the full protection of the office to any compatriots being affected." Further, he said that the problem that underlay the riots should be considered "as a manifestation of racial segregation but that instead of limiting itself to useless discussions on this theme, [he preferred] to demonstrate his interest in mediating concrete actions that would lead to negotiations that will have positive results." He also indicated that, as a result of the riots, the Mexican government had decided that the future departure of *Braceros* (Mexican nationals working in the United States as part of a joint, wartime agreement) to the United States "would be predicated on their not suffering any discrimination."[34]

About a month after the end of the disturbances, the Mexican government sent a memorandum to the U.S. State Department outlining anti-Mexican incidents that had taken place in the United States.[35] A day later, Castillo Najera met with Cordell Hull, the secretary of state assuring him that "the matters discussed in the memorandum would receive appropriate attention."[36] As a result, a meeting took place in Washington on July 28 in which representatives of the Mexican government and the U.S. Department of Justice discussed the various incidents of mistreatment of Mexicans in the United States. All such discussion, however, involved anti-Mexican incidents that had taken place in Texas; the Zoot-Suit riots were not even slated for discussion. The Justice Department offical said that if the Mexican ambassador learned of any specific cases of the mistreatment of persons of Mexican descent but not citizenship (referred to in the translation as "*doble nacionalidad*" or dual citizenship), he should communicate the basic facts to the Justice Department.[37] This clearly left the door open for the Mexican govenment to present cases of mistreatment of Mexican Americans, as well as Mexican nationals, to the Justice Department. Indeed, during the height of the riots, the Mexican Consulate had been approached by representatives of Los Angeles Committee for American Unity with an offer to help gather affidavits of victimized Mexican Americans and Mexican nationals. But this offer was turned down, and there is no evidence that any cases were ever brought forward.[38]

REACTION OF THE LATIN AMERICAN PRESS

Latin Americans had other concerns regarding the Zoot-Suit riots, these reflecting a diversity of class and political interests. Aside from the diplomatic exchanges previously discussed, other sources that yield insight into the mentality of the Latin American public were the editorials and articles that appeared in the popular media. Of course, one should be suspicious of relying too closely on newspapers as true reflections of public opinion. In both the United States and Latin America, the "public opinion" expressed in newspapers is and always has been influenced by political and economic pressures, usually by concerns over advertising. In Latin America and Mexico, the government has had a long interventionist tradition vis-à-vis the news: over the decades they had developed subtle and not so subtle ways of influencing what made it to print. For one thing, most reporters depended on government stipends to supplement their meager paychecks; and many newspapers depended on government subsidies in addition to advertising revenue.[39]

In Mexico, there is some evidence that the federal government sought to control the media during the Zoot-Suit disturbances. The reaction to the riots by Mexican nationalists threatened to embarrass the Camacho administration's pro-United States stance.[40] As noted, the secretary of foreign relations became a target for mass demonstrations and critical media comment. Leftists demanded that the government take a strong position against the North American racism seemingly revealed by the riots. Additionally, the U.S. government, through its embassy officials in Mexico City, sought to "control" anti-American sentiment by urging restraint in circulating news stories on the riots originating in the United States.[41]

Nevertheless, during the months of June and July 1943, the *Secretaria de Relaciones Exteriores* forwarded the accumulated newspaper clippings to Mexican consulates throughout Latin America. The Mexican government also collected clippings from the local Mexico City press. It is diffi-cult to generalize regarding journalistic reactions to the riots: there was a great diversity of emphasis. The first major article to appear in the Mexico City press was one critical of the Pachuchos, in *La Prensa* on June 14, 1943. The headline read, "Without being Truly Mexicans, They Are an Affront to Our Republic."[42] The article went on to say that the Pachuchos (also called *Tarzanes*) were "a real affront to our country" and that "they are almost always mestizos of Mexican and Negro, or Mexican and Chinese or Filipino; the great majority of them are not by birth or nationality Mexi-cans." The article stated that these "vagabonds" were illegitimately trying to get the protection of the Mexican government. This was the first nega-tive Mexican interpretation of the Pachuchos to appear in print. Its gen-eral thrust, that the Pachucos were not "real" Mexicans, would reappear again in the popular media and in academic treatises. The theme of racial degeneracy, however, does not seem to have continued.[43]

Other Mexico City periodicals seemed to distance themselves from the Pachuchos as Mexicans but were also critical of the North American rac-ism that had produced the riots. *El Excelsior*, perhaps the most widely read newspaper in the capital, published a piece in June under the headline "No Mexican Has Been Injured in Los Angeles."[44] The article reported that the U.S. State Department had assured the Mexican government that no Mexi-can citizen had been affected by the riots. The U.S. authorities had prom-ised rapid compensation for any damages to Mexican nationals, but as of yet, not a single Mexican citizen had come forth to request reparation. The article went on to quote Eleanor Roosevelt, who said that the Pachucho riots probably had their origins in long-term discrimination against Mexi-cans in that part of the country. *El Popul*, another Mexico City newspa-per, reprinted a translation of an article written by Carey McWilliams for *The New Republic*.[45] This was an analysis by one of the leading champi-ons of the Mexican youths in Los Angeles. He blamed the riots on chronic discrimination, poverty, journalistic sensationalism, and police racism. McWilliams pointed out that no more than half of those assaulted during the episode had been wearing a Zoot Suit; that, contrary to police public pronouncements, there were no Zoot-Suit gangs in Los Angeles in an or-ganized sense; and that "98 percent of the Mexican youth in Los Angeles is American-born, American-raised, American-educated."[46] After the riots ended, the Mexican press continued to analyze the implications thereof. By late June, *Excelsior*, was blaming the riots on racism and the pernicious influence of William Randolph Hearst's Yellow Journalism. *Excelsior*'s columnist wrote: "As our readers already know, the riots were a typical case of racial discrimination, a branch of the vile prejudice that the Hitlerites and their accomplices have elevated to a supreme law of human society.[47]

Border regions in northern Mexican states were especially concerned as to the significance of the riots. In Nuevo Leon, Monterrey's *El Norte*, on June 22 compared the beatings of Mexicans in Los Angeles to the activities of the Nazi's in Europe. The editorial pointed out that Article 30 in the Mexican Constitution provided that "every person is a Mexican citizen whose parents are Mexicans, whether they are born within or without the Republic. . ." and criticized the Mexican government's lack of action after the riots. They called on their government to "formulate an energetic protest to the American Government for the outrages and brutalities committed on our Countrymen."[48]

It took only a few days for Latin American newspapers outside Mexico to learn about the riots through the wire services. The clippings gathered by the Mexican *secretaria de relaciones* were probably not all the articles that appeared, but they formed a good cross section. On June 10, *El Crisol,* a daily newspaper in Havana, Cuba, reported that there was a "civil war" between American soldiers and the "Chucheros" (Pachuchos).[49] The next day, the Havana paper reported that Nelson Rockefeller, the coordinator of inter-American affairs, had sent a personal delegation to Los Angeles to seek a solution to the crisis. This article was accompanied by a photograph of people, evidently Zoot-Suiters, running through the streets with men in uniform in pursuit. While there was recognition of the fact that the "Chucheros" were of Mexican origin, the Cuban newspaper did not emphasize it. They seemed to believe that the Pachucos were some kind of organized guerilla force. They reported that Manuel Lopez Romero, "the reputed boss of the Chucheros in Arizona," had been sentenced to five years in prison after being convicted of more than 100 assaults. The idea that there could be a "boss" of all the Pachuchos in Arizona gave the impression that they were some kind of large-scale organized criminal gang.[50] Subsequently, *El Crisol* reported that the "Chucheros" had sent representatives to the police with a white flag to ask for peace, reinforcing the image of the riots as a war between armies.[51]

Confusion and lack of understanding regarding the events in Los Angeles shaped the Latin American media's puzzlement over how to interpret the Pachuchos. In some cases, they simply republished the Mexican media's views, as in the case of El Salavdor's *Diario Latino,* which reprinted the analysis of Mexico City's *El Universal:*

> The first Mexican immigrants in California never wanted to become citizens but the majority of their children were made so by birth, at the same time their grandchildren did not accept their north American nationality through ignorance, thus creating an extraordinary undefined generation. Statistics show that this thrid generation of Mexican descent in California do not know Spanish and are ignorant about Mexico.[52]

The Mexican ambassador to El Salvador collected many more stories appearing in local newspapers, all of which seemed to follow the lead of the Mexican press in emphasizing the non-Mexicaness of the Pachuchos.[53]

The reaction to the riots in the presses of other Latin American nations emphasized the racial overtones of the civil disturbances. *El Dia* in Quito, Ecuador, ran a story with the headline, "In the City of Los Angeles There has Been One of the Biggest Race Riots of Recent History.[54] Lima, Peru's *Las Novedades* ran a long article emphasizing the racial aspects of the riots, noting that white Zoot-Suiters had not been attacked. They also criticized the Mexican Foreign Office for their slow reaction to the riots.[55]

Still other newspapers expressed concern over possible Fascist involvement in the affair. This concern mirrored the fears of some in California. In late June, Senator Jack Tenny urged the California legislative committee to investigate the possible involvement of members of the Communist party, the Nazi Bund, and Fascist organizations in the riots.[56] Representatives of the Mexican government also had suggested that Fascist provocateurs were involved in the riots, and this was picked up in the media. *Ahorra* in Caracas, Venezuela, editorially demanded that the United States clearly explain the situation to Latin Americans, suggesting that the riot, "could be the beginning of a Nazi-fascist campaign to take advantage of the situation."[57] Peru's *La Novedades* reprinted the report of Mexican Ambassador, Adolfo de la Huerta, in which he expressed full confidence in the abilities of U.S. officials to conduct an impartial and honest investigation into the affair, yet opined that they would "undoubtedly find the work of Fascist agents who have been active everywhere trying to destroy continental solidarity."[58] Finally, *El Avance* (Cuba) reported that the Mexican Foreign Office had declared that "there were no reasons to believe that the Sinarquista Party (A Mexican Fascist party) has intervened in any way what-soever into the recent disturbances."[59]

CONCLUSION

The international implications of the Los Angeles Zoot-Suit riots were that they served to heighten Latin Americans' awareness of racial attitudes within the United States regarding Mexicans and Latin Americans. While only a small number of Latin Americans probably read or knew about the riots, they served as an introduction to the status and problems of the ethnic Mexican colony within the United States. There is no evidence that the journalistic responses collected by the Mexican government were ever transmitted to the U.S. State Department, but undoubtedly the U.S. government was painfully aware of the propaganda coup that their servicemen and citizens had handed the Axis Alliance. The English-language *Inter-American Monthly* made the authorities aware, if they had not already been so, that "the Latin-American press used the riots as a basis for attack on the United States Racial Policy" and that Latin American journalists "decried the violence as a type of Hitlerian racial intolerance. . . ."[60] The threat of fracturing or seriously damaging the wartime alliance between the United

States and Mexico, or of giving the Axis propaganda to win the sympathies of the Latin American public, made the U.S. government take the riots very seriously. Besides a local and state investigation into the causes of the riots, the F.B.I. was to find out if there had been foreign agents involved. Special instructions had been issued to military commanders, and within a few days Los Angeles became off-limits to military personnel.

Ten days after the conclusion of the Zoot-Suit riots in Los Angeles, massive race riots against African Americans exploded in Detroit. Eventually, 23 persons were killed, 530 injured, and 1,300 arrested in what up to then was the bloodiest urban race riot of the twentieth century. Yet this civil disturbance did not occupy the attention of the federal government or international journalistic community to the same extent as did the Los Angeles riots of 1943. Because of the need for wartime hemispheric alliance, what otherwise might have been merely more anti-Mexican episode in California history became an international incident of some importance.

The fact that the Mexican government did not intervene more strenuously on behalf of its nationals, some of whom undoubtedly were victims of the violence, is understandable in terms of the new relationship that the Mexican government hoped to forge with the United States. Good relations with the North Americans were essential in order to continue with Mexico's economic progress. Anti-Pachucho sentiment expressed in some Mexico City newspapers also served to rationalize a policy of non-intervention. Mexican American youth were stigmatized as being traitors to their culture (not speaking good Spanish, for example) and, paradoxically, to their adopted country (by not being loyal U.S. citizens). The message from some media critics was that even if the Pachucos were Mexican citizens, they were not worth the protection of the Mexican government. The government seems to have agreed. No protests or claims for compensation were forwarded to the Justice Department by Mexican officials, even though the former clearly had left the door open for those of Mexican descent to do so.

Nevertheless, the Zoot-Suit riots made the Mexican and Latin American public acutely aware that there was an ethnic culture of Mexican descent within the United States, one victimized by racism and discrimination. Unfortunately, this knowledge often came with an additional message: that this ethnic culture (Mexican Americans) was not worthy of respect by respectable Mexicans. It would be several decades before the Mexican intelligentsia would begin to transcend the negative stereotypes first made so prominent by the Zoot-Suit riots of 1943.

Beyond this international effect, the Zoot-Suit riots were important in the civil rights history of Mexican Americans in California. More than 200,000 Mexican Americans joined or were drafted into the armed services during World War II, and for them, the Zoot-Suit riots were proof of the continuing contradictions in American society. After the war, these veterans, mindful of the many discriminations they had endured before and during the war, along with the widely publicized events of the Zoot-Suit riots, would not be willing to continue with the status quo in ethnic relations. These men and women would go on to create many of the organizations that seriously challenged segregation and discrimination in the 1950s. The dramatic image of the Pachuco in a Zoot Suit would later become an icon of the 1960s Chicano Movement's cultural declaration of independence. Indeed, one of the major events of the Chicano movement was the production of Luis Valdez's play and later film, *Zoot Suit,* an artistic statement about the injustices of the World War II era and the Pachucos' relevance to contemporary Chicanos. In the end, the Zoot-Suit riots, as understood in film, song, and community memory, would become significant as part of the ethnic awakening among Chicanos.

Notes

1   See Rudolfo Acuna, *Occupied America: A History of Chicanos* (New York, 1988), 255-258. The Sleepy Lagoon case and the growing hysteria surrounding Pachuco "gangs" in Los Angeles in the year prior to the riots were important as well. See the classic study by Williams, Carey McWilliams, *North From Mexico: The Spanish- Speaking People of the United States* (1949; New York: Greenwood Press 1968), 247–251.

2   While there are a number of interpreters of the Zoot-Suit phenomenon, serious historical studies of the riot itself have been minimal. The only published monograph is that of Mauricio Mazon, *The Zoot-Suit Riots: The Psychology of Symbolic Annihilation* (Austin, 1984). In this book Mazon reviews the historiography of interpretation of the Zoot Suiters (115–121). Other histories are unpublished dissertations, master's theses, and special reports and papers of the: *California Legislature, Joint Fact-Finding Committee on Un-American Activities in California,* Second report (Sacramento, 1945); Marilyn Domer, "The Zoot-Suit Riot; a Culmination of Social Tensions in Los Angeles" (M.A. thesis, Claremont Graduate School, 1955); Dale, Drum, Report on Pachuco Gang-Activities in the City of Los Angeles (Los Angeles, 1951); Alfredo Guerra Gonzalez, "Mexicano/Chicano Gangs in Los Angeles: A Sociohistorical Case Study" (Ph.D. Diss., UCLA, 198 1); Ismael Dieppa, "The Zoot-Suit Riot: A Culmination of Social Tensions in Los Angeles" M.A. thesis, Claremont Graduate School, 1955); Solomon James Jones, "The Government Riots of Los Angeles, June 1943"(M.A. thesis, UCLA, 1969).

3   The classic critique of the Pachuco appears in Octavio Paz, *The Labyrinth of Solitude: Life and Thought in Mexico* (New York, 196 1), Ch. 1; For contemporary interpretations of this phenomenon, see Beatrice Griffith, *American Me* (Boston, 1948), 15–28; George I. Sanchez, "Paychecks in the Making," *Common Ground* IV (Autumn, 1943), 13–20; Ruth D. Tuck, *Not With the Fist: Mexican-Americans in a Southwest City* (New York, 1974); also Ralph H. Turner and Samuel J. Surace, "Zoot-Suiters and Mexicans: Symbols in Crowd Behavior," *American Journal of Sociology* 62 (1956), 14–24.

4   Maurcio Mazon, *The Zoot Suit Riots: The Psychology of Symbolic Annihilation* (Austin: University of Texas Press, 1984), p. 69–70.

5   Quotes in *Mazon*, p. 70.

4   Carey McWilliams, *North From Mexico,* 249.

7   *Mazon*, pp. 15-30.

8   Ibid., p. 53.

9   Ibid., p. 74.

10   Alfredo Elias Calles to the secretaria de relaciones exteriores, 10 June 1943, "Disturbios Raciales en Los Angeles, California," Archivo de la Secretaria de Relaciones Exteriores, Mexico City, File 11165 1–1 [hereafter cited as SRE Archives]. This telegram is reported by Jones as being sent on June 8. See Solomon James Jones, "The Government Riots of Los Angeles, June 1943" (M.A. thesis, UCLA, 1969), 38. Consul Elias Calles knew firsthand of the riots. He had attended a meeting on June 7, 1943, of the Citizens' Committee for LatinAmerican Youth, spon-

sored by the County Board of Supervisors. At this meeting, the details of the initial days of the riot were recounted.

11 Adolfo de la Huerta to C. Lic. Ezequiel Padilla, June 10, 1943, SRE Archives.

12 The issue of citizenship or nationality was basically a political one, since the Mexican Constitution (Chapter 11, Article 30, A 11) stated "they are Mexican by birth: Those who are born abroad of Mexican parents, of a Mexican father and foreign mother, or of Mexican mother and unknown father." My translation of *Novedades* Jane, 22 1943, p. 1. If any victim was United States-born of Mexican parents, he was considered a Mexican citizen by the Mexican Constitution until he renounced his citizenship.

13 Coded cablegram from the secretaria de relaciones exteriores to the Mexican Embassy, Washington D.C., June 14, 1943, in SRE Archives.

14 *Los Angeles Daily News,* June 6, 1943, 9; quoted in Solomon Jones, "The Government Riots of Los Angeles, June 1943," (M.A. thesis, UCLA, 1969), 37.

15 Ibid.

16 *Los Angeles Examiner,* June 10, 1943, p. 9.

17 Ibid., June 9, 1943, p. 11.

18 *La Opinion,* June 12, 1943, p. 1.

19 Memorandum of Conversation, Cordell Hull, Department of State, June 15, 1943, Purport File No. 811.4016/596.

20 *Los Angeles Examiner,* June 13, 1943, 4:4. Just before the issuance of this statement, Philip Bonsal, an official in the Department of State, transmitted a brief report on the status of the "Zoot Suit" disturbances to the Secretary Hull. In this report, Bonsal indicated that U.S. Ambassador Messersmith had learned that Foreign Minister Castillo Najera "had been forced by public opinion and necessity to defend himself and the President from adverse newspaper comment to make a strong statement regarding the "zoot suit" incidences." He further noted that as yet, neither the Mexican consul in Los Angeles nor the mayor of Los Angeles knew of any Mexican nationals who had been involved in the disturbances. See Philip Bonsal to Mr. McGurk, Department of State, June 17, 1943, p. 2, Purport File No. 811.4016/585.

21 Ibid., June 17, 1943, p. 4 in Jones, 39; the next day, Hull phoned Mayor Fletcher Brown and reiterated that no Mexican national had suffered damages.

22 Domer, 110.

23 On the day of the publication of the Mexican Government's position on the riots, Vicente Lombardo Toledano gave a lengthy statement, characterizing the riots as "a deliberate attempt to destroy the unity and harmony between the Americans and Mexicans living in California and to destroy the Good Neighbor Policy . . ." He reviewed the growing hysteria in Southern California regarding Pachuco gangs and compared it to the tactics of the Nazis. See Messersmith to Hull, June 16, 1943, "Memorandum of Conversation with Mr. Bonsal of the Department with regard to the Pachuco Incidents in Los Angeles and Clippings from *Excelsior,* Purport File No. 811.4016/567. For the Mexican government's internal handling of the affair, see "Circular a nuestras misiones diplomaticos," June 17, 1943, SRE Achives.

24 The other instructions are alluded to in the communique by Juan Maneul Alcaraz Tornel, the Charge d'affaires in Peru to the SRE on June 22, 1943. The instructions were No. 51444 given on June 17, 1943. Despite these instructions regarding discretion, there were leaks. On June 22, 1943, for example the Lima newspaper *Las Novedades* published an article which was a reprint of the Mexican Ambassador's report on the riots to his government.

25 *Excelsior,* June 13, 1943, p. 4.

26 *Hollywood Citizen News,* June 22, 1943, p. 5; quoted in Jones, 39.

27 *Novedades,* June 20,1943, p. 1.

28 *The Inter-American,* July 1943, 6.

29 Ibid.

30 *Excelsior,* June 26, 1943 , p. 6:3a.

31 *The New York Times,* June 26, 1943, p. 28; quoted in Jones, 39-40; The Inter-American, August 1943, 5.; for a detailed report on the student disturbances, see Memorandum, June 26, 1943, from American Embassy to United States Department of State, Purport file no. 811.4016/590.

32 *Excelsior,* June 26, 1943, p. . This committee was perhaps the first nongovernmental organization in Mexico to recognize the realities surrounding the Mexican American communities in the United States.

33 *La Opinion,* June 19, 1943, p. 1.

34 Ibid., June 16, 1943, pp. 1, 8.

35 Memorandum no. 4253, July 23, 1943, Mexican Embassy to Department of State, Purport file no. FW 811.4016/673.

36 Memorandum of Conversation, Secretary of State Hull and the Mexican ambassador, July 24, 1943, Purport file no. FW811.4016/637.

37 Memorandum, July 28, 1943, Mexican Embassy in Washington and the Justice Department, SRE Archive.

38 Memorandum to Director Re: Mexican Youth Gangs, I I June 1943, 3, SIZE Archive. The Los Angeles Committee for American Unity was classified as a Communist front and its activities were closely monitored by the FBI. On June 8, 1943, for example, the FBI agent reported that they had met and promised to send a telegram to the Confederacion de Trabadores Mexicanos (CTM) in Mexico urging them to make protests to Washington regarding the treatment of Mexicans. "Los Angeles Committee for American Unity," FBI Report, Los Angeles 14 June 1943, 3.

39 See the discussion of this in Michael B. Salwen and Brice Barrison, *Latin American Journalism* (Hillsdale, NJ, 1991).

40 See, for example, Herbert S. Bursley, conselor of Embassy Mexico City, to Cordel Hull, Secretary of State June 26, 1948, purport file 811.4016/590. Bursley reports: "The Mexican Government had endeavored to persuade, apparently with considerable success, the local papers to treat the disturbances in Los Angeles and the race riots in Detroit as calmly as possible."

41 Here see the previously cited memorandum, Amabassador Messersmith to Secretary of State, June 19, 1943, "Disturbances in Los Angeles Involving Mexicans."

42 *La Prensa,* June 14, 1943, p. 1. This and other Latin American newspaper articles subsequently cited are in the SRE file 11165 1 -1 and are clippings, some of which did not include the page number.

43 The most famous critique of the Pachuco is the well-known first chapter in Octavio Paz's, *The Labyrinth of Solitude: Life and Thought in Mexico* (New York, 1961) which ironically used the Pachuco as an archetype for exploring Mexican identity. The theme of the Pachuco as an embarrassment and an affront to "decent" Mexicans was made by the Mexican American historian Manuel Servin in "The Post-World War II Mexican Americans, 1925–1965: A Nonachieving Minority," in *An Awakening Minority: The Mexican Americans,* Manuel Servin, ed. (Beverly Hills, 1974), 168. For Mazon, both Paz and Servin illustrate the theme of annihilation: "Both managed to sever the connection between zoot-suiters, and the cultural identity of Mexicans," 116–117.

44 *Excelsior,* June 17, 1943, p. 1

45 *El Popular,* July 10, 1943.

46 *New Republic,* June 21, 9143, 819.

47 *Excelsior,* June 23, 1943.

48 *El Norte* (Monterrey, Nuevo Leon), June 22, 1943.

49 *El Crisol,* June 20, 1943.

50 Ibid, June, 14 1943.

51 *El Crisol,* June, 14 1943.

52 *Diario Latino,* June 14, 1943 reprint of an article in *El Universal* (n.d.) SRE Archive.

53 News clipping were forwarded from *Diario de Hoy,* June, 23 1943; *Prensa Grafica,* June 14, 15 and 24, 1943; *Diario Latino,* June 12, 14, 24, 1943; *Nuesto Diario* (Guatemala) June 25, 1943.

54 *El Dia,* June 13, 1943.

55 *Las Novedades,* June 20, 21, 1943.

56 The final report of this committee concluded that Mexican Sinarquistas had played no role in the riots but that the Communists probably had. See Marilyn Domer, "The Zoot Suit Riot; A Culmination of Social Tensions in Los Angeles" M.A. Thesis, Claremont Graduate School, 1955, 102; quote from *Hollywood Citizen News,* June 21, 1942.

57 *Ahorra,* June 22, 1943.

58 *Las Novedades,* June 27, 1943.

59 *El Avance,* July 9, 1943.

60 *Inter-American Monthly,* August 1943, 5 quoted in Jones, 39.

CHAPTER TEN

Vintibusiness California Style: The Wine Industry, 1769 to the Present

Victor W. Geraci

Wine enthusiasts witnessed an amazing first year of the new millennium as wineries merged, small wine businesses profited from buyouts, and consolidations created huge international wineries. Seeking to emulate and compete with the giant corporations, the California wine industry tooled up for an agribusiness explosion. In the first quarter of 2000, two of California's largest wineries planned expansions to secure a better foothold in the global wine economy. Jess Jackson, a proprietor of Kendall-Jackson Wine Estates, started the frenzy with his March purchase of Matanzas Creek winery in Sonoma County.[1] Not to be outdone, the Napa Valley–based Robert Mondavi Corporation expanded its California, Chilean, and French empire with a $12.6 million minority share purchase of the Tuscan winery Tenuta dell'Ornellaria.[2]

Yet, these sales paled in comparison to those conducted in a single week in August, with three transactions that totaled over $2 billion. The buying frenzy started with the Foster's Brewing Group purchase of Napa Valley–based Beringer Wine Estates for $1.5 billion, followed on the same day with the announcement of the $95 million purchase of R. H. Phillips Vineyard by the Vincor Corporation of Canada. Two days later the flurry of activity continued, as the Wine Group of San Francisco purchased six brands from Sebastiani Vineyards, thereby creating the second largest wine producer in the United States.[3] Now, the Robert Mondavi Corporation went on a second shopping spree, purchasing Sonoma Valley's Arrowwood Vineyards and Winery for $45 million and announcing plans to establish a high-end winery in the Languedoc region of France.[4] The wine giant then made a deal with the Walt Disney Corporation to create a wine-oriented attraction at Disney's new fifty-five-acre "California Adventure" addition to Disneyland.[5]

While these developments were rapid and spectacular, the rise of California wine making to global status unfolded over the course of two and one-half centuries. Therefore, perhaps the history of the wine industry in California is best understood within the context of the state's agricultural history. Like agriculture in general, the wine industry in California took advantage of the state's Mediterranean climate and was propelled by a remarkable system of irrigation, a willingness of agriculturists to experiment with new plant varieties and embrace scientific techniques, and an economy that, over time, fostered large capital investments, cooperative marketing schemes, and a firm commitment to research and development of agribusiness.

MAJOR THEMES IN CALIFORNIA AGRICULTURE

California agriculture evolved from a sporadic and subsistence-level horticulture practiced by certain Indian groups to the large Spanish- and Mexican-era *ranchos*, culminating with the classic model of American commercial agriculture. Anthropological evidence leads most historians to believe that local indigenous inhabitants began to settle in the region more than 11,000 years ago and that by the mid 1700s the region supported

The vineyards of Zaca Mesa Winery in the Santa Ynez Valley of Santa Barbara County. *Photograph by Kirk Irwin, copyright © Kirk Irwin.*

about 310,000 persons who supplemented their diets with minimal agriculture. The mild climate, plentiful game, and natural plant resources of the area made large-scale farming unnecessary.

European farming practices were introduced to the region in 1769 by Spanish priests and soldiers and initially developed into a system of large ranchos dedicated to growing wheat and raising cattle to feed and furnish the staffs and occupants of forts and missions, as well as to provide hide and tallow exports to Spain. By 1800, inhabitants of the Spanish settlements had added "mission agriculture" (the padres relying heavily on the labor of Indian converts to cultivate vegetable gardens, fruit orchards, and vineyards) to the agricultural tradition. Yet, this pastoral system fell into disrepair by the 1820s, when the secularization of the missions by the Mexican government saw Church-owned lands pass slowly into the hands of private, non-Spanish landholders.[6]

After statehood in 1850, California agriculture underwent a 150-year growth spurt that culminated in the state becoming the largest producer of farm goods in the United States by 1948. It retained its status as a world-class agricultural region throughout the last half of the twentieth century. Today, California farmers cultivate more than 200 specialty crops and products, making the state the most diversified producer of farm goods in the world. Indeed, most economic experts consider California, in the words of agricultural historian Lawrence J. Jelinek, a "Harvest Empire."[7]

This remarkable productivity and diversity emanated from a combination of five base factors. First and foremost, California's Mediterranean climate (generally rainless summers and mild, wet winters that make for an exceptionally long growing season), when supplemented with a statewide irrigation system to overcome an uneven distribution of winter rainfall, provided ideal growing conditions for a combination of fruits, nuts, winter vegetables, cotton, and rice. A second factor has been the experimentation with many foreign crops from the time of the first Spanish contact in the 1760s to the present. Wealthy gentlemen farmers, through simple trial and error as well as the adoption of the latest scientific methods, continually planted new crops and invested in expensive new technology to keep production and profits high. A third major factor has been the advantage of an adequate and inexpensive harvest labor force, first Indians living on or nearby the missions and ranchos and later immigrants from Asia and Mexico, as well as other regions of the United States. In the last half of the twentieth century, social concern for migrant workers, coupled with the rise of farmworkers' unions, fostered a shift to a dependence on mechanized production and harvesting systems. The fourth piece of the matrix evolved as farmers developed advanced marketing and distribution systems. Initially isolated from the rest of the American marketplace, California farmers quickly took advantage of the post-1869 transcontinental railroad boom by developing effective marketing cooperatives, stimulating the expansion of shipping routes, encouraging the deployment of refrigerated railway cars, utilizing new canning and drying techniques for perishable crops and products, and borrowing new corporate marketing and fiscal strategies to supply national as well as international markets.

Lastly, and in many ways most important, has been the rise in California of large-scale farms and corporate farm/factories functioning as industrialized agriculture: this has been labeled as "agribusiness." From the Spanish rancho system, with its large land-grant properties, emanated a California tradition that by the 1920s helped concentrate land ownership and foster what historian Cary McWilliams calls "Factories in the Fields."[8] The size of farms continued to grow and by the 1990s more than 60 percent of the total agricultural production sprang from less than 10 percent of the state's farmers. Most historians consider the California wine industry as illustrative of these five general tenets as played out in the Spanish, Mexican, and American eras.

CALIFORNIA WINE TRADITIONS

European expansion into the Western Hemisphere during the Age of Discovery transported centuries of wine tradition from the Old to the New World. Once in North America, French, Italian, Spanish, and German settlers grew a new wine industry through 300 years of trial and error. Throughout this great wine experiment American vintners faced and overcame government policies (that wavered between complete support and prohibition), urban sprawl, boom and bust cycles, and the intense competition proffered by foreign winemakers. Historically, the most successful wine businesses were those that in some fashion stabilized a cyclic market by integrating farmers and winemakers into a vertical (control of all aspects of production, distribution, and sales) and horizontal (consolidation of similar businesses) vintibusiness.[9]

The story of California viticulture (the science of grape growing) and viniculture (the study of winemaking) is a four-part one that reflects the five major themes in California agriculture. It begins with the Spanish and Mexican occupation between 1769 and the 1840s, when small regional producers supplied a limited amount of wine for local consumption. In the second era, California statehood (1850) through prohibition (1918), the industry exploded with promise and patterned itself after the big business tenets of Gilded Age capitalists by utilizing vertical and horizontal integration.[10] In the third phase, initial successes crumbled between 1918 and 1945, as moral crusaders nudged the nation into abstinence, and wine markets collapsed due to the effects of the Great Depression and the subsequent world war. In the final phase, 1945–2000, after the long forced hiatus of prohibition, the Great Depression, and World War II, the American wine industry underwent a renaissance financed by the entrepreneurial energy and capital of wealthy professionals (doctors, lawyers, dentists, college professors, retirees, and CEOs). From the 1950s through 1970s, a new breed of professional wine industrialists converted wine farms into modern vintibusinesses that thrived by blending consumerism, agribusiness, government policy, science, and education.[11]

The wine industry, like American business in general, developed an economic Pax Americana capable of profiting from what historian Olivier Zunz characterizes as a business relationship between national wealth, personal freedom, and well-being. California winemakers assumed their rightful place in what *Time* and *Life* publisher Henry Luce described as the "American Century," and they prospered in what Zunz characterizes as a middle-class consumer movement enhanced by corporate managers, engineers, social scientists, and scientists.[12]

Quest for New World Wines

Viticulture arrived in the Americas during the Age of Discovery (1500–1750) as European immigrants brought their wine-drinking traditions to the New World. These early explorers found that the Native American peoples had no knowledge of wine or, for that matter, any fermented spirits. Thus, European explorers and colonizers spent three centuries attempting to quench their thirst for wine by introducing viticulture to South Africa, Australia, New Zealand, Chile, Argentina, and the United States.

Early colonial American growers quickly found that European wine-grape varieties fared poorly in the climatic conditions of New England. This proved to be a problem, since English merchants originally had hoped that American wine would free them from a dependence on French, Spanish, and Italian wines. Subsequent wine trials in the agricultural southern colonies of Virginia, North Carolina, South Carolina, Georgia, Louisiana, and Florida failed. Undaunted, colonial wine entrepreneurs then unsuccessfully attempted both viticulture and viniculture in the pre-Revolutionary colonies of Maine, Maryland, Pennsylvania, and New Jersey. This quest to produce wine continued with westward migration and finally paid off with commercial successes in Missouri, Ohio, and New York.[13]

Grafting American to Spanish Viticultural Traditions

By 1800, Spanish priests, soldiers, and citizens had planted vineyards and produced wine on the other side of the American continent (in the Alta California region of Mexico). These vineyards grew grapes from vines cloned from European varietals and produced sacramental wine for the Catholic mass, wine for table use, and wine for commercial trade at presidio, pueblo, and mission settlements.

Early Spanish land settlement policies that encouraged the growth of viticulture continued with the Mexican colonization law of 1824 and the *Reglamento* of 1828. Subsequently, hundreds of secularized land grantees throughout California composed a wealthy landowning class (*Dons*) that utilized vast tracts to raise cattle (for the hide and tallow trade) and maintain small subsistence agriculture for everyday food and wine needs. Consequently, wine became a major part of the California agricultural scene throughout Spanish, Mexican, and *Californio* settlement.[14]

California's annexation by the United States in 1850 allowed for the marriage of the American winemaking experience (East and West) and catapulted American wines into the international marketplace. New excitement for the possibility of an American wine industry prompted Senator Stephen A. Douglas of Illinois in 1851 to state enthusiastically that the "United States will, in a very short time, produce good wine, so cheap, and in such abundance, as to render it a common and daily beverage."[15]

CALIFORNIA TAKES THE LEAD

At the time of statehood, southern California, specifically the Los Angeles region, led the nation in winemaking. Production topped 500,000 gallons per year, a figure that bested Guernsey County, Ohio, the former United States leader. Large commercial wineries in the Los Angeles area grew under the entrepreneurial know-how of men such as Benjamin D. Wilson (a Tennessean who married into a Mexican family and made a fortune in cattle, real-estate, and wine), Jean-Louis and Pierre Sainsevain (nephews of Jean Vignes, viticultural pioneer from France), and Matthew Keller (Irish immigrant, agricultural author, and vinyardist). These wineries primarily produced sparkling wines, *Angelica* (sweet wine), and *Aguardiente* (Brandy).[16]

Successful winegrape growing and favorable governmental policies encouraged the expansion of viticulture to Santa Barbara, Monterey, San Diego, Sacramento, Napa, and Sonoma Counties and provided the backdrop for much of the wine industry's initial success. California agricultural reports boasted that the number of grapevines statewide had increased eightfold between 1856 and 1862. Eager to encourage the growth of this new, and newly viable, industry, the California legislature excluded vineyards from taxation in 1859, thereby instituting a long tradition of assistance to the state's grape growing (both wine and table grapes) industry. Further government support came in 1861, when the state legislature in conjunction with the State of California Commissioned Agricultural Society pledged to find the "ways and means best adopted to promote the improvement and growth of the grape vine in California." Agoston Haraszthy, widely considered the father of the California wine industry, took advantage of the supportive mood and traveled throughout Europe collecting more than 100,000 cuttings from 1,440 wine varieties for experiment in California. From these cuttings, Haraszthy propagated hundreds of thousands of rooted vines in his Sonoma County Buena Vista Rancho.[17] During this same period, even with the planting of more than 14 million more grapevines, wine production could not keep up with the demand from thirsty consumers. Thus, U.S. merchants between 1858 and 1861 imported in excess of 500,000 gallons of wine annually.[18]

Despite its booming fame, the California wine industry wavered as post–Civil War competition from successful wine industries in Missouri, Ohio, and New York intensified. In an attempt to take advantage of the growing competitive market, unscrupulous commercial wineries sent young, poorly processed, and altered wines into the marketplace. Proprietors of these marginal wineries picked grapes before ample sugar levels developed, resulting in inadequate fermentation and poor-tasting wines. To make matters worse, unsanitary cooperage and hurried harvests promoted inclusion of rotten berries in the crush, introducing harmful bacteria and increasing spoilage. As consumer demand increased, low-priced European wines poured into the American market and eastern vintners began to place California labels on their inferior wines.

Over the next three decades, a new breed of educated leaders moved to rebuild public trust and expand the wine industry. These innovators, interested in truth in labeling, lobbied state legislators and won passage of the Wine Adulteration Act of 1862, which regulated preservatives and taste additives. At this point, wine experts pushed to rebuild California as a premium wine-producing region based on the advantages of growing of grapes in the Bay Area, in a moderate climate and in close proximity to urban populations. Leaders like George Husmann, Missouri viticulturist, nurseryman, writer, and professor of horticulture, trained a new generation of professional winemakers and growers. Husmann's 1863 book, *An Essay on the Culture of the Grape in the Great West,* and his 1866 publication, *The Cultivation of the Native Grape, and Manufacture of American Wines,* addressed the problems of grape growing in the western United States. Husmann so believed in the promise of California as a producer of quality winegrapes that in 1883 he took his growing expertise to the Napa Valley, where he planted a vineyard. Another industry leader, Theodore Hilgard, a lawyer, judge, and man of letters from the primarily German community of Belleville, Illinois, came to California with his son Eugene. The young Hilgard went on to become a professor of agriculture and viticulture at the University of California, Berkeley, and the director of the college's Agriculture Experiment Stations.[19] Under this new cadre of leaders, the wine industry quickly moved into every county of the Bay Area, finding the greatest success in Sonoma and Napa.[20]

The commitment to improving the industry deepened throughout the 1880s. With the help of the University of California and independent grapegrowers, the state authorized a Board of State Viticultural Commissions in 1880. This group promoted the marketing of California wines at state and national fairs and World Expositions. Continued remediation of quality issues increased with the research and development programs run by F. T. Bioletti, University of California Professor of Agriculture, at the Berkeley experiment stations.[21]

In a strange twist of events, it would be destructive insects and diseases that helped resolve many of the state's wine quality problems. Phylloxera (root lice), which initially helped California winemakers in the 1870s by destroying virtually all of the winegrape vines in France, turned up in California's vineyards in the 1880s. Adding to the problem was the devastation of the Los Angeles vineyards by Anaheim or Pierce's Disease (a plant virus carried and transmitted by insects). In the long run, pests and diseases actually benefited the industry by purging the state of its inferior Mission grapevine variety and simultaneously acting as a mechanism to rid the state of many marginal and disreputable growers and producers. Capital   to combat the blights and replant the state's vineyards came from wealthy agricultural investors. Los Angeles's troubles shifted the industry's entrepreneurial energy to the northern part of the state, where cool climate, "premium" winegrapes could flourish. The few remaining vineyards of southern California shifted to the production of table grapes (fresh fruit), raisins, and sweet after-dinner wines.[22]

California winemakers found ways to compensate for the cyclical convulsions of boom and bust markets during three depressions that flattened the national economy near the middle of each of the three post–Civil War decades. Indeed, the historical cycle of boom (high consumer demand and high profit) and bust (sudden overcapacity and collapsed prices) in the industry forced California winemakers to form cooperative marketing organizations and vertically integrate business structures. In 1894, seven well-financed San Francisco wine merchants, in an attempt to integrate the wine business vertically from vine to store, founded the California Wine Association (CWA). The CWA membership specialized in bulk-blended wines and by 1902 had grown to include the proprietors of more than fifty wineries. By 1894, a second cooperative, the California Wine Makers Corporation, horizontally integrated growers to sell winegrapes to larger wineries. Organizations such as these helped stabilize the industry and between 1890 and 1910 facilitated the doubling of California wine production to 45 million gallons per year.

At the turn of the century, the wine industry mirrored the state's other farming and food-processing industries. It was a time when new consumer demands resulted in expansion, technological advances drove up productivity, food processing was approached scientifically, and better distribution systems and modern marketing techniques enhanced sales. State and federal governments funded agricultural research and development at state universities. Farmers shared their knowledge (gained through trial and error) by way of conversations, journals, and treatises. They prospered as they formed trade associations to oversee marketing needs. Then the federal government expanded the influence of the United States Department of Agriculture (USDA) with the 1862 Morrill and 1867 Hatch Acts, which allowed the costs of research and development to be funded and carried out by state and federal agencies. This spirit of innovation, long characteristic of winemaking, became intense in California.[23]

California's wine industry, like its peers in specialized crop agriculture, grew rapidly with the swelling urban markets and rising consumer incomes. Enthusiasm for the future of the California wine industry seemed bright as the twentieth century began. The state's population soared to 1,485,000 persons, and national wine consumption grew to .3 gallons per-capita per-annum. By 1910, this demand, while still low by European standards, had grown sufficiently to consume the 50 million gallons of wine produced yearly. California's share of the national wine market had grown from 50 to 88 percent, its only serious rivals being European wineries. The industry's entrepreneurial energy flowed through the more than 100 commercial wineries of the San Francisco Bay region. And California wines were available in markets in the eastern United States, as well as in Asia, South America, and Europe.[24]

PROHIBITION, DEPRESSION, AND WAR SHIFT CONSUMER PREFERENCES

High hopes collapsed with the passage of the Eighteenth Amendment to the United States Constitution in 1919. The so-called dry forces stunned American wine drinkers and producers when their century-long anti-alcohol movement achieved national success with a Prohibition Amendment and its subsequent implementation through the Volstead Act. In the end, Prohibition slowed down American alcohol consumption, ended an era of working-class saloons, and served as one of the more successful alliances of the upper and middle classes to legislate morals and habits.[25]

The new laws of the land did not end all alcohol manufacturing. Federal agencies issued permits for the production of vinegar, sacramental wine, medicinal wines, industrial alcohol, flavorings, and home winemaking. In short order, home manufacturing of wine skyrocketed. Such production jumped from an estimated 50 million gallons per year before prohibition to 76.5 million gallons per year during it, as home winemakers legally made 200 gallons per year for family use. Herbert Hoover's Wickersham Commission counted over 45,000 legal permits in California alone and in 1931 concluded that "it appears to be the policy of the government not to interfere with it." Remarkably, the national per capita wine consumption climbed from .47 gallons per year in the fifty years before prohibition to .64 gallons per capita per year during prohibition.[26]

While this wine consumption increased, the commercial wine industry collapsed. The number of bonded American wineries fell to fewer than 140 in 1932, from a high in 1919 of more than 700. Grape growers, on the other hand, prospered as the price for red grapes used for homemade wines jumped from $25 per ton to more than $82 per ton in 1921. Despite prohibition, wine traditions persisted, as more than 750 winegrape growers attempted to stabilize the industry by forming the California Vineyardists Association in 1926.

By 1932, most Americans had tired of prohibition and a wet California legislature, a wet United States Congress, and a wet newly elected president, Franklin D. Roosevelt, approved the legal manufacture and sale of 3.2 percent beer and 12 to 14 percent sacramental wine, this a sweet, carbonated beverage. The Roosevelt administration also allowed doctors to prescribe wine medicinally. Consequently, wine production tripled between 1932 and 1933. On December 5, 1933, the nation repealed prohibition.[27]

Regretfully, the legacy of prohibition haunted the wine industry for decades, as California winegrape growers had converted their premium vineyards to produce thick-skinned varieties of grapes that could withstand shipment to home winemakers in the eastern United States. Those Americans who had continued to drink wine had learned to accept cheaper, sweeter, and lower quality table wines. Furthermore, each state now established its own liquor laws. Worse yet for the industry's future was the belief held by many Americans that the consumption of any alcohol was immoral.

POST-PROHIBITION

With the repeal of prohibition, California's grape growers increased production and began to rebuild their industry with the aid of new scientific viticultural knowledge and techniques. Like early agricultural pioneers, California's wine farmers took advantage of the state's ideal growing climate and cheap sources of labor. Nevertheless, one by-product of prohibition was that most consumers had switched their preferences from dry to sweet wines with high alcoholic content. (The nation's wine consumers had preferred dry wines by a 2 to 1 ration in 1900, but had switched to sweet wines by a 4 to 1 margin by the time prohibition had ended.) This resulted in an expansion of the sweet wine production in California's Central Valley, where the number of bonded family wineries doubled in 1933.

California's now-legal wine industry became one of the few business enterprises to expand during the Great Depression. Over 380 United States wineries reopened, yet they faced cooperage shortages, cash-strapped consumers, and different alcohol regulations in each state. In 1935, California wineries addressed these problems with the formation of the Wine Institute (in San Francisco) which quickly boasted a membership of 188, or 80 percent, of the state's wineries. Further cooperative rebuilding of the industry came in 1938, when the California Department of Agriculture helped establish the Wine Advisory Board, which mandated membership for all 733 of the state's wineries and assessed a per-gallon tax to finance a national California wine advertising campaign. With the help of the government, science, and modern business techniques, California had re-established its wine industry.

Nevertheless, this re-established industry did not grow smoothly during the post-depression and World War II years. Small wineries faced with depression-era shortages of capital were forced to embrace outside investors and takeovers by large eastern liquor companies such as Seagram's, Schenley, and National Distillers. It appeared that the California wine industry had consolidated overnight. Yet, by midcentury, the impatient distiller corporations had abandoned wine making and the state's wineries were once again mostly owned by resident entrepreneurs.

CALIFORNIA'S WINE REVOLUTION

After World War II, California commercial wineries reentered the national and international wine marketplace, after a twenty-five year hiatus, by adapting to and then recultivating the tastes of a growing number of consumers. Like California agriculturists in general, wine farmers learned to market their products and promote a relationship between themselves, the government, and the universities. Over the next two decades, American consumption of flavored sweet wines increased from 100 million gallons in the mid-1940s to 145 million gallons in the mid-1950s. Further changes occurred in 1958, when government regulations legalized "pop" wines, which contained enough carbon dioxide to produce a soft pop upon opening the bottle. This led the way to the popularity of light fruit wines by the late 1960s. By 1971, more than 41 million gallons of "pop" wines were sold yearly.[28] Grocers filled store shelves with brand names such as Boone's Farm, Annie Green Springs, Sangria, Ripple, Bali Hai, Key Largo, Spanada, Tyrolia, and Thunderbird. Meanwhile, Americans' rising disposable incomes led to increased wine consumption and enticed vintners to begin bottling their own wines for retail sale, rather than merely shipping them as bulk products to be bottled by national wholesalers.

Within a single generation, American wine increased in both quality and prestige and quickly rose to prominence in the world wine market. Between 1964 and 1974, the number of California bonded wineries grew from 231 to 311 and winegrape acreage more than doubled, from 136,758 acres in 1965 to a 1974 high of 322,044 acres.[29] The increase was led not by new pioneers, but by the eight largest wine companies, which increased their hold over the market from 42 percent in 1947 to 68 percent in 1972.[30]

The crucial moment of self-realization for the California wine industry came with the famous Bicentennial (1976) blind tasting of French and California wines in Paris, France. In what *Time* magazine called "The Judgement of Paris," French wine experts named Napa Valley's Stag's Leap Wine Cellars 1973 Cabernet Sauvignon and Chateau Montelena's 1973 Chardonnay superior to French Bordeaux and Burgundy competitors. Most important, the tasting inspired many American winemakers to raise their standards and, in the words of winewriter Paul Lukacs, to "begin thinking of 'world class' as a goal."[31]

In the long run, changed attitudes resulted in a new California style of winemaking that grew to dominate the worldwide industry.[32] U.S. percapita wine consumption jumped dramatically, from 1.51 gallons in 1963 to a 1971 high of 2.37 gallons per adult.[33] Not only did consumption increase, but consumers also began to switch their preferences to premium table wines in an attempt to achieve social status, the perceived serenity of the "good life," and improved health. By 1972, dry table wines topped 50 percent of all wines consumed and wineries began to market aggressively to the emerging market.[34] Wine's historic social and religious symbolism helped provide legitimacy to the 1960s accumulation of eclectic social movements that sought simpler times amidst the chaos and injustice of the postwar world. Wine entrepreneurs quickly took advantage of these Cold War fears and promoted tours that provided a romantic, pastoral experience for the visitors.[35] Added to this new consumer trend was a national shift towards health consciousness that increased interest in table wines in 1972 after Dr. Salvatore P. Luca, professor of preventive medicine at the University of California, described how wine could be used as a natural tranquilizer, cholesterol reducer, source of vitamins, and digestive aid.[36]

The explosive new interest in wine prodded California winemakers, with the help of universities, to produce large amounts of more affordable premium wines and redefine "the best" as the products of the new California wine style that utilized science to produce fruit flavored wines from quality grapes. This new California style, fostered by enologists (wine scientists) from the University of California at Berkeley and Davis, ushered in an era of varietal-designated and vintage dated wines. In short order, these university programs produced graduates that successfully lessened the amount of poor quality wines. Consistent, high quality wines became the norm, as agricultural scientists found ways to cool or control fermentation overheating and introduced superior yeasts that improved taste, color, and clarity of the wine.

Vintibusiness wine farmers now began to adopt the general tenets of agribusiness by seeking governmental incentives and investing heavily in land, machinery, and facilities (buildings and showrooms) and by developing new kinds of grapes and techniques. A favorable 1960s–1970s tax climate for investors helped the industry expand. Furthermore, federal, state, and local tax concessions made it advantageous for individuals and companies to invest in vineyards and wineries. And the wine industry offered investors the potential for considerable growth in an inflationary period. As in the past, the industry drew capital from professionals and entrepreneurs.

These revolutionary changes lead to an unprecedented growth of the industry in the 1960s and 1970s, which in turn required a high level of investment in land and technology. This new wave of entrepreneurs adapted the business techniques of large corporations to a fragmented industry, thereby centralizing or merging small companies to form wine, alcohol, and food-processing corporations. These new, large wineries instituted marketing techniques that included the popular press, television, and radio. They also promoted tourism to wine country, building tasting rooms and hosting vineyard events to help spur an expanding interest in wine and winemaking and boost sales to new heights.[37] One result of this growth was an ever-increasing need for more vineyard land. Wineries, seeking to produce more premium winegrapes, began to look beyond the traditional wine-growing counties of Napa, Sonoma, and Mendicino to new vineyard lands in the Central and South Coast regions of California.[38]

NAPA SEEKS PREMIUM WINEGRAPES

Bay Area wineries and grape growers followed the traditional historic trend of large-scale California agriculture by responding to grape shortages with new local vineyards. But rapid urban expansion following World War II had encouraged many farmers to sell their land to eager real estate developers as its value rose. The result was escalating land prices in the very regions best suited for growing winegrapes. After half a decade (1960–1965) of unprecedented urban sprawl, concerned agriculturalists moved to counter the loss of prime agricultural lands that threatened the vineyards of the San Francisco Bay Area. Winemakers argued that vineyards provided a sense of community, helped secure economic diversity, preserved historic and aesthetic values, and secured open space for recreational and health benefits.[39] In response, Bay Area counties patched together local laws that exclusively zoned land for agricultural use and encouraged wineries to expand. Statewide, farmers and environmental activists temporarily joined forces to lobby state lawmakers for a means to curb the loss of agricultural lands and open spaces. Legislators, in turn, passed the California Land Conservation Act of 1965 (called the Williamson Act) and the Property Tax Assessment Reform Act of 1966.[40] These laws established a voluntary county participation program designed to give property tax incentives to save valuable farmland.

These policy measures slowed the conversion of California farmland to urban uses and promoted the sale of land for viticulture. Over the course of the next decade, small winegrape growers cashed in on inflated land prices by selling vineyard lands to a new generation of gentleman farmers from the cadre of professionals looking to invest in the latest version of the good life—the wine industry. These high-income investors purchased land, planted grapes, and under the existing tax laws avoided paying taxes by simultaneously writing off all invested income and capital improvements to vineyards as losses. This system created a tax dodge whereby wealthy investors suffered no permanent economic loss even as vineyards functioned in the red. The window of opportunity for this kind of legal money laundering lasted until the 1976 Tax Reform Law, which amended the Internal Revenue Codes to exclude vineyard investments as a viable tax write-off.

In a move reminiscent of the major themes of California agriculture farmers, grapegrowers, ranchers, and investors experimented with mixing one agricultural endeavor with another in order to create efficient high-profit businesses. Consequently, this era saw the conversion of row cropland, dairies, and fruit and nut lands to vineyards. At the same time, non-winegrape growers capitalized on the grape shortage by selling table and raisin grapes for bulk wine juice. Ranchers, on the other hand, planted vineyards as a way to achieve an agricultural diversity capable of stabilizing earnings while avoiding a measure of profit-eating property taxes. Investors, seeing an opportunity for short-term profits, also got caught up in the mystique of the wine lifestyle and sought to counter inflation through investment in vintibusinesses. By the early 1970s, the demand for vineyard land reached a fever pitch. In an effort to quench the nation's thirst, marketers quadrupled foreign wine imports, from 14,369,000 gallons in 1964 to 51,394,000 gallons in 1974. Economic reports verified concerns that the United States wine industry was woefully short of premium winegrape acreage. In 1973, Professor Maynard Amerine of the University of California at Davis correctly predicted that 150,000-acres of new vineyards would be planted throughout the state over the next several years.

The search for new winegrape lands heightened throughout California as economic projections from the Bank of America and The Wine Institute predicted continued growth of the wine industry. The news encouraged developers, grape growers, bankers, insurance companies, and gentleman farmers to move into action and reach out to agricultural scientists from the University of California at Davis and California State College at Fresno for the research and development technologies to guide the expansion of the California wine industry.

MARKETING THE WINE LIFESTYLE

California agriculturalists historically established ways to develop new marketing and distribution systems to increase sales and raise profit margins. The California wine industry carried on this tradition when it successfully tapped into America's post–World War II middle class, a group newly freed by its car-culture and flush with newly realized disposable income. Americans sought new and exciting ways to relax and a leisure culture was born. Throughout the 1960s and 1970s, many of these upscale consumers planned vacations and short escapes to various "back-to-nature" destinations: one such spot was the family wine farm—where visitors might sample different wines while taking in the relaxing vineyard atmosphere—to enjoy the good life at its source. Visitors marveled at the artistry of individual and family winemakers; some even dreamed of one day owning their own wine business. Throughout the 1980s and 1990s, the enophile dance, that between consumer and winemaker, continued as tourists faithfully flocked to visit and revisit what appeared to be quaint family wine businesses. In reality, the image of a family wine farm, with its vineyard, tasting room, polished landscaping, and tour, had become a calculated part of an advertising and promotional strategy for large wine enterprises. Unbeknownst to many a visitor was the fact that regional wine escapes had become a complex combination of agriculture, industry, and tourism orchestrated by vintibusiness corporations.

Nevertheless, and regardless of their design, visits to vineyards and wine-country tours were truly enjoyable and, overall, the late 1980s and early 1990s were good years for the California wine industry. Wine as a business not only survived a flurry of neoprohibition (modern anti-alcohol forces), label disclosure laws, taxation, and restrictive advertising policies, but it also continued to grow on an average of 5 percent annually.[41] Again, increased production failed to quench consumer demand and the resulting domestic wine shortages, aided by a strong U.S. dollar (as compared to European currencies) resulted in increased importation of foreign wines. By 1982, the United States imported over $750 million of wine annually.[42]

Strong foreign footholds in the United States wine market forced industry officials to complain that American wines could not compete with the products of foreign wineries supported by their respective subsidies and tariffs. Many predicted that this unfair playing field would eventually spell the downfall of the entire American viticultural industry. As foreign competition increased, many winegrape growers and vintners counted on the California Wine Commission, a marketing consortium funded with a graduated tax on wineries, and its Wine Institute to promote the state's $6 billion industry and help equalize domestic and international markets. In 1983, California wine officials sent John Deluca, president of the Wine Institute, to Washington, D.C., to lobby for government policies that would "reduce, and eliminate barriers to trade on a basis which assures substantially equivalent competitive opportunities for all wine moving in international trade." And with the help of Representative William Thomas (R-Bakersfield), Congress proposed the Wine Equity Act.[43]

Regretfully, the inability of American winemakers to act as a unified group resulted in rejection of the Wine Equity Act. Internal struggles in the

California Wine Institute, between large and small wineries, detracted from the organization's ability to pressure federal officials for a protective policy. Smaller vintners perceived that larger corporations controlled the wine commission and manipulated market shares and political influence for themselves. In an attempt to effect equity on the commission, member winemakers sought to dismantle the apportionment of voting power, determined by levels of production, and let up a battle cry of "one winery one vote." The infighting continued, resulting in 1990 in the dismantling of the commission and no policy for the limitation of foreign wine imports.[44]

CONTINUED BAY AREA EXPANSION PLANS FALTER

Notwithstanding foreign competition, the consumption of California wines continued to rise and northern wineries again attempted to meet consumer needs by increasing vineyard acreage. This time, however, expansion efforts in the Bay Area faltered, as large wineries and growers encountered stern resistance from former environmental allies seeking to protect rural land from hordes of tourists and auxiliary tourist industries (hotels, motels, shops, and restaurants). These land stewards had good cause for concern. By the late 1980s, Napa County tourism had risen to 2.5 million visitors per year and dozens of new wineries had sprung onto the scene.[45] Fearing the harmful effects of even more visitors and new wineries on the agriculture and health of the area, Napa County planners curbed the growth of wineries by requiring that 75 percent of all grapes processed in the county had to have been grown in Napa vineyards. And since Napa land values had risen 58 percent to over $55,000 per-acre between 1987 and 1990, new vineyard planting had become cost prohibitive. Unable to expand through massive vineyard planting, Napa vintibusinesses created satellite vineyards and operations in Monterey, Santa Barbara, Santa Cruz, and Temecula.

THE SCIENTIFIC SOLUTION

Even as the possibilities to expand Napa vineyards dwindled, many northern wineries looked to the historic lessons and trends of the agricultural history of the state to maximize vineyard production through science and technology. Most turned to their old government and university research and development partners. By 1991, U.C. Davis bragged that 75 percent of the people in the California wine industry had completed at least some of their training in the campus's viticulture and enology programs.[46]

But industry leaders failed to remember that over time federal and state support for the wine industry had wavered between encouragement and outright prohibition. In the 1980s, growers and vintners faced downsizing in state- and federal-government funded research programs. Adding to the problem was neoprohibitionist pressure on politicians to deny funding for research for alcohol-related industries.

In 1990, governmental research and development in support of the wine industry collapsed with the passage of the Agricultural and Food Policy Act, thus ending six decades of federal price-support policies for traditional food crops and the wine industry.[47] In response, Bob Hartzel, president of the California Association of Winegrape Growers, testified before the USDA subcommittee on Information, Justice, Transportation and Agriculture that since Congress passed the 1990 Excise Tax (which raised retail taxes on wine from 17 cents to $1.07 per gallon—a 529 percent increase) grape growers contributed more to the U.S. treasury than did the producers of any other agricultural crop and therefore deserved research money.[48] This form of governmental support of the wine industry never rematerialized, and eventually most research programs and new technology costs shifted solely to vintibusinesses themselves.

Without government support, many wine businesses found alternate, in-house ways to conduct research and development. Large wineries like Mondavi and Gallo developed their own research programs and hired scientists for their private labs. Many smaller wineries joined together to form the American Vineyard Foundation, pooling their resources to fund public viticultural investigations. Yet, by the mid-1990s, only one in six California wineries contributed to the foundation.[49] Despite the lack of a unified effort, most wineries simply realized that healthy vines produce more and better-quality grapes. Therefore, improved plant health took on more immediacy in light of the protracted winegrape shortages and new outbreaks of phylloxera and Anaheim Disease.[50]

An Industry for the New Millenium

The two-century-old California wine industry has become a major agricultural contributor to the U.S. economy. In 1997 the American Wine Industry provided roughly 207,000 jobs, paid $3.2 billion in wages, directly contributed $12.4 billion to the Gross Domestic Product, and paid slightly less than $500 million in federal taxes. From 579 wineries in 1975 to a 1999 high of 2,081, today only two states (North Dakota and Alaska) have no commercial wineries. California continues to lead the nation, hosting 1,056 wineries and producing more than 80 percent of American wine annually.[51]

Despite these impressive figures, American wineries continually failed to meet increased consumer demands. Wine wholesalers and vintibusinesses responded by importing increasing amounts of New Zealand, Australian, Chilean, Argentinean, South African, French, Spanish and Italian wines.

Yet, long-term projections for continued growth in the domestic wine industry have never dimmed. John Love, World Agricultural Outlook

Board (USDA) predicted that, ". . . a robust economy—providing more discretionary income—is the key to continued growth in consumption." Love also predicted continued growth of wine consumption through the year 2010 at a rate of 2.5 percent—down slightly from 3 percent over the last half of the 1990s.[52] Confident Wall Street Investors viewed this growth as promising and continued to invest in California vintibusinesses such as Beringer Wine Estates, Brown-Foreman Corporation, Chalone Wine Group, Golden State Vintners, Ravenswood Winery, and Robert Mondavi Corporation, to name a few.[53]

From this story evolved an American agricultural industry, centered mainly in California, capable of withstanding economic gluts and shortages while remaining competitive in the international marketplace. As an agribusiness enterprise the wine farm became deeply rooted in the five major themes in California agricultural history—climate, experimentation, entrepreneurial investment, the ability to build new markets and distribution networks, and development of small concerns into efficient agribusinesses. For wine growers, perhaps the most relevant historic lesson has been that the most successful wine businesses have been those that have, in some fashion, united grape growers and winemakers into what modern economists call vertical integration or vintibusiness.

Notes

1 Daniel Sogg, "Two Wine Empires Expand in California," *Wine Spectator*, May 15, 2000, 12.

2 Daniel Sogg and James Suckling, "Mondavi Buys Into Tuscany's Ornellaia," *Wine Spectator*, April 30, 2000, 12.

3 James Laube, "Consolidation Sweeps Wine Industry: Three Major Deals Total Nearly $2 billion," *Wine Spectator*, October 31, 2000, 14–15.

4 James Laube, "Mondavi Buys Arrowood for $45 million," *Wine Spectator*, September 15, 2000, 10; and Dana Nigro, "Mondavi Wins OK for Groundbreaking French Estate," *Wine Spectator*, September 30, 2000, 14.

5 Dana Nigro, "Mondavi Winery to Open at New Disney Park in February," *Wine Spectator*, November 15, 2000, 18.

6 For a good basic introduction to this era refer to; Frank Adams, "The Historical Background of California Agriculture" in Claude B. Hutchison, ed., *California Agriculture* (Los Angeles: University of California Press, 1946), 1–49. For the era between the Mexican period and California Statehood refer to Paul W. Gates, *California Ranchos and Farms 1846–1862* (Madison, Wis. : The State Historical Society of Wisconsin, 1967).

7 Lawrence J. Jelinek, *Harvest Empire: A History California Agriculture*. 2nd edition (San Francisco: Boyd and Fraser Publishing Company, 1982), passim; Ann Foley Scheuring, *A Guidebook to California Agriculture* (Los Angeles: University of California Press, 1987).

8 Carey McWilliams. *Factories in the Field: Migrants and Migratory Farm Labor in California* (Boston: Little, Brown, and Company, 1942).

9 The term vintibusiness, coined by the author, refers to the agribusiness phenomenon whereby vertical integration of grape farming, wine production, and wine distribution falls within the control of an agricultural corporation.

10 Descriptions of the American merger tradition can be found in Naomi R. Lamoreaux, *The Great Merger Movement in American Business, 1895–1904* (New York: Cambridge University Press, 1985). Descriptions of the California wine business tradition can be found in Vincent Carosso, *The California Wine Industry 1830–1895* (Berkeley: University of California Press, 1951); Charles L. Sullivan, *Napa Wine: A History from Mission Days to Present* (San Francisco: The Wine Appreciation Guild, 1994).

11 Discussions of the modern agribusiness techniques used by vintibusinesses can be found in James T. Lapsley, *Bottled Poetry; Napa Winemaking from Prohibition to the Modern Era* (Los Angeles: University of California Press, 1996); Ernest and Julio Gallo with Bruce Henderson, *Ernest & Julio: Our Story* (New York: Random House, 1994); and Robert Mondavi with Paul Chutkow, Robert Mondavi, *Harvests of Joy: My Passion for Excellence* (New York: Harcourt Brace and Company, 1998).

12 Olivier Zunz, *Making America Corporate 1870–1920* (Chicago: The University of Chicago Press, 1990); Olivier Zunz, *Why the American Century?* (Chicago: University of Chicago Press, 1998).

13 Discussions of the history of American winemaking can be found in Leon D. Adams, *The Wines of America*, 4th edition (New York: McGraw-Hill Publishing Company, 1990), and Thomas Pinney, *A History of Wine in America: From the Beginnings to Prohibition* (Berkeley: University of California Press, 1989).

14 Gary L. Peters, "Trends in California Viticulture," *The Geographical Review* 74 (October 1984), 463; Gates, *California Ranchos and Farms, 1846–1862*, ix.

15 W. J. Rorabaugh, *The Alcoholic Republic: An American Tradition* (New York: Oxford University Press, 1979), 105.

16 Gates, *California Ranchos and Farms*, 64; Carosso, *The California Wine Industry*, 7–8; Irving McGee, "Jean Paul Vignes, California's First Professional Winegrower," *Agricultural History* 22 (1948), 176–181; and Charles L. Sullivan, *A Companion to California Wine: An Encyclopedia of Wine and Winemaking from the Mission Period to the Present* (Berkeley: University of California Press, 1998), 298–299, 168, and 171–173.

17 Brian Mc Ginty, *Strong Wine: The Life and Legend of Agoston Harazthy* (Stanford: Stanford University Press, 1998).

18 Gates, *California Ranchos and Farms*, 66–69.

19 Eugene W. Hilgard, *Report of the Professor of Agriculture to the President of the University* (Sacramento, California: State Printing Office, 1879); George Hussmann, *Grape Culture and Wine Making in California: A Practical Manual for the Grape Grower and Wine Maker* (San Francisco: Payot, Upham and Company, 1888); and Maynard A. Amerine, "An Introduction to the Pre-Repeal History of Wine," *Agricultural History* 43 (April 1969), 259–268.

20 Maynard A. Amerine, "The Napa Valley Grape and Wine Industry," *Agricultural History* 49 (January 1975), 289–291.

21 Frederic T. Bioletti, *Agricultural Experiment Station Berkeley, California*, "Grape Culture in California, Its Difficulties: Phylloxera and Resistant Vines, and Other Vine Diseases," (Sacramento: Superintendent of State Printing, 1908); Frederic T. Bioletti, *Agricultural Experiment Station Berkeley, California*, "Grape Culture in California: Improved Methods of Wine Making," (Sacramento: Superintendent of State Printing, 1908); Frederic T. Bioletti, *Agricultural Experiment Station Berkeley, California*, "Grape Culture in California; Yeasts From California Grapes," (Sacramento: Superintendent of State Printing, 1908).

22 Victor W. Geraci, "The El Cajon, California, Raisin Industry: An Exercise in Gilded Age Capitalism," *Southern California Quarterly* 74 (Winter 1992): 329–354.

23 Eric E. Lampard, *The Rise of the Dairy Industry in Wisconsin 1820–1920* (Madison, Wis.; The State Historical Society of Wisconsin, 1967), passim.

24 Muscadine, *The University of California/Sotheby Book of California Wine*, 383, 414, and 419; Pinney, *A History of Wine in America*, 374.

25 General readings in the after effects of prohibition can be found in: Thomas M. Coffey, *The Long Thirst; Prohibition in America: 1920–1933* (New York: Norton and Company, 1990); David E. Kyvig, *Law, Alcohol, and Order: Perspectives on National Prohibition* (Westport, Connecticut: Greenwood Press, 1985); David E. Kyvig, *Repealing National Prohibition* (Chicago: University of Chicago Press, 1979); Gilman M. Ostrander, *The Prohibition Movement in California, 1848–1933* (Berkeley: University of California Press, 1957); John C. Burnham, "New Perspectives on the Prohibition Experiment of the 1920s," *Journal of Social History* 2 (Fall 1968), 51–68; and John C. Burnham, *Bad Habits: Drinking, Smoking, Taking Drugs, Gambling, Sexual Misbehavior, and Swearing in American History* (New York: New York University Press, 1993).

26 Victor W. Geraci, "Grape Growing to Vintibusiness: A History of the Santa Barbara, California Regional Wine Industry, 1865–1995," Ph.D. Dissertation University of California Santa Barbara, 1997, 208.

27 Stanton Peele, "The Conflict between Public Health Goals and the Temperance Mentality," *American Journal of Public Health* 83 (June 1993): 805–810.

28 "Pop Wines . . . Something for Everyone," *Los Angeles Times Home Magazine,* October 15, 1972.

29 "U.S. Wineries Savor Success at Home," *Los Angeles Times,* February 23, 1979.

30 Richard Bunce, "From California Grapes to California Wine, the Transformation of an Industry, 1963–1979," *Contemporary Drug Problems* (Spring 1981): 57.

31 Frank J. Prial, "Wine Talk: A Coda To the 1976 France vs. California Rivalry That Changed Some Attitudes," *The New York Times,* May 22, 1996.

32 K. S. Moulton, "The Economics of Wine in California," in *Muscatine, The Book of California Wine,* 380–405.

33 Gavin-Jobson Publication, "The Wine Marketing Handbook, U.S. News and World Report, 1972," 14, 74, 89; and Frank Braconi, Morton Research Corporation, *The U.S. Wine Market: An Economic Marketing & Financial Investigation* (April 1977, A Morton Report, Merrick, New York): 4–5, 14–18, 37–57, and 89–98.

34 Ibid.

35 Robert C. Fuller, *Religion and Wine: A Cultural History of Wine Drinking in the United States* (Knoxville: The University of Tennessee Press, 1996), 8–9.

36 Nathan Chroman, "Wine: What the Doctor Ordered," *Los Angeles Times,* 11 May 1972, 18.

37 Irving Hoch and Nickolas Tryphonopoulos, *A Study of the Economy of Napa County, California* (University of California; California Agricultural Experiment Station Giannini Foundation of Agricultural Economics Research Report Number 303, August 1969), passim.

38 Charles L. Sullivan, *Napa Wine; A History from Mission Days to Present* (San Francisco: The Wine Appreciation Guild, 1994), 234–305.

39 Donald Joseph de la Peña, "Vineyards in a Regional System of Open Space in the San Francisco Bay Area: Methods of Preserving Selected Areas," Master's Thesis in City Planning in the College of Environmental Design; University of California, Berkeley, 1962, passim.

40 Rebecca Ann Conard, "The Conservation of Local Autonomy: California's Agricultural Land Policies, 1900–1966," Ph.D. Dissertation, University of California, Santa Barbara, 1984, passim.

41 Dale M. Heien, "The Impact of the Alcohol Tax Act of 1990 on California Agriculture," A position paper sponsored by the United Agribusiness League; Irvine, California, July 1990.

42 Jeff Mapes, "Reagan Tells Congress No on Wine Equity Act," *The Wine Spectator,* December 16–31, 1983, 19.

43 Jeff Mapes, "Reagan Tells Congress No On Wine Equity Act," *The Wine Spectator,* December 16–31, 1983, 19; James Suckling, "Wine Legislation Attempts to Curb Tariff Barriers," *The Wine Spectator,* June 1–15, 1983, 2.

44 "Rapid Changes In Wine Commission Legal Dispute," *Wines and Vines,* April 1990, 14; Dan Berger, "Small Wineries Beat Giants, Kill Marketing Power," *Los Angeles Times,* May 25, 1990; Lawrence M. Fisher, "Smaller Wine Makers Gain Clout," *Los Angeles Times,* June 16, 1990.

45 Marc Frons,"Tasting Wines At Their Scenic Sources," *Business Week,* May 15, 1989, 157.

46 Richard S. Street, "Wizards of Wine," *The Wine News,* June/July, 1991,14–17.

47 R. G. F. Spitze, "A Continuing Evolution in U.S. Agricultural Policy," *Agricultural Economics* 77, 1990, 126–139.

48 Phyllis van Kriedt, "Hartzell Explains the Consequences of the 1990 Excise Tax Increase," *California Wineletter,* September 2, 1993.

49 Mike Winters, "U.S. Wine/Grape Researchers Decry Money Woes," *Wine Business Monthly,* May 1997, 1, 14–18.

50 "Infestations & Tight Money Will Shake-Out Wine Industry," *California Wine Tasting Monthly,* April 1993, 7.

51 Steve Barsby & Associates for Vinifera Wine Growers Association. "The Economic Contribution of the Wine Industry to the U.S. Economy, 1997," *Wine Business Monthly* 6, August 1999, 29; and Kim Marcus. "U.S. Winery Total Grows at Fast Pace," *Wine Spectator* 24, September 15, 1999, 21.

52 John Love, "The Long Future of U.S. Wine Value," *Wine Business Monthly* 6, August 1999, 34–37.

53 Abby Sawyer, "The Wine Industry on Wall Street: As Business Booms an Increasing Number of Wineries Consider Public Stock Offerings," *Wine Business Monthly* 4, December 1997, 1,10.

INDEX

California History: A Topical Approach
Developmental Editor and Copy Editor: Andrew J. Davidson
Production Editor: Lucy Herz
Proofreader: Claudia Siler
Cartographer: Jane Domier
Indexer: Margie Towery
Cover designer: De Pinto Graphic Design
Printer: Sheridan Books